LEARNING TO BE LEARNERS

A MATHEGENICAL APPROACH TO THEOLOGICAL EDUCATION

Les Ball

Learning to be Learners
A Mathegenical Approach to Theological Education
Les Ball

SCD Press
PO Box 1882
Macquarie Centre NSW 2113
scdpress@scd.edu.au

© Les Ball 2022

ISBN-13: 978-1-925730-31-9 (Paperback)
ISBN-13: 978-1-925730-32-6 (E-book)

Leslie James Ball asserts his right to be recognised as the primary author of this work.

Key words: integrative learning; mathegenical pedagogy; taxonomical curriculum; theological education; theological world view

Cover design and internal layout and design: Lankshear Design Pty Ltd.

LEARNING TO BE LEARNERS

A MATHEGENICAL APPROACH TO THEOLOGICAL EDUCATION

Les Ball

SCD Press
2022

Publications associated with SCD Learning & Teaching Theology Conferences

1. Les Ball, *Transforming Theology. Student Experience and Transformative Learning in Undergraduate Theological Education* (Preston, Vic.: Mosaic, 2012). Second edition: Macquarie Park, SCD Press, 2022.
2. Les Ball & James R. Harrison (eds.), *Learning & Teaching Theology. Some Ways Ahead* (Northcote, Vic: Morning Star, 2014). Second edition: Macquarie Park, SCD Press, 2022.
3. Yvette Debergue & James R. Harrison (eds.), *Teaching Theology in a Technological Age* (Cambridge: Cambridge Scholars Publishing, 2015).
4. Les Ball & Peter G. Bolt (eds.), *Wondering About God Together. Research-Led Learning & Teaching in Theological Education* (Macquarie Park, NSW: SCD Press, 2018).
5. Peter G. Bolt & Peter Laughlin (eds.), *God's Exemplary Graduates: Character-Oriented Graduate Attributes in Theological Education* (Macquarie Park, NSW: SCD Press, 2021).
6. Les Ball, *Learning to be Learners: A Mathegenical Approach to Theological Education* (Macquarie Park, NSW: SCD Press, 2022).
7. Peter G. Bolt & Peter Laughlin (eds.), *Testing Us Testing God. Assessment in Theological Education* (Macquarie Park, NSW: SCD Press, 2022).

CONTENTS

Acknowledgements   vii

Introduction: Why 'Mathegenical'?   ix

Part 1: **A WORLD VIEW FOUNDATION**

   1 *The Shaping of a World View*   1

Part 2: **THE ARCHITECTURE OF CURRICULUM**

   2 *Curriculum Principles and Design*   35

   3 *Constructing Curriculum*   69

   4 *Curriculum Review and Development*   99

Part 3: **PERSPECTIVES ON PEDAGOGY**

   5 *Influences and General Principles of Theological Pedagogy*   115

   6 *Focus on Teacher or Learner – Pedagogy or Andragogy?*   143

   7 *Focus on Learning – A Mathegenical Approach*   159

   8 *Integrating Pedagogy – Bringing It All Together*   179

Conclusion: How Then Should We Teach?   209

Bibliography   214

Index   221

ACKNOWLEDGEMENTS

Of the vast number of valued students and colleagues who have so often shown me how I can improve my teaching, some stand out as having invested so much of themselves in my personal and professional development that has led directly to the compilation of this book.

Dr Stan Nickerson, my first theological college principal, appointed me as the Academic Dean at the Baptist Theological College of Queensland. There, he fostered my engagement with curriculum planning and management, with a free hand to initiate reforms and lead faculty, always with his wise and trusted hand guiding and supporting. Without Stan's mentoring, my theological career would simply never have been. Professor Stephen Smith, my final theological college principal, brought me out of planned retirement with the directive, 'Do whatever you want to make us all better teachers'. With freedom to innovate and Steve's constant facilitation, along with the combined excellence and insights of the teaching faculty at Australian College of Ministries, my thinking on theological education was refined and crystallised to produce this book. I went to these colleges to shape their faculty; I came away from them very much shaped by those faculties.

I have also had the rare benefit of having my wife, Dr Carol Ball, as a mature age student in my theological classes, then as a theological teaching colleague and author, and now as an insightful critic and commentator on all aspects of this book. Her unique perspectives on student response to my ideas and practices, her direct observations and assessments of my teaching and faculty leading, and her constant prodding and coaxing to ensure I persevered in various projects have all been instrumental in the emergence of this book.

INTRODUCTION: WHY 'MATHEGENICAL'?

How should we teach? This question has engaged educational theorists and practitioners for generations. Until around the 1960s, the issue of pedagogy was treated as a field that pertains to the formal education of children, since they were the main recipients of formal education. Methods of teaching were geared predominantly to direct instruction of essential content shaped and delivered by a knowledgeable teacher. Students were expected to absorb the content that was commonly drilled into them as the necessary training for good citizenship or social utility that was the goal of their education. Pedagogical theory was concerned with how such learning could be most efficiently delivered. As higher levels of secondary and then tertiary education emerged far more broadly in the post-World War II era, such a basic teaching method was extended to those higher levels. In tertiary education, that led to the teacher term of 'lecturer', which summarised the prevailing pedagogical mode.

When I began my university studies in the 1960s, we students sat in a tiered lecture theatre of 300 first-year English I students being lectured by an erudite expert for three hours a week in English poetry, then a further three hours in English prose, and a two hour lecture on English drama, with regular weekly tutorials of fifteen to twenty students, in which a tutor would generally deliver a paper on a related topic and engender some class discussion of well-prepared questions. Even those who went to the highest level of a major in English III sat in a class of eighty students being lectured and tutored along similar lines. The emphasis was very strongly on direct instruction and relatively passive reception in fragmented blocks of discrete fields with no structural inter-relation, coherence or application to personal settings. Yet I developed an enduring love of Shakespeare and the wonders of the English language throughout this process. From today's perspective, it is difficult to envisage how such an outcome could result from such a process. But somehow it worked.

It was not long after that decade that this sort of process came under harsh criticism as being based on a pedagogical approach that failed to relate to tertiary students as adults. In the 1970s, Malcolm Knowles popularised the concept of andragogy ('leading adults' as distinct from pedagogy: 'leading children') as a way of addressing the fundamental differences between how a child learns and how an adult learns. His first significant publication on this issue was entitled *The Modern Practice of Adult Education: Andragogy versus Pedagogy* (1970). The very title of that work suggested a conflictual comparison between the inadequacies of pedagogy for adult learning against the preferred ideals of andragogy. He structured his ideas on contrasting sets of basic assumptions about adults that necessitate a different approach to learning and teaching. These assumptions highlighted the contrast in areas such as the learners' need to know, the learners' self-concept, the role of the learners' experiences, readiness to learn, and motivation. The common thread in these assumptions is the extrinsic aspects of pedagogical motivation and disposition to the learning of children as contrasted to the intrinsic aspects of andragogical motivation and disposition of adults. The influence of Knowles's work led to a growing contest between pedagogy and andragogy because they seemed to be incompatible ideologies. Further, practising teachers began to see that not all adult learning was naturally suited to some andragogical principles and, on the other hand, some andragogical principles were applicable in lower levels of education. That Knowles acknowledged such problematic issues is evident in the successive revisions of titles of the numerous editions of his work, with the 1980 subtitle being *From Pedagogy to Andragogy* and the 1984 edition *The Adult Learner: A Neglected Species*. The posthumous 2005 edition, compiled by associates of Knowles, includes an acknowledgement of the problem of adopting an ideological position rather than being pragmatically selective.[1] Knowles's conceptualisation of andragogical principles has had a marked impact on tertiary educational thought and practice, yet the adversarial nature of much of the ensuing dialogue has not always been edifying.

The following decades were characterised by a polarisation of a content-focused pedagogy (teaching children what they need to know) and student-focused andragogy (guiding adults to know what they want to know). This

---

1   Knowles et al., *The Adult Learner*, 69.

conflict has led generally to the ascendancy of andragogical principles, which rightly treat tertiary students as adults but have largely failed to see that, in an ordered society, even adults need guidance. In such a society, a licence to drive a vehicle is an adult opportunity, but there are rules governing the right application of that opportunity that are necessary. In all human relations, there are ethical codes that promote healthy relationships or curb unhealthy relationships among its members. So too in education, we are treating adults, yes, but adults who need the appropriate balance of freedom to determine and explore and structured guidance to reach the heights of their capabilities. An approach that focuses too intently on direct instruction can stifle creativity and produce cloned puppets, while an approach which focuses too intently on adult licence and self-direction can lead to chaos and the production of anarchic rebels. While both approaches have admirable intentions, such extreme outcomes are not desirable. Consequently, I suggest that we need to go beyond the pedagogy v. andragogy debate and find a different paradigmatic approach to teaching and learning. After more than fifty years as a teacher, I have come to advocate the paradigm of teaching learners to be learners—with all the best elements of direct instruction and individual exploration and creativity—as a helpful umbrella under which to conduct our educational business.

The theme of this book centres around the concept of producing lifelong learners who are proficient to confront and to master the ever-changing world into which they will be released upon graduation. Throughout the book, I present the notions of world view, curriculum, and pedagogy (as generally understood) as the three hand-in-glove building partners in the educational enterprise. The element of world view is a necessary starting and finishing point for the grounding of that 'sense-making' part of learning. It stems from the understandings brought to the learning enterprise by the learner as well as the operational and conceptual dispositions of the teachers and the institution. It is as the learners wrestle with the platforms that undergird their beliefs, values, and relationships that they affirm, modify or revolutionise their understandings. Learning that is unrelated to world view awareness and appreciation is hardly likely to lead students to make sense of that learning.

Curriculum is a relatively low priority in much tertiary educational literature, especially as it relates to theological education, yet it provides the raw building blocks on which the whole undertaking is based. Curriculum is also the blueprint that guides the construction in an ordered way so that all blocks will fit securely and purposefully into the final construction. Curriculum thus provides the structural integrity and ordered design of the entire complex of learning. In this book, the positioning of curriculum after world view and before pedagogy is intentional, as that is the order in which they should logically be considered. A curriculum that does not arise organically from a principled concept of how we make sense of things (our philosophical, theological, historical, and educational world view) will be a 'hit and miss' affair. Similarly, to proceed directly to pedagogical methods without first structuring a well-conceived curriculum is very much a 'cart before the horse' approach. The role of curriculum is essentially architectural.

Once curriculum has been planned, pedagogy plays the role of craftsperson in the building process. It is the art by which the whole edifice is crafted. It works the building blocks efficiently and sensitively into the complex construction whose ultimate purpose is the attainment of those desirable graduate attributes that evidence the dynamic learning capabilities required for successful life after graduation. Pedagogy is that craft that skilfully leads students to the highest levels of learning that they can reach and positions them to go on to even higher levels.

Thus, the process of learning is an educational excursion by which the student attains increasingly higher levels of learning throughout the course. There are stages of such attainment throughout the course which can be regularly identified, and graduation provides an opportunity to pause and reflect on the particular stage attained. But graduation is not the real end goal of the excursion. From there, the graduate is equipped to explore and to scale ever higher peaks of learning discovery. Teachers need to teach so that learners learn to be learners. That is a mathegenical approach to education, especially higher education, and most poignantly, theological education.

This book emerges from a graduate course delivered to teaching faculty in the Sydney College of Divinity. As such, the overarching tenor of the book is that of an experienced teacher in dialogue with professional colleagues, rather than a declaration of firmly held positions. While the book addresses key questions that need answers, it does so by prompting consideration and professional discussion of those questions. Such consideration may profitably be conducted in isolation. However, the ideal way of achieving this end is to read the book in association with collegiate faculty, within an 'iron sharpening iron' environment. In that way, the answers that emerge will be more specifically aligned with and thereby will serve the precise context in which the professional teaching is being conducted. That is, the book is designed primarily for those who are actively engaged as teachers in theological education, who wish to enhance their professional theory and practice as theological educators.

This work is structured around three pivotal areas of concern to all theological educators, as noted above: world view considerations, curriculum design, and pedagogical delivery. In keeping with the dialogical ethos mentioned above, the individual chapters of the book are designed to facilitate (though not necessarily require) professional peer engagement. Accordingly, each chapter incorporates a number of critical reflections to serve as prompts for such dialogue within a given context. Alternatively, the critical reflections may be used as a means of individual extension of the chapter's content to that same local context. In whatever setting the book is used—individual or group—the goal of such insertions is constantly to attain that local professional contextualisation of theory applied to specific practice.

PART 1

A WORLD VIEW FOUNDATION

1 | THE SHAPING OF A WORLD VIEW

In a recent interview on the topic of theological education, Rowan Williams, former Archbishop of Canterbury, observed that 'theological education is about the world that faith creates, or the world that faith trains you to inhabit' and that doing theology is 'making sense of (people's) lives'.[1] Those sentiments convey something of the importance of appreciating both the world that we have inherited and the world that we now inhabit. Theology may well be the understanding of a divine God, but it is an understanding shaped by and expressed in the context of a living humanity. Theological educators and their institutions have themselves been shaped and conditioned to understand and express both their theology and their educational agenda by their contextual philosophical, theological and historical heritage. 'The world' is also the context in which theological graduates will move and work. Accordingly, we commence our study by a consideration of those 'first principles' that combine to establish a coherent world view so we may understand clearly those worlds we have inherited and now inhabit. This world view thinking will pervade all aspects of our theological educational program, so it is well to ensure at the outset a good grasp of its characteristics and role.

A. PHILOSOPHICAL PRINCIPLES OF THEOLOGICAL EDUCATION

This section will explore the philosophical bases on which we ground our teaching of theology, which are often unspoken but always pervasive. All

---

[1] Williams, 'Theological Education Is for Everyone'.

teachers are heirs of a particular philosophical tradition and culture and often we seek—consciously or otherwise—to perpetuate that tradition and its associated culture. While that is neither irresponsible nor wrong in itself, such an observation requires us to be critically aware of the breadth of philosophical perspectives that influence our approach to teaching. That is, we need to be able to locate ourselves in a philosophical milieu and to have a critical appreciation of that milieu's strengths and limitations. Such a grounding is the first element in this treatment of the fundamental principles of theological education because it is the conceptual point of departure for any educational enterprise.

What Are We Trying to Do?

If we aim at nothing, that is what we are most likely to hit. A fundamental principle of any project—educational or otherwise—is to know what we are trying to achieve. As a basic starting point, we need to consider and to articulate what we are seeking to do as theological educators.

> *Critical Reflection.* Take a few minutes to think over what you are personally aiming to achieve as a teacher. Try to express, in a sentence of no more than around twenty words, your 'big picture' aim as a theological educator.

Consider first the aims of education in general. In the ancient world of the Greek philosophy of Aristotle and Plato, a central motif was that of *paideia* as a combination of all forms of cultural education. It was focused on the conscious development of 'virtue' or excellence of character. Hence, the purpose of education was the forming of a child to conform to established norms of excellence and devotion to the gods, which required knowledge of the truth, including the right pattern of theology, with virtuous conduct flowing naturally from such correct knowledge. Life skills were valued, but only so far as they enhanced virtuous character and conduct. A similar strand runs through the Jewish thought of Philo and Josephus, in which virtue is expressed as the fruit of *paideia* as it purifies the soul and promotes the highest goal of piety and godly conduct.[2] In this world, the imperative of education was 'training the child in the way he should grow', with a focus on imbuing the child with the knowledge

---

2 Wright, '"Integration" in the Ancient World', 22–31.

of the established virtues needed for noble adult living in their ordered society.

In the Western world (and probably most others in culturally varied ways), education has become more stratified. Now, the objective of primary education is essentially utilitarian, seeking to equip educands with the necessary skills and values to be a successfully surviving member of society, in terms of basic communication and computational skills, relational capacity, and socially determined values. Secondary education is aimed at developing individual perspectives and specialised interests related to adult development and roles, with a focus on gainful vocational preparation and social membership as good citizens. Tertiary levels of education have increasingly adopted the goals of specific vocational or professional preparation and development to fill respected roles in society, whether by personal contribution or in an employed career. Arching over all this is the dominant utilitarian objective of equipping people to be virtuous and competent members of a well ordered and culturally proficient society. Such pervasive aims drive virtually everything that happens in any educational program, from content to teaching methods, from curriculum design to cultural activities, from staff selection to student appointments, from resourcing to community engagement. The mechanics vary, but the principles are consistent.

> *Critical Reflection.* Pause for another moment. Can you see such principles at play in your personal education that you underwent prior to becoming a teacher? How did they (or other principles) drive your educational program?

When it comes to the governing principles of Christian education, do such aims still apply? In many ways, they probably do. The obvious difference is, of course, in the implied understanding of terms such as 'society' and 'values'. Christian education seeks to impart the necessary knowledge, skills and values to be a virtuous and competent member of society, with 'society' essentially becoming 'church', however that is to be defined. Whether it is aimed at instilling the needful knowledge of Jesus and his teachings as a platform for lifelong belief and practice or at applying biblical teaching deductively to personal or social problems, educands are meant to be equipped to fill a role as good Christian citizens, in social settings such as family, church, and wider societal relationships. But is there more than the simple substitution of 'christianised' terms involved? Is there a dimension of the informal curriculum that is concerned with the inherent person in the learning process, irrespective of utilitarian outcomes? Where does the development of 'being' stand in a tension with the development of 'doing'? When we start exploring this dimension, we are immediately discomforted by the loss of visibility—we can readily observe what people can do, but we encounter a haze when we try to observe what they are. Consequently, there is often a default reversion to the 'doing' philosophy, with a quest for a demonstration of doctrinal knowledge and ethical conduct rather than the more elusive goals of personhood. But does difficulty of observation justify neglect of what is vital? This is one of the issues we will constantly encounter throughout our teaching—and throughout this book.

> *Critical Reflection.* What do you value most in a student: theological orthodoxy, performative skills, personal character, or other? How do you prioritise what you deem most important in your teaching? At what cost does this priority come?

If the broad aim of Christian education is to produce virtuous Christian character and conduct, what is the distinctive aim of theological education? Because this is a core focus throughout this book, I will raise just a brief but, I think, essential philosophical issue here. I suggest that each of us will basically belong to one of two often contending philosophical camps when it comes to our driving aim of theological education. Is the aim of theological education conservative or progressive? Is it to guard the faith or to grow the faith? Is it the transmission of a received heritage or a regeneration of spirit? Is it to defend the faith and its historic expression or to challenge the faith and to create new expressions? Are we aiming to form learners into the pattern of good Christianity or are we aiming to transform learners into whatever pattern they can become, even if that is not our preferred pattern? One of the constant challenges in our teaching will be to come to grips with the tension between curating and cultivating the faith. Both elements have strong claims and even stronger advocates. Where we ultimately tend to stand will shape very much our approach to curriculum design, content, and delivery, so we need a deep understanding of this fundamental philosophical issue.

> *Critical Reflection.* This is a vital tension for you to address at all points of your theological teaching. Can you articulate ways in which you as a theological teacher may maintain the integrity of the received faith while fostering an individual (and potentially variant) expression of that faith?

A philosophy of education, then, is the articulation of a systematic scheme of thought that can guide practice. The challenge for the Christian (and thereby theological) educator is to render that philosophy explicit in the process of teaching. Robert Pazmino is a voice from a now somewhat removed past, yet that voice speaks as clearly now as it did earlier. Pazmino writes about Christian education in general, but the philosophical principles he propounds may be applied equally well to theological education. He suggests that philosophy is a foundational conjunct with Bible and theology because together, they provide cultural universals to guide belief and practice. Education, he claims, arises from a culture's philosophical roots. The challenge for a Christian educator is to articulate and sustain a philosophy of education that is consistent with a Christian world view. As a guide, he lists five classic characteristics of such a world view.

1. It has a *holistic* goal, trying to see every area of life and thought in an integrated fashion.

The notion of integration pervades the rest of the principles. If integration—of all aspects of thought and being—is a goal, then the learning process will be geared to that end rather than having a focus on blocks of content or discrete skills. It is as learners comprehend how all elements 'fit together' that they grow in making sense and in appreciating the worth of the education on offer.

2. It is a *perspectival* approach, coming at things from a previously adopted point of view which now provides an integrative framework.

Again, there is an integrative progression in the evolving world view of the learner. All tertiary learners come from a conditioning background that has shaped their perspectives. Those perspectives need to be recognised, understood, and respected so that new ways of thinking may be accommodated or, as appropriate, be allowed to modify or replace previous perspectives.

3. It is an *exploratory* process, probing the relationship of one area after another to the unifying perspective.

Exploration involves taking and guiding the learner on a journey of discovery that will involve new encounters and will yield new insights and understandings. Yet it is important that these new attainments be held in an accommodating cohesion lest intellectual and personal chaos ensues.

4. It is *pluralistic* in that the same basic perspective can be articulated in somewhat different ways.

The 'different ways' place the focus on the individual learners to have the freedom and the developing capacity to form and to express perspectives in their own ways according to their own life contexts. This can be invigorating for the learner, but it may simultaneously be discomforting for the teacher, especially if the learner's new perspectives turn out to be significantly different from those of the teacher.

5. It has *action outcomes*, for what we think, what we value and what we will do.[3]

It is probably a truism to say that an education that has no demonstrable outcome has little if any real value. The practical outworking of this principle is that learners need to be given opportunity to formulate and to express in word and action just what these outcomes are in terms of their personal situation.

Throughout all these principles, there is a clear focus on the personal integration of new experiences and new learnings in the life and thought of the learner. This is the hallmark of Christian education in the eyes of Pazmino.

> *Critical Reflection.* Think of your current or recent teaching of a particular class. How does (or may) this set of characteristics relate to that teaching? Would you amend this list of characteristics in shaping your personal philosophical approach?

Thus, Pazmino has provided a useful set of principles that may undergird a general approach to Christian education in generic terms. Stephen Brookfield is a secular college teacher who brings the focus onto general principles of tertiary education, applicable to any program regardless of content. His emphasis is once again on the learner *qua* learner. In his book *The Skillful Teacher*, he enumerates four core philosophical assumptions of effective college level teaching.[4]

---

[3] Pazmino, 'Philosophical Foundations', 81–110.
[4] Brookfield, *The Skillful Teacher*, 15–26.

1. **Skilful teaching is whatever helps students learn.**

In starting with what he admits may well be a trite truism, Brookfield acknowledges the complexity of its implementation in a class of variable learners. What aids one learner may well hinder another. Yet there is a need to be creative and flexible to promote as much learning for all students as possible. This requires discerning 'reading the room' to gauge the nature and diversity of the learners in order to match various approaches to teaching and learning. He presses the need for the teacher to be constantly asking, 'Will doing this help the students learn?'.

2. **Skilful teachers adopt a critically reflective stance toward their practice.**

A significant part of this critical reflection is the need to view classroom activity through the various lenses of participants, especially those of the learners. There is a fundamental integrity in modelling such critical awareness to students, but it also has the value of genuine respect for the persons of the student body, which is itself conducive to their growth as learners. Perhaps such continuous critical reflection is most important where it is least common, namely, among middle- to late-career teachers whose ways have been well established but whose teaching can imperceptibly become remote from the realities of student lives.

3. **Teachers need a constant awareness of how students are experiencing their learning and perceiving teachers' actions.**

This is an extension of that critical reflectiveness. Many teachers receive student feedback on their teaching and general levels of overall student satisfaction with the programs. However, some of the most significant components of such students' surveys are those comments that reveal how much, or how little, notice is taken of the ways in which students perceive the teacher's actions and relationships with them. It is easy to dismiss such observations as uninformed or as 'outliers' and so they need not be acted upon, but it is wise to keep in mind that how students feel about their experience in the classroom is as much a determinant of their likely success in learning as any expert knowledge or pedagogical skills of the teacher.

4. **College students of any age should be treated as adults.**

Perhaps another truism, but tertiary students *are* adults. However, that does not mean they are fully mature or experienced in all aspects of life, especially in matters of approaching a new discipline. So, they are not looking so much to their teachers to be best friends or colleagues, nor equal co-learners with equal authority in their programs—they want them to be effective guides in their learning. They will want teachers to be authoritative but not authoritarian; they want teachers to be respectful towards them by attempting earnestly to discover and address their concerns and difficulties; they want to know that what they are being asked to learn and to do is of significance and value to their personal lives and various aspirations.

As Pazmino emphasised the pervasive element of integration in Christian education, Brookfield's core assumptions focus clearly on the person and perspectives of the adult learners who enter tertiary education. The ever-present need is for them to be viewed as *learners* who are seeking to grow as persons in their life journey, under the guidance of expert and caring teachers who can lead them reliably and respectfully as adults into the new world of experience that is their course of learning. Such a philosophical understanding of the centrality of the person of the learner in the tertiary educative process will largely influence the teacher's approach to the teaching task. If the learners are not learning, is the teacher really teaching?

> *Critical Reflection.* How do you 'read the room' of your students to discern their perspectives on your teaching and their learning? Are there places in your teaching in which you have acted significantly on the results of such awareness to modify your ensuing teaching? What effect (if any) did this have—on you and on the learners?

From a broad understanding of general principles undergirding Christian education and a more focused set of core assumptions about tertiary teaching and learning, we can proceed to narrow the focus more specifically to consider some philosophical principles pertinent to tertiary theological education. Ervin Budiselić's article, 'An Apology of Theological Education', is written from an evangelical perspective, which dismisses the notion of elitist theological education and focuses on the kind and quality of desirable education. The article presents a survey of the historical development of theological education and contemporary challenges and concludes by arguing for the primacy of the Bible as the foundation and practical ministry as the goal of authentic theological education.[5] This combination of biblicism and pragmatism pervades much of

---

5   Budiselić, 'An Apology of Theological Education', 131–154.

the theological educational goals in evangelical traditions, while Catholic traditions tend to take a more philosophical approach, yet the two approaches are not radically different in outcome.

Recent work by Peter Mudge and Dan Fleming is representative of the more philosophical approach. In a two-part composition, entitled '"To Take You Where You Do Not Wish To Go": Extending the *Telos* of Online Theological Education', they offer a philosophical discussion of the ultimate end—the *telos*—of theological education.[6] They suggest three broad goals that are shared by theological institutions and that are critical in the articulation of that institution's *telos*:

1) that they will draw on the intellectual tradition of which they are a part
2) that they will seek to demonstrate a degree of excellence in teaching and in research according to the disciplines proper to their educational focus
3) that they will seek to respond to the specific concerns and needs of their student body as well as the world of which they are a part.

The ensuing discussion of *telos* stems from its Aristotelian roots as refined by Aquinas in the concept of 'flourishing', that is, the attainment of the best 'goal' or 'end' of some entity, be it animal or human, that is embodied in its living to its full potential according to the kind of creature it is. The discussion then moves to Newman's idea of the end goal of the university, which is based on the belief that the chief quality of an educated person is not simply a set of special knowledge or expert skills, but the enhanced capacity for judgement in the application of such knowledge and skills, in both individual personhood and societal relations. This involves the student in being not obsessed by a curriculum but geared towards the cultivation of a certain quality of mind. Thus, the *telos* of flourishing derives from the quest for truth, beauty, and goodness and other virtues, all based on the premise of a connected theology. Ultimately, the *telos* of theological education is viewed as the 'end persons' involved in the process.

What both evangelical (Budiselić) and Catholic (Mudge and Fleming) perspectives have in common is the focus on the human quality and growth of the learner on the basis of a cohesive (biblical or philosophical) theology, which is manifested in active and integrated outcomes, in service and relations. When we combine the general emphasis on integration, the pedagogical emphasis on the centrality of the learner and the learner's perspectives, and the desire for the

---

6   Mudge & Fleming, 'The "Who" of the Teacher Who Teaches', 106–122.
    Mudge & Fleming, 'The "What" of the Institution That Teaches', 123–139.

flourishing of the educated learner, we can formulate a cohesive philosophy of tertiary theological education that is geared to the development of a well-integrated learner with an enriched capacity for critical reflection, articulate communication of a philosophically cohesive world view and creative application in all dimensions of living as a theologically connected individual in both person and work.

> *Critical Reflection.* Is the desire for learners to 'flourish' a conscious component of your approach to teaching? Can you identify any specific evidence of such development in some learners? Are you comfortable if your students flourish in ways that are not expected or even desired by you?

B. THEOLOGICAL PRINCIPLES OF THEOLOGICAL EDUCATION

In Section A, we examined undergirding philosophical assumptions that shape our approach to teaching theology. Within that philosophical climate, there is a theological world view that perhaps even more deliberately influences that teaching. In this section, we will examine various elements of that theological world view as they impinge on our teaching, both philosophically and pragmatically. We will note that there is a two-way interplay of theological philosophy and educational practice, with both dimensions exerting significant influence on the other—what we think theologically shapes our teaching (and, in fact, may even be betrayed by our teaching; how we teach has a theological impact on learners (which may not always be the intended impact). Finally, we need to have a theological appreciation of the role of both Scripture and the Holy Spirit in our processes as theological educators.

The Theological Imprint on Theological Teaching

Underlying our world view as theological educators is a basic set of explicit or implicit theological understandings, which we do well to acknowledge and, when appropriate, to review. An essential starting point is to *understand theological education in relation to the* missio Dei. While most of us could clearly articulate a vision of the mission of God in the church, even such a formed understanding requires continual review.

The Roman Catholic Church has at times been charged with ultra-conservatism, but recently, Pope Francis, in his typically progressive vein, has offered a challenging and fresh vision of what theological education should—indeed must—be in the world of today and tomorrow. In his invigorating foreword to his constitutional statement issued in 2017 (which I recommend to the reading of Catholic and non-Catholic alike), he declared:

> This, then, is a good occasion to promote with thoughtful and prophetic determination the renewal of ecclesiastical studies at every level, as part of the new phase of the Church's mission, marked by witness to the joy born of encountering Jesus and proclaiming his Gospel, that I set before the whole People of God as a programme in *Evangelii Gaudium* [Joy of the Gospel].

This is followed by his call for such renewal as it relates to theological education, which warrants attention by all contemporary theological educators:

> The time has now come … to impart to ecclesiastical studies that wise and courageous renewal demanded by the missionary transformation of a Church that 'goes forth' (4).
>
> *The theologian who is satisfied with his complete and conclusive thought is mediocre* [my emphasis]. The good theologian and philosopher has an open, that is, an incomplete, thought, always open to the *maius* [the 'greater thing'] of God and of the truth, always in development (5).

Four fundamental criteria for a renewal and revival of the contribution of ecclesiastical studies to a church of missionary outreach are indicated:

- contemplation of the face of God, revealed in Jesus Christ as a Father rich in mercy;
- wide-ranging dialogue … for experiencing in community the joy of the Truth and appreciating more fully its meaning and practical implications … dialogue with Christians of other Churches and Ecclesial Communities … maintaining 'contact with scholars of other disciplines, whether these are believers or not';
- inter-disciplinary and cross-disciplinary approaches carried out with wisdom and creativity in the light of Revelation … the vital intellectual principle of the unity in difference of knowledge and respect for its multiple, correlated and convergent expressions

> ... ensuring cohesion together with flexibility, and organicity together with dynamism ... show[ing] its effectiveness in relation to the fragmented and often disintegrated panorama of contemporary university studies and to the pluralism—uncertain, conflicting and relativistic—of current beliefs and cultural options
>
> ... thinking capable of formulating a guiding synthesis ... to overcome the 'fatal separation of theory and practice' ... in the unity of science and holiness;
>
> - 'networking' between those institutions worldwide that cultivate and promote ecclesiastical studies ... the model for approaching and resolving problems 'is not the sphere... where every point is equidistant from the centre, and there are no differences between them', but rather 'the polyhedron, which reflects the convergence of all its parts, each of which preserves its distinctiveness'.[7]

There is so much to ponder in this papal document that it bears repeated visiting. When we teach theology, do we teach the systematic facts about God, or do we incorporate opportunities for seeing the face of God? How effectively does our teaching about God communicate a personal awareness of God? Does our theology teaching lead learners into the presence of God? Regardless of what theological nuances may pervade our understandings, such considerations are surely core to the development of a learner's capacity for God-knowledge. Francis's second point about dialogue in community is also significant in the teaching of theology. Given the very social nature of Christianity and its much-valued expression of *koinonia*, how much effort do we invest into developing such communal dialogue as a means of learning? If we exhort individual learners to be the best they can be, but fail to embody such striving in a communal sense, what is the theological impress made on the learner? It bears repeating that such individualism lies behind the aspect rated most lowly by student reviews of theological teaching (as also in other fields), namely, the limited opportunity to develop group relations as members of a learning community, as peers in a working and growing dynamic. Yet, such individualism is not limited to the student body. It also manifests itself in an institutional philosophy that can lead to fragmentation, even competition, among faculty, departments, and colleges. Francis's call for interdisciplinary cohesion leading to creative synthesis has as much to do with a

---

7 Holy See. *Francis Apostolic Constitution*, 8–10. While the Foreword (1–10) is in focus in this chapter, the whole Constitution will no doubt be of vital importance, especially to Catholic faculty.

theological mindset as it has to educational efficiency. To enlarge the scope of the learners' world view and theological horizons, such other-oriented philosophy will extend naturally to that networking beyond local parameters, which will take the learner to a fuller expression of self than is possible within the limited constraints of one institution. Such considerations are vital in the communal theological growth of the learners so they may take their place capably in the outworking of the divine mission through theological education.

While Pope Francis is operating within the philosophical framework of Catholicism, a not dissimilar emphasis emerges from an evangelical emphasis on Scripture-based theology. Mark Bailey addresses the overarching goal of theological education in terms of its theological purpose expressed as theological reflection and wisdom pertaining to a responsible life in faith. He frames his approach on fidelity to God-revealing Scripture, and so remaining faithful to God and his word is a core plank in his theological platform. The formative principles he espouses originate from that authority of Scripture, with its dual role of revealing truth and refuting error. While doctrinal fidelity plays a key role as an agency of learning, Bailey proceeds from there to a discussion of how theology is a call to the church to make God the centre of all its priorities. His theological framework—and hence, his foundation of theological education—is shaped around an orthodox view of Scripture and a Christ-centred trinitarian faith derived from the Bible and endorsed by the historical councils of the church, which is consistently purposeful in its goal.[8]

From a less doctrinal and more relational perspective, Darren Cronshaw focuses more on the avoidance of that cult of individualism in learning and promotes the idea of relationality, or communal dialogue in Pope Francis's terms, as a major theological component of theological teaching. He adopts the position that individualism is contrary to authentic ministry and that Christianity is at its theological core relational. Building on this premise, Cronshaw applies the concepts of relationality to the person of the theological teacher as a major consideration in both theological modelling and personal growth in education. He analyses the ways theological teaching is understood as relational sharing of one's life in various directions—sharing of that life with God, with colleagues, with students, and with the world. These are the aspects of relational teaching that pervade Cronshaw's thought, with the overarching goal of fostering deep and dynamic learning in authentic Christianity.[9]

---

8 Bailey, 'The Foundation and Shape of Theological Education', 23–42.
9 Cronshaw. 'The Relational Teacher', 338–351.

Critical Reflection. (Where) is there space in your teaching for the elements of:

- contemplation of God
- dialogue in community
- interdisciplinary cohesion and synthesis
- active networking?

If such space cannot realistically be a part of all units, how may they be achieved across a discipline or an entire curriculum, and thereby relate to the missio Dei?

A second theological consideration is the *theological impact of our educational philosophy.* How we approach the educative task conveys as much about theology as any of the curriculum content. If we present from a position of unquestionable authority (whether located in the position of a teacher or in the interpretation of a text), we are making a theological impress on the learner. The way we treat and relate to learners says much about our theology of humanity. In identifying the graduate attributes that we are seeking to foster, we declare our theological values. Even the way we structure our learning activities—for example, if they favour a particular learning style or emphasise individual over communal learning—will be a part of the theological shaping of the learners. Of course, the assessment of student work is inevitably perceived as an evaluation of the personal worth of the student. Norman DeJong's *Education in the Truth* suggests a hierarchy of questions to be addressed in formulating a philosophy of education. These questions also throw light on the theological impact of our educational philosophy on the theological formation of the student.

1) *Basis of authority.* What is the basis in which all thinking rests?
2) *Nature of persons.* What or who are persons?
3) *Purposes and goals.* What are the purposes and goals in education?
4) *Structural organisation.* In what structures and by what agents are these purposes and goals to be realised?
5) *Implementation.* With what resources, tools and methods will the purposes and goals of education be implemented?
6) *Evaluation.* How well are things being done?[10]

---

10 DeJong, *Education in the Truth*, 61–63.

Clearly, the position of authority adopted by teachers will be imbibed more naturally by the learner than all the theoretical concepts that may be presented. Teachers need to be aware not only of where their fundamental sense of authority lies—in the institutional appointment, in the formal position of master teacher, in scholarship, in Scripture, in philosophy, in ecclesiastical tradition, in society or in personal philosophy—but also of the impact on learners of the degree to which they tenaciously hold to that authority in their teaching practice. Aligned with such attitudinal perspectives is the attitude of the teacher to the persons of the learners. Are they blank pages to be filled with the teacher's scholarship and wisdom? Are they images of God who are growing beings whom the teacher is both privileged and responsible to influence? The authority of the teacher is one thing. The authenticity of the teacher in relations with learners is another. These two dominant elements in the above hierarchy shape all the subsequent considerations and are of vital importance in the theological impress on the student of the person, perspective and teaching style of the teacher.

> *Critical Reflection.* What is the basis of authority in your teaching—the teacher, the scriptures, the church's teaching, scholarship, or other? What impact does this stance on ultimate authority convey to your learners?

In all our teaching of theology, it is well also to keep constantly (and explicitly) in mind the continuous role of the Holy Spirit in the call and equipping of the teacher and the active involvement in the learner's growth. Teachers who are themselves Spirit-led learners will be more effective agents of Spirit-led growth in learners. When students imbibe that exemplary lesson, they will have learned a theology of ministry from their teachers' teaching.

Gary Newton begins his treatment of the role of the Holy Spirit in the teaching process with a summary review of the theological dimensions of the Spirit's direct role in teaching. From there, he focuses on the role of the Spirit in the personal and professional preparation and continuous calling of the teacher for the task of leading students in their theological journey. He addresses the irony that, although the Holy Spirit is typically acknowledged as the major catalyst to the educational process of learning and Christian growth, the Spirit's role is often overlooked or simply taken for granted, with all the implied neglect that accompanies such perspectives. Newton's argument is that, if we do not actively seek the Holy Spirit's cooperation in our teaching, that teaching will lack spiritual power and will fail to accomplish spiritual results. A teacher of theology needs to have confidence in the call and giftedness to perform the task and to sustain and empower that teaching. A continuing closeness to God becomes a way of life for the spiritually gifted leader. A commitment to excellence in preparation and the development of ever more effective teaching methods is a natural and ongoing outcome of such giftedness, calling, and spirituality. These are the Spirit-endowed qualities of an authentic teacher of theology.[11]

Dana Harris brings the focus onto the Holy Spirit's impact on the learner. She commences with the statement that, ideally, the goal of theological education is not limited to degree acquisition, but also includes some spiritual formation. Thus, she rejects the false dichotomy that is commonly created between theological education and spiritual formation. Harris is concerned with the nexus of instruction in the faith and spiritual formation, a nexus that is often sought but not always clearly visible or sustainable. Her aim is to show how theological education and spiritual formation are organically connected and that spiritual formation is an essential part of theological education. She examines the nature of both components, acknowledges the challenges involved in seeking their integration and offers some practical suggestions for implementation. There are numerous potential areas for spiritual engagement and learner development within formal educational delivery, be that on campus or online, but they all stem from two main bases: the nexus of spiritual formation and self-awareness, and a holistic view of God, self, and community. When learners are progressively led to a clearer appreciation of their own standing before God and the inherent limitations of their own selves; when they are exposed to the diversity of global views of God—then, they will more completely integrate the theological curriculum and their personal transformation. That is, as learners grow in their understandings and appropriations of theology, biblical studies, philosophy, and history, they are also being shaped spiritually by this study.[12]

> *Critical Reflection.* In what ways, if any, can you identify the calling and equipping of yourself by the Holy Spirit as a teacher in your current role? How significant is this in establishing confidence in and commitment to your task? How is this conveyed to your students? What structural components in your teaching encourage spiritual development in your students?

---

11 Newton, 'The Holy Spirit in the Educational Process', 125–129.
12 Harris, 'Theological Education and Spiritual Formation', 78–89.

Occasionally, there is proffered the argument that formal academic study is not necessary in the Christian life because the Holy Spirit is sufficient for all growth. However, we can readily find a clear *biblical mandate for theological education* as a collegiate exercise involving appointed teachers and dedicated learners. There are copious biblical references that we could adduce, but we need not resort to proof-texting for support. In a previous work, I have advocated for a biblically based transformative learning to be at the heart of the theological educative process. That advocacy was based on the imperative injunction in Romans 12:2 that exhorts a continuous process of personal transformation by means of the progressive renewal of the mind, in which 'renewal' implies not merely a filling of the mind, but a change of perspective of some kind, in character and conduct, involving the alignment of a person's moral and spiritual vision and thinking to the mind of God. As well as such individual development, the notion of the corporate and communal nature of Christianity requires a communal and relational expression of theological understandings and principles, within a holistically integrated world view. Thus understood, theological education involves more than the responsibility to preserve and perpetuate theological dogma (though it surely does include this). Additionally, it must view the person of the learner as a central focus in the overall theological process, since it is in the dynamic embodiment of theological understandings in the theologically integrated person that genuinely relational biblical transformation is manifest.[13]

To draw this section towards a conclusion, it is helpful to stand back a little to discern an overall theological impress that overlays virtually all theological institutions. One way of doing this is to examine the typical 'model' of theological delivery that bests fits our institution and the inherent theological perspective that shapes such a model. In asking the question, 'What makes something theological education?', Brian Edgar ranges across elements such as content, purpose, methods, ethos, and context. He notes that some forms of theological education stress one or other aspect more than another and may insist that one or other is absolutely fundamental. In such emphases, a theological imperative is involved. It is sometimes articulated, sometimes assumed, sometimes unconsciously imbibed, but in all cases, we do well to identify that imperative and either commit to it or adapt it as deemed appropriate. Edgar's work helpfully maps out the similarities and differences in four broad approaches to theological education. It reviews David Kelsey's bipolar approach to

---

13 Ball, *Transforming Theology*, 144.

theological education ('Athens' v. 'Berlin' models, with their respective emphases on the classical gaining of theological wisdom v. the enlightenment quest for rational enquiry and vocational utility) and Robert Banks's missional approach ('Jerusalem' model, which views theology as the outworking of mission with the goal of global conversion). He then extends these models to reach a fourth, confessional model that he labels a 'Geneva' model (with its emphasis on knowing God through the use of the creeds and the confessions, the means of grace, and the general traditions that are utilised by a particular faith community).[14] Bruce Allder has followed this sort of geographical categorisation by suggesting a further extension, namely, an 'Emmaus' model, with an emphasis on developing discipleship in community, with a central motif of journeying with others in a community of faith living in a diverse world and an emphasis on discipleship as lifelong learning within such a context.[15] While such 'models' typologies are broad and in places overlapping, they serve well to provide a typological map that can locate specific theological education programs and institutions and their emphases, thus providing a useful tool for self-awareness and reflective self-critique.

Finally, under the heading of theological principles (and no doubt as a reflection of personal authorial leaning), can we extrapolate some *biblical guidelines for theological education?* I suggest that such guidelines relate to the persons, the substance and the process of the educative enterprise. The primary persons are obviously the teacher and the learner. If a person is to assume the role of theological teacher, that person needs to be assured of both calling and equipping: the one grounds confidence (in what is a highly responsible role), the other develops competence (in what is a highly complex task). If a person is to be a theological learner, that person needs to be committed to the task, to be willing to take direction, to be open to growth in belief, practice, and character, and to contribute to the developing community of learning. All persons need to be aware of the continuous role of the Holy Spirit in calling, enabling, and growing. The substance of theological education needs to balance two dimensions of preservation of the faith as handed down by faithful forebears and the growing of the faith for its contemporary expression in mission. This requires a pervasive tension of respect for tradition and challenges to customs. In light of this tension, the processes of transmission and furtherance of

---

14 Edgar, 'The Theology of Theological Education', 208–217.
15 Allder, 'Theological Education Models Reconsidered'.

knowledge, development of academic and ministerial skills, and the formation of values and character are highly significant operational considerations. Biblical guidelines do not provide a 'cookie cutter' pattern for theological education. Rather, they posit a genuine respect for the value of all persons in the process, discernment in the selection, ordering, and treatment of contents and the need for integrity in all processes. Returning to the words of Pope Francis:

> [T]he development of peoples, essential for attaining justice and peace worldwide, 'must be well rounded; it must foster the development of each man and of the whole man'.[13] It also speaks of the need for wise men in search of a new humanism, one which will enable … [human persons to] find themselves'.[14] *Populorum Progressio* thus interprets with prophetic vision the social question as an anthropological question, one affecting the fate of the entire human family.[16]
>
> *Critical Reflection.* Can you articulate your own succinct set of biblical or other theological guidelines for teaching theology in your context?

C. HISTORICAL PRINCIPLES OF THEOLOGICAL EDUCATION

It is another of those truisms that theological understanding does not happen in a vacuum but is conditioned in its expression by its historical context. The same can be said of theological education. Its goals and approaches have been historically shaped by the context in which it evolved. While a knowledge of 'how things were done in the past' may seem detached from today's enterprise, it may be helpful to pause to review just how, despite all the historically shaped variations, there are some significant common strands that run through the whole history of theological education. By doing so, we are better placed to appreciate what elements are traditional in our approaches and why they remain significant, what we may have lost in the changes and how we may remediate that loss and what things we need to ensure we do not inadvertently perpetuate to the detriment of our current purpose. That is, an historical awareness assists us to discriminate between the essential and the peripheral in our educational mandate. We turn now to that evolving nature of theological education through history.

---

16   Holy See, *Francis Apostolic Constitution*, 3.

As we traverse the centuries, we will note a continuous dual thread of maintaining the integrity of Scripture and a commitment to theological fidelity, despite the great variations in methods of seeking those ends. As in many historical developments, theological education through the ages has been marked by a series of tensions that were not always maintained in balance. The prevailing intellectual climate of the time witnessed fluctuating swings in the quest to balance science or reason on the one hand with faith and subjective experiential religion on the other. Various hermeneutical approaches emerged as a result of these tensions, which became manifest in the associated models of theological education. In all such models, there were clear strengths, yet also patent shortcomings. We do well to analyse these models to extrapolate the good that in many ways has engendered much of our approaches to intellectual inquiry and learning today.

Historical Review of Theological Education

a. The Early Church

The Apostolic and Post-Apostolic period focused on the close reading of biblical texts. However, it was the approach to interpretation of those texts that would shape formal theological education. Essentially, the Bible was taken as a source book for theology, worship, and spirituality. This early church period was dominated by the need to counter the numerous emergent heresies within the embryonic church and to establish an articulate orthodoxy. *Irenaeus* (c130–200CE) appealed to tradition with his 'Rule of Faith' (with the bishop as the arbiter of orthodoxy) and so interpretation had to be in accord with the traditions of the church leaders, in an approach summed up as 'authoritative exegesis'. In light of the embryonic phase of the evolution of doctrinal orthodoxy in the face of the proliferation of diverse and divisive views, there was a natural emphasis on authoritative teaching of doctrine at this stage, with a heavy emphasis on the 'official' interpretation of biblical texts as endorsed by the bishop. Conversely, *Origen* (c185–254CE) was located in the more philosophically speculative milieu of Alexandria, where he developed a complex system of allegorical interpretation of layers of meaning to be interpreted at different levels. Yet even here, the approach was essentially the authoritative leading of students in the way of the particular school of interpretation. By the third century, formal schools had developed, with an eclectic mix of philosophy, rhetoric, and theology, which were viewed as the mainstays of advanced education. Such schools were particularly prominent in the two educational epicentres of Alexandria and Antioch, which provided the main stimulus for the ensuing Christological controversies that racked the church. Generally, Alexandria upheld the rule of faith interpreted by mystical allegory, while Antioch tended to emphasise rational analysis and historical development of Scripture. But in both centres, the main approach to learning was catechetical, which gave rise to numerous important creedal confessions, adherence to which became the touchstone of orthodoxy.

The influence of *Augustine* (354–430CE)—the 'father of Christian theology'—cannot be overstated for the development of theological education. While staunchly upholding the rule of faith, he skilfully integrated faith and reason. Augustine's first principle of interpretation specifies that it aims to lead readers to love God and other people: proper interpretation seeks to cultivate a proper, ethical, and devout Christian life. The first approach to understanding the text is to take it at a literal historical level, the 'real meaning' intended by the writer. However, when that is unclear or vexed, an allegorical meaning is to be sought. He developed three interpretive principles for determining such allegorical meaning: consult what other clear biblical passages say on the subject; consult the 'rule of faith' or traditional teaching; when these two are in conflict, consult the context to determine which of them commends itself. His method profoundly influenced all later hermeneutics and theological education, particularly notable in the work of Aquinas, Erasmus, and Luther, and undergirds much modern biblical exegesis. Further, his commitment to the monastic life as the arena of his own learning strongly influenced the formation of such theological communities as learning centres, a forerunner of the 'leisured study' of later theological institutions. In Augustine, we can observe the beginnings of modern exegetical method and the emergence of the sense of communal learning as the ideal of theological education.

> *Critical Reflection.* To what extent can/should the 'rule of faith' shape theological teaching today? How do various ecclesiastical traditions align with this? Is there such a pervasive 'rule' that plays out in your institution?
>
> *Critical Reflection.* How can we re-capture the ethos—even if not the form—of 'leisured study' within a community (such as in a monastic centre) in today's vastly different society? Is it still appropriate in our more technologically connected world?

b. The Medieval Period

In the cultural unity engendered by the Carolingian renaissance, the movement known as 'Scholasticism' emerged, and flourished during the eleventh to the fourteenth centuries in Western Europe. The Schoolmen (so called) were teachers of philosophy and theology, first among the monastic orders, and later (from about 1200 on) in the universities. Their main agenda was to reconcile reason and faith, philosophy and revelation. Their method was the first to use the system of organised textbook theology, coupled with a dialogical, or thesis, method of discovering truth. As such, they can be viewed as the forerunners of modern dialectical philosophy and empirical scientific method, as well as systematic theology. Key figures in Scholasticism were Anselm of Canterbury (c1033–1109, Archbishop of Canterbury, 1093–1109) and Thomas Aquinas (1224–1274).

Anselm's basis of teaching is as follows. Faith should precede understanding but understanding can in turn deepen faith through reason—'I do not seek to understand that I may believe, but I believe that I may understand: for this I also believe, that unless I believe I will not understand'. He produced a famous ontological 'proof' of God's existence, derived from the Platonic concept of reason. Peter Abelard (1079–1142) advanced this approach further in his famous *Sic et Non* (*For and Against*) (1122), in which he arranged contradictory statements from Scripture and the church Fathers to force students to reconcile them. Essentially, Abelard sought to understand his faith by the use of his reason. Others, such as Peter Lombard (especially in his *Book of Sentences*) and Thomas Aquinas were to use a similar critical dialectical method. Such a dialogical system of education can be observed clearly in the emphasis on critical reasoning and evidence-based argumentation that features so strongly in our contemporary educational principles, especially in the upper regions of higher education.

Aquinas, a Dominican, was the greatest philosopher and theologian of the medieval church and spent most of his life as a teacher at the University of Paris. He perfected the Scholastic method of enquiry and brought new dimensions to the use of reason—reason can only tell what God cannot be (similar to the Chalcedon Definition of 451); therefore, what is left gives an idea of what he is, that is, God's existence can be established philosophically. He claimed that there is no contradiction between faith and reason, so long as rational enquiry is properly conducted. Aquinas distinguished between faith, opinion, and knowledge—faith requires an act of assent, and is stronger than opinion, but less than knowledge since it lacks full comprehension. The influence of 'Thomism' has been enormous on both Catholic and Protestant thought and theological education, especially in the last 100 years.

It is worth noting that the medieval schools were not focused on practical ministry training, with pastoral service not featuring prominently. Rather, the emphasis was on philosophical and contemplative enquiry, which accounts for the importance of this movement to the rise of universities in medieval Europe, not all of which were devoted to theology.[17]

c. The Reformation Period

The Renaissance heralded a hitherto unparalleled era of questioning of the status quo, with an emerging ethos of humanism that saw dignity in the human individual quite apart from the authority of received tradition and social structures. The question tended to change from 'what must we do in an ordered society?' to 'why should we do this in our society?' This evolution from 'what' to 'why' is integral to an understanding of the general educational and specific theological reformation that it ushered in via the Reformation. Major contributors to theological educational approaches included Desiderius Erasmus (Dutch humanist scholar, 1466–1536), Martin Luther (German monk and university teacher, 1483–1546) and John Calvin (French Swiss theologian, 1509–1564).

Erasmus can be viewed as the chief founder of modern biblical criticism and hermeneutics. His insistence on returning to the original languages, and his historical understanding of ancient texts, introduced the philological element that has ultimately developed as a dominant motif in grammatical textual hermeneutics, that is, a more critical-historical and grammatical approach to exegesis, to arrive at a spiritual meaning. Luther, ably aided by his indispensable ally Philip Melanchthon, rejected the authoritative base of church tradition and leadership as well as what he termed the empty speculation of medieval allegorisation. He affirmed, with Aquinas, that Scripture had one essential meaning, the historical as expressed in the text. This textual meaning is to be discerned by applying the standard rules of grammar in the light of Scripture's original historical context. Thus, the groundwork for grammatical-historical exegesis was cemented. Calvin developed the grammatical-historical method of Erasmus and Luther, focusing the place of meaning in the historical interpretation

---

17 For an introduction to some key aspects of scholastic thought, refer to the selection of readings in one of the numerous collections of historical church documents, such as H. Bettenson and C. Maunder (eds.), *Documents of the Christian Church*; H. T. Kerr (ed.), *Readings in Christian Thought*, Part II; or A. E. McGrath (ed.), *The Christian Theology Reader*.

and developing the spiritual message from the text. More influentially than anyone else, Calvin insisted that the only true meaning was that intended by the historical author, and he stridently condemned interpretation that sought to reach beyond that.

In the face of such largely Protestant impulses, the Roman Catholic position solidified by way of restricting theological education to seminaries as spiritual communities that would provide theological and ministerial training. Thus, the system of separating ministerial formation from the broader theological educational system developed and remained very much the form until Vatican II in the twentieth century. The advent of Protestantism engendered a renewed emphasis in the Council of Trent (1545–1563) on the role of tradition and the sacraments within the Roman Catholic Church.

> *Critical Reflection.* What aspects of Scholasticism and the Reformation remain valid for today's theological education? Do you see them evidenced in your own teaching? Are there elements you could gainfully add to your teaching approaches? Are there any elements that persist but that need to be modified or even removed?

d. The Enlightenment and Beyond

The eighteenth-century period of the Enlightenment presented a major challenge to Christianity (and Christendom), with serious questioning of authority (especially of the church), tradition (in social structures, science, and theology) and the role of reason: 'reason' became almost deified. In many ways, this was not so much a revolutionary twist but was rather the convergence of those developing fore-running influences of rationalism, humanism, and critical questioning, which combined to generate the seemingly unstoppable rise of secularism. This form of secularism was, in its own way, an evolution from the former Christian humanism of the Reformation to a secular humanism that rejected the notion of supra-rationalism. Two major thinkers who influenced greatly the emergence of enlightenment thinking in theological education were Immanuel Kant (1724–1804) and Friedrich Schleiermacher (1768–1834).

Kant reacted against the notion of the sufficiency of 'natural religion' and developed a dialogue between philosophy and theology. His thinking on epistemology (*Critique of Pure Reason*) and ethics (*Critique of Practical Reason*) led to a 'critical' re-examination of the rationalism and empiricism of the eighteenth century and opened the way for the more speculative, philosophical theology of the nineteenth century. Reason, he said, pertains to phenomena (appearances of things), not to noumena (things-in-themselves): 'I have therefore found it necessary to deny knowledge in order to leave room for faith'. In his later work (especially *Religion Within the Limits of Reason Alone),* both the rational and the ethical merge to give his own ingenious and controversial interpretation of Christianity: essentially a religion of ethical duty, with Jesus as the archetype of ideal humanity.

Schleiermacher's theology was marked by a strong emphasis on the subjective element in Christianity. The basic thesis of his reconstructed theology was derived from Romanticism: a reaction against the strictures of regulated forms and content (especially in literature and art). This led to a cult of the individual, whose superiority is drawn from emotions, imagination, and creative powers, rather than from the intellect. He developed a very subjective religion, the heart of which consists in a certain quality and structure of the religious affections of which theological statements are but the verbal expression. Therefore, all doctrines must be shown to be related to the religious self-consciousness, a principle that involves a radical transformation of doctrines such as creation, original sin, and the divinity of Christ, to name just a few. The main aspects of Schleiermacher's theology are: (1) revelation is knowledge of God through corporate experience, not a body of doctrine propositionally revealed, and (2) redemption is an increase in God-consciousness.

Such forms of radical individualism and subjectivity influenced theological education deeply and came to its climax in nineteenth-century liberalism. The Tübingen School (from the University of Tübingen) became the centre of nineteenth-century German radical biblical criticism, under the leadership of FC Baur (1792–1860). The Tübingen School teaching was characterised by an anti-supernaturalistic attitude to history and tendency criticism in the interpretation of biblical writings, which anticipated to a degree the later development of Redaction Criticism. Baur's was an anti-theistic, non-supernatural approach to history and Christian origins. A more radical shift in biblical studies came with David Strauss (1808–1874) and his concept of 'higher criticism', with its radical interpretation of the historical and theological backgrounds of biblical documents in place of 'lower criticism' with its research in the biblical texts and versions. Strauss developed the key concept of 'myth' or '*mythus*', a technical term designating what was non-historical in the Bible though not necessarily untrue religiously or theologically. That is, the Gospel records of Jesus' life, sayings and miracles are taken as historically untrue, but they communicate a great deal of legitimate theological interpretation. Such concepts as these were to influence greatly the course of nineteenth- and twentieth-century liberalism, which has dominated theological scholarship, and thus, education of the modern period. Though it is not wise to reduce any set of philosophical concepts to a simplistic statement, nonetheless the following ideas may provide a useful summary of the main elements of liberal theology and biblical study:

i. an eagerness to discard old orthodox forms if judged to be irrational in the light of modern knowledge or irrelevant to what was regarded as the central core of religious experience
ii. a confidence in the power of human reason when guided by experience
iii. a belief in freedom
iv. a belief in the social nature of human existence
v. a faith in the benevolence of God and the goodness of creation
vi. enthusiastic endorsement of critical scholarship.

Critical Reflection. How far does Enlightenment thought influence your theological teaching? To what extent can such thought be viewed as both an improvement on previous traditions of learning and a weakening of such learning? Are there points at which such broadly pervasive Enlightenment thought generates tensions in your teaching? If so, how do you resolve them?

e. Contemporary Ideologies

Over the past fifty years or so, there has been a marked development of recasting theological education from emerging ideological perspectives. Groundbreaking theological works such as Paulo Freire's *Pedagogy of the Oppressed* (1968) and Gustavo Guttierez's *A Theology of Liberation* (1971) set the scene for numerous critical hermeneutical approaches to both biblical interpretation and the role of theological education. Freire advocated that teaching should challenge learners to examine power structures and patterns of inequality within the status quo, with education viewed as a means to transform oppressive structures. Guttierez viewed theological education as a means of fighting oppression and promoting social justice. Since then, many other expressions of social ideology have been articulated, with perspectives ranging across the spectrum of political, economic, ethical, gender, ethnic, and other special interest groups. Such philosophical-theological perspectives have been supplemented by developments in transformative educational theory, with various applications of the learning theory popularised in the work of Jack Mezirow in the 1970s and beyond. Here, the role of education is to transform the learner's world view by means of disorienting dilemmas that necessitate a new perspective. A specifically Christian application of such elements pervades the work of John Hull in the 1990s and 2000s (for example, 'Christian education and the reconstruction of Christian faith', 2006), wherein he posits a theology of resistance as the undergirding concept of Christian education of adults. This educational approach takes Mezirow's disorientation a step further to the point of disruptive inclusion. Hull presents the societal structures that oppress, and hence, exclude from successful society the poor and the oppressed not as barriers to be overcome but as identifiers to be resisted and re-imagined as opportunities to establish a revised sense of inclusion. That is, the stigmatic markers of their social exclusion are to be critically re-interpreted as badges of a positive identity.

All these ideological approaches have had various expressions in theological education in terms of its purpose, its curriculum, and its pedagogy. Yet they all have one basic thing in common: the liberation emphasis on education, especially theological education, as a means of attaining inclusion and advancement of all people groups on an equitable basis and the elimination of social barriers and oppression. So it is that Hull's pedagogy of resistance, for example, fits well in a context of a group's sense of 'otherness' or marginalisation. Those who feel alienated or 'other' can thereby establish a newly identified sense of belonging and validation. However, care is needed that we do not impose a pseudo-sense of 'otherness' to effect some preconceived need for radical change. Worse still is the potential to impose a sense of guilt on those who do *not* feel that they are 'other' but in fact already have a clear sense of self and their belonging. The 'outsider' needs to be allowed to gain and enjoy belonging, but the 'insider' need not be made to feel guilty. All have the right to a positive self-awareness and sense of belonging.

> *Critical Reflection.* Are there specific ideological approaches that influence your teaching programs? How much do these influences shape the content and methods of those programs?

f. Australian Theological Education[18]

A helpful review of historical developments in Australian theological education is presented in the publication edited by Andrew Bain and Ian Hussey, *Theological Education. Foundations, Practices, and Future Directions*.[19] Bain's chapter, entitled 'Theological Education in Early Christianity: The Contribution of Late Antiquity', provides background by analysing the characteristic emphases of theological education in the period of the early church, with particular note of the later patristic writers' concern for character development and scriptural immersion. Bain also suggests that some of the characteristics of the period commonly viewed as negative may, in fact, be of constructive value for the task today.[20] In particular, he draws parallels between the patristic period's methods and the educational needs of today, noting the fact that learners were not turning inward and away from pagan learning but were relating critically to it as members of the wider society, with a strong emphasis on the foundational role of Scripture in theological education, commonly expressed and learned in the context of community ministry. Such a nexus of elements has become a marked feature of contemporary theological education, especially in evangelical quarters, in which the focus is on equipping learners to be ministers in dialogical engagement with their wider society.

Following Bain in the same publication, Graeme Chatfield takes up the historical analysis of the various models that emerged in sixteenth-century Europe, a period that is foundational for Protestantism. Chatfield reviews the emergence and ethos of three expressions of theological education: universities, seminaries, and vernacular. He does this by relating the models to key figures of the Protestant Reformation, with a final note of how similar issues have recurred in contemporary Australia. Of particular note here is the way the historical polarisation of the classical 'academic' academy (mainly in universities) and the more 'spiritual' theological and Bible colleges has gradually waned as the colleges have tended to merge into the academy, with a consequent blurring of any distinctives, especially in curriculum matters. That is a point worth noting and its impact warrants consideration.[21]

---

18   This sub-section is geared to the primary context of writing, namely Australian theological education. While the specific details are local, the overall thrust is comparable with many other postcolonial Western nations' development in various local expressions.
19   Bain & Hussey, *Theological Education*.
20   Bain, 'Theological Education in Early Christianity', 47–59.
21   Chatfield, 'Models of Western Christian Education and Ministerial Training', 60–73.

The third chapter from this publication is a historical review of the Australian scene. Rather than a chronological review, this chapter adopts a thematic approach, which provides a series of snapshots of theological education from the perspectives of students, faculty, pedagogical approaches, and developing relationships. In the concluding remarks on the contemporary scene, the chapter indicates some probable directions and potential challenges that are currently emerging.

Some major themes to have emerged in Australian theological education can be summed up as follows.[22] With origins in the mid-nineteenth century as essentially in-house denominational training for clergy, theological education in Australia has had two discernible periods in its development. For one hundred years, the approach was the relatively classical education along British or Roman lines, with a set curriculum of Bible, Theology, Languages, Church History, and Philosophy. Programs were designed and delivered on the basis of full-time face-to-face lecture delivery to a small number of mainly male candidates for ordained ministry. Theology was excluded from Australian universities and so the denominational theological colleges were established to meet the need for a continuing supply of clergy. This led to a widespread system with a narrow limitation of personnel, curriculum, and teaching style, based on lectures to ready recipients under the direction of the churches. From the 1960s, the scope broadened with the emergence of interdenominational evangelical Bible colleges and the opening within many denominational institutions to lay, part-time, and female students. With access to governmental financial support from the 1990s, there has been a rapid increase in enrolments, including in several universities that now include theology programs. As with the Australian educational scene in general, there has developed a greater emphasis on vocational outcomes which, in terms of theological programs, means ministry in its many forms. Thus, curriculum has expanded, and teaching methods have become more creative, with a far greater emphasis on ministry and interpersonal skills and a correspondingly reduced emphasis on the classical components to address the demand that graduates be 'fit for purpose' (that is, ministry purpose) upon graduation. There have been associated social, political, and financial challenges, but the most recent educational challenge has emerged from the identification of the need for integration of the increasingly fragmented approach to program delivery.

---

22   See Ball, 'A Thematic History', 88–100.

g. And Today?

In introducing his book *Theology, Church, and Ministry: A Handbook for Theological Education*, David Dockery asserts that, throughout its history, the church has maintained a commitment to theological education that takes seriously the responsibility for such education to help people develop a theologically informed way of viewing the world, and to make Christian responses to life using Christian strategies and motivations for ministry. From his review of the historical developments within theological education, he concludes that theological education in the twenty-first century must carry out the essential teaching task commissioned by the risen Christ (Matt. 28: 19–20), centred on the threefold goals of building up the church, leading the church to maturity and leading the church to unity. Theological institutions, therefore, have a responsibility to prepare ministers for the issues they will encounter in the churches while remaining focused on the classical disciplines of theology. Theological education must be academically sound, grounded in the Scriptures, Christ-centred, and ministry and mission focused. In such terms, Dockery captures the ethos of much of the general aspiration of contemporary theological education, with its responsibility to prepare graduates for the issues they will encounter in the churches while remaining focused on the classical disciplines of theology. Inherent in all this is the need to develop well-integrated learners, who are not marked by narrow specialisation of knowledge or skills, fragmentation of thought or practice or disconnection from the church or its surrounding society.[23]

Kevin Lawson, writing at the end of the twentieth century, noted some significant developing trends and opportunities the church faces at the beginning of the twenty-first century, with ramifications for both Christian education in general and theological education in particular. He noted the increasing splitting of more focused educational ministries, such as children's ministry, youth ministry and others, to which colleges are responding by offering more focused (and, I suggest, potentially more fragmented) programs of study than previously. The advances in digital technology and the rapid growth of Christian music and other popular cultural forms are being progressively explored for educational purposes, largely in terms of resourcing and modes of delivery, but (I suggest) we should also note the deeper impress of such developments on the human development of learners. Finally, he noted the accelerated secularisation of (Western) society, which is causing Christian parents to turn away from secular

---

23 Dockery, *Theology, Church, and Ministry*, 3–22.

education forms, but which we should also note increases the responsibility of theological education to meet such a rising challenge.[24]

So then, the contemporary scene of theological education globally involves a complex contemporary quest for integration of so many competing and at times directly conflicting goals. There is the need for expert theological knowledge and analysis and a corresponding need for the skills to communicate in a technologically changing and increasingly diverse world. There is a demand to equip learners for social engagement and the contextualisation of their learning. There is the desire to maintain the traditions and core tenets of Christianity and for effective engagement with a wide spectrum of Christian thought and expression. There is a growing sense of ecumenical learning and appreciation, especially in the face of alarming and rampant secularism (in the churches and in broader society). In some ways, theological institutions are struggling for survival, yet they must constantly strive to make progress in their mission. Two words that seem apposite to our age of theological education are 'complexity' and 'challenge'. Theological educators need to work together to address such perennial issues.

> *Critical Reflection.* What are the key challenges you are facing today in your teaching? What strategies do/could you employ to meet those challenges?
>
> *Critical Reflection.* Review the historical approaches to theological education. In what ways do the various approaches enhance the nexus between scholarship and faith development? Are there any newly appreciated elements from this review that you can effectively incorporate into your teaching? If so, what benefit would that achieve for learners?

D. A FINAL WORD

Considerations of world view often tend to become rather hazy concepts. From the above discussion, it is clearly a very complex phenomenon. We tend to assume that the things we take for granted in our world are in fact the natural

---

24 Lawson, 'Historical Foundations of Christian Education', 17–25.

order of things, yet all our common approaches and values have been shaped by a long evolution of philosophy, theology, and culture. As theological educators, we need to be astute—and clear—in defining where we stand and how we make sense of our lives in the face of and in relation to an environmental context that may conflict with our personal position. There is a need to appreciate both the ambient world view of the world we inhabit and the embodied world view by which we make sense of our faith-based world. That there is a distance between the two has always been the situation of the church. The role of theological education, therefore, is sometimes to provide learners with an apologetic defence of its position, but more commonly, to help them to establish a bridge to span the gulf. As learners—and teachers—become more aware of the core elements of the various dimensions of world view, they will become better equipped to promote dialogue and enhance their growth as capable lifelong learners.

PART 2
THE ARCHITECTURE OF CURRICULUM

2 | CURRICULUM PRINCIPLES AND DESIGN

Curriculum is arguably the core of any theological institution's *raison d'être*, its distinctive and defining characteristic. Curriculum provides the chassis upon which educational programs ride and decisions around curriculum are a priority to address before attempting any form of delivery. Curriculum is the shape of the course of studies: the selection, location and sequence of the individual blocks of study that comprise the overall program of learning. However, despite much recent progressive thinking on education, many theological curriculum structures are almost 'set in stone' as they seem simply to perpetuate the structures and content inherited from (the teachers') past educational experience. While there is much common dissatisfaction expressed about things such as a crowded curriculum, a fragmented curriculum and an often-irrelevant curriculum, there has been remarkably little attention paid to any notion of a radical overhaul of curriculum—perhaps it is in the 'too hard' basket both politically and culturally. While curriculum design and development are often the special province of a select group of senior faculty members, all teachers need to be aware of the ramifications of the curriculum they are delivering for the effectual outcomes of the study program. Accordingly, in this section, we will first explore various considerations that influence curriculum in theological education, then we will suggest a number of general guiding principles of curriculum. We will conclude with a more focused analysis of managing curriculum design, delivery, development and review. In this way, we seek to gain a deeper understanding of the significance of the somewhat intangible but always present factors, such as the institution's philosophical tradition, which is the essential starting point of curriculum, and the desired graduate outcomes, which are the desired end of curriculum. The main thrust of this and following chapters is to discern the vital role of curriculum in fulfilling the purposes of these two elements.

A. THE PERVASIVE INFLUENCE OF PHILOSOPHICAL TRADITION ON CURRICULUM

In his development of principles that guide curriculum design, Fritz Deininger begins from a consideration of the 'calling and ethos of the institution', followed by the 'educational philosophy of the institution'.[1] It follows from this that a fundamental principle of curriculum design is that all elements should align with and contribute to the overall mission and ethos of the institution. There are two key terms in that statement: *mission* and *ethos*. It is obvious that curriculum designers and deliverers need to be fully cognisant of and committed to the overall mission of the institution, else disjunction and discord will ensue. However, the ethos of the institution, developed through the institution's traditions—sometimes over a long history—has perhaps an even greater impact than the explicit mission statement on the way curriculum is designed and delivered. Most theological institutions are created to serve a larger institutional body and are rarely in a position to be totally autonomous in their curriculum design. Consequently, an understanding of the influence of the philosophical tradition of that wider body is a primary consideration in curriculum development.

The history and the structure of the wider body and the educational tradition of the teaching body will have a determinative bearing on curriculum. Even when officials of the wider body are not directly or formally involved, the philosophical and educational traditions are powerful influencers. Table 2.1, with typical Australian bodies, suggests some general ways in which different kinds of organisational ethos influence the development of curriculum. The inference we can draw from this table is the more hierarchical the control, the less the potential for local innovation; the more local the control, the greater the potential for local innovation.

---

1   Deininger & Eguizabal, *Leadership in Theological Education Volume 2*, 11–36.

Table 2.1: Theological Education: Who rules? So what?[2]

Dominant Influence	Typical Institutions	Impact on Curriculum Content and Delivery
Global ecclesiastical regulation	Roman Catholic, Orthodox, Nazarene	Global ordination rules set limited parameters of courses. Strong priority in content and delivery given to needs of seminary/ordination candidates.
National/state hierarchical ecclesiastical systems	Anglican, Uniting Church, Presbyterian	Ordination requirements for candidates dominate curriculum content. Strong distinction in delivery between candidates and general (non-ordination) students.
Congregationally autonomous ecclesiastical traditions	Baptist, Churches of Christ (typically within teaching consortia because of small size)	Ordination requirements are accommodated but not exclusive. No discrimination between ordination and general students in delivery. Greater local college flexibility in curriculum decision-making.
Locally independent colleges	Pentecostal Colleges, Bible Colleges	Technically not limited by external requirements, but commonly connected to a local church or other informal local network. No discrimination between ordination and general students. More freedom to develop and innovate at college level.
University regulation	Public universities (ACU, CSU, Flinders, Murdoch), Private universities (UD, UNDA)	Legally separate from church control (and explicitly not faith-based in the public universities), yet strongly influenced by requirements of participating churches (specifically Roman Catholic, Anglican, Uniting Church). Curriculum is subject to university regulation, commonly demanding rationalisation of offerings and paring down of (typically) small classes. Innovation prompted by churches is slow and limited.

2 Derived from Ball, *Transforming Theology*, 45.

> *Critical Reflection.* What influence on your college's curriculum content and structure does the philosophical tradition of your wider institution have?

However, it is not just the wider body that has such influence. The philosophical grounds of the college itself also shape approaches to curriculum. How a college views its role will establish a baseline for all curriculum considerations. Traditionally, theological colleges have largely viewed their roles as *conservators of important tradition.* Such a philosophical perspective places great value on the primary educational domain of transmission and reception of special and/or new knowledge, of the preservation and perpetuation of traditional knowledge and wisdom. The past half-century or so has witnessed the emergence of a more *entrepreneurial* approach to theological education, with an increasing emphasis on marketable skills (of ministry) and critical skills (of methods of data processing), with an eye to meeting the market and its identifiable needs. Within this philosophy, method rather than content typifies the curriculum. Most recently, theological colleges have moved towards expressing their ideal as *transformers*—of both individuals and society. Such a philosophical perspective views the role of curriculum as being to form a person by means of personal appropriation of concepts that become a part of the person's identity and thereby shape the whole of one's life.

Table 2.2: Institutional Ethos and Curriculum

Institutional Ethos	Philosophical Emphasis	Curriculum Focus
Conservator	Preservation and perpetuation of traditional knowledge and wisdom	Knowledge transmission and retention
Entrepreneur	Marketable and critical skills	Skills of data processing and application
Transformer	Individual and societal reform	Concept integration and appropriation

All three philosophical positions will focus on a particular approach to curriculum emphasis, which will be shaped to align with those philosophical traditions. Each will place a high value on a particular domain of learning, with associated learning characteristics prominent in the delivery of curriculum, as well as in pedagogy, as we will examine in later chapters. Typically, a college will ascribe theoretically to 'all the above' but in practice, the dominant philosophical ethos will determine the weight given to various curriculum elements.

> *Critical Reflection.* Can there be a coherent philosophical perspective in a federal type of consortium? What is the dominant philosophical perspective of your college? Is there consonance or dissidence between your college's dominant ethos and that of your accrediting body? To what degree does your personal philosophical perspective align with such institutional tradition?

Where We Are and Where We Could Be

While it is arguably core to theological education, it is arguable also that curriculum is the 'poor cousin' of theological education consideration. There has been very little serious attention paid to theological curriculum, despite the fact that it is what students have enrolled in to be better equipped to fulfil their aspirations, however those aspirations are understood. Yet while these aspirations have become progressively more diverse and sophisticated, the traditional classical curriculum still dominates, with some tinkering only in matters of subject combinations and majors, and the limited incorporation of practical ministry or fieldwork units, but nothing on the core elements of curriculum. Curriculum is somehow the sacred cow of theological education, despite common criticism of shortcomings of graduate outcomes. For more than a decade, there has been much criticism of the fragmentation and overload in curriculum, with the teaching of discrete and seemingly disconnected disciplines, quite removed from the context of any ministry or other vocational setting. Bain and Hussey have summed up much of the concern about the effectiveness of theological education, and by implication of its curriculum, as 'a failure to produce skilled leaders in ministry formation', which is the particular reference of their analysis.[3] As with many others, they also note Perry Shaw's observation that 'curricular reform is one of the most pressing needs facing theological education in the twenty-first century'.[4] Accordingly, our focus now is on some underlying principles of curriculum design and delivery that will

---

3   Bain & Hussey, 'Five Years On', 136.
4   Shaw, *Transforming Theological Education*, 17.

provide a framework for any further consideration of such a significant topic.

A fundamental and indeed a primary consideration is the issue of the primacy of content vis-à-vis the learner. In some ways, this lies at the core of what it means to teach learners to be learners, the central objective of this book. Acknowledging this tension and how we address it warrant frank discussion at the outset because our response to this issue will shape our overall approach to all elements of curriculum design as much as it does our pedagogy.

Traditional curriculum has been content centred: that is, it has been driven by the attempt to teach in a limited time (typically three or four years) all the theology necessary for adequate ministry. The stated aims of most theological education providers are typically expressed in terms of the systematic acquisition of the traditional content areas of theological studies—Scripture, Theology, Church History, Philosophy—to provide 'a thorough and comprehensive grounding in the principal areas of theological studies' and, occasionally, as a theological base for ministerial practice. In general, undergraduate and many postgraduate coursework awards feature a strong emphasis on a first year devoted to introductory surveys in various sub-disciplines and a heavy concentration of biblical and theological studies throughout the course, with a relatively lesser emphasis on practical units and even less on personal developmental units. There are many strong reasons for such a structure, as students consistently state that they are wanting to be immersed in Bible and theology as a major part of their enrolment. There is also the passionately held commitment to the faithful transmission of the tenets of the faith long held sacred and that form the backbone of the historical church of which the contemporary church is a living part. There are other intrinsic factors involved, including the overall institutional ethos and the ecclesiastical tradition of the constituting body, often a distinctive church denomination that seeks to further its stated mission. In recent times, there has evolved the additional extrinsic factor of external or governmental accreditation, which relies heavily on benchmarking of both standards and structures. All these forces are at play in the construction of the curriculum, and all are valid elements that need respect and engagement. However, the combination of these forces tends to lead to uniformity and stagnation in curriculum design and development, as there is a tendency to fit everything into the safety net of 'what we have always done'.[5]

Such sound reasoning notwithstanding, there are serious shortcomings in such a content-driven curriculum. The essence of the sacred content needs to be

---

5   See Ball, *Transforming Theology*, 33–49, for a general overview of the Australian scene.

maintained, but the way it is incorporated needs review. The ambitious futility of seeking to provide a comprehensive—or even an adequate—core of knowledge and how to communicate that knowledge in a variety of ministerial contexts all in such a limited time frame has often been noted, but rarely addressed. Obvious flaws emerge when we consider who determines and selects (and thereby limits) the 'necessary' content, the relevance of typical sequencing and structure of studies, the regular complaints about gaps in the curriculum and the ad hoc nature of attempts to fill those gaps, and the inbuilt obsolescence of much industriously prepared content. It is traditional and comforting to base curriculum on predetermined and relatively fixed content, but this very comfort generates the fragmentation and non-contextualised teaching so often lamented. Students learn to recite much knowledge, but there remains doubt as to how far they progress in learning to be effectual independent and agile learners beyond the limited corpus to which they have been exposed.

A content-centred curriculum seeks to draw the learner into the world of theology. Conversely, a learner-centred approach seeks to infuse theology into the world of the learner by placing the emphasis on the learner as the centre of the educative process. Such an approach sits more logically into the desire to produce learners in theology. After all, the aim of theological education is to produce theologically grounded and competent people rather than walking theological encyclopaedias. However, a learner-centred approach has its difficulties, which include the loss of control over correct and revered doctrine, the impracticality of individually tailored programs and the lack of consistency and reliability of knowledge outcomes. Further, many theological institutions are strongly governed by church mandates to incorporate specified content for clerical accreditation, so curriculum development is circumscribed by such external controls. So, how can a learner-centred approach work to produce capable learners while retaining fidelity to the historical church and its requirements?

First, let us be clear that content matters—there can be no such thing as a content-less curriculum. In a former career as a high school English master, I experienced three decades of evolving educational philosophy, which saw the transition from a syllabus based on formal grammar, Shakespeare and classical literature to an obsessively learner-centred approach that sought to 'educe' from within the learner what was already latent, and so encouraged students to choose topics and themes of exploration, with no concern for compositional formalities or classics. Over a period of around fifteen to twenty years, we progressed from having a high degree of literate competence and literary awareness among students, albeit within a limited range, to a situation in which a newly appointed head of an English department had never learned basic grammar or syntax, had never read any Shakespeare and knew only those topics of transient sociological interest in a past day. So yes, content matters—it always has done and always will do.

If, as Rowan Williams suggests, doing theology is making Christian sense of the learners' lives, it will be at times challenging to both the learner and the institution, since sense is not always a comfortable or convenient thing for either. As Williams added, theological education is not about supplying a set of perfect answers but is rather about establishing a human 'locatedness' on the basis of theological insights. This requires that learners be allowed to grow at their own rate in a safe and nourishing environment.[6] The sort of thinking expressed by Williams respects the integrity of theological knowledge, but it does so in its service of the dynamic growth of the learner, not as a static body to be absorbed. It places the focus less on systematic content mastery and more on personal graduate attributes. In such an approach, the predominant factors of what to teach and how to teach intersect, a junction that is of integral concern to curriculum development.

> *Critical Reflection.* Which of these content v. character tensions are present in your institution? How are they managed? What primary driver shapes your personal approach to delivering the curriculum (or that part for which you are or are likely to be responsible)?

A curriculum designed with the learners' growth in focus plays an important role in developing such character-oriented graduate attributes, not as an adjunct to academic purpose, but as a central plank in the academic program. To achieve this, curriculum design needs first to be aware of—and strategically to avoid—the typical de-motivational elements of curriculum, such as a lack of adequate preparatory skills development for successful study in theological fields, a heavy overload in introductory units of academically and personally challenging content, a lack of perceived connection to the contemporary student's prospective world in terms of applied content and learning processes and a pervasive fragmentation of course units with a subsequent lack of integration of content knowledge, practical skills and personal values. Then, it needs to be aware of—and strategically to incorporate—three typically salient areas of learners'

---

6   Williams, 'Theological education is for everyone'.

perceptions of course units, which provide strong motivation for perseverance and success in learners' growth. These perceptions are that:

- *the unit is important:* to personal development, to ministry enhancement, to vocational pathway
- *the unit is do-able:* within their learning capacity, with adequate resources and skills tuition to set up for success
- *the unit is enjoyable:* engaging the learner actively, engaging with the learners' lifestyles and personal attributes.

These qualitative considerations need to be embodied in effective curriculum design in which the learners' development is in focus. The balance between preserving and perpetuating a body of sacred content and the concurrent development of a learner's personhood is not a conflictual contest but a curriculum necessity.[7]

Balance is one thing, but sequencing is another. A common approach to curriculum structure is to provide an introductory first year of foundational units (generally on the basis of broad surveys of biblical, theological, historical and/or language components, but occasionally including some practical introduction) followed by several semesters of more focused topics dominated by the study of specific biblical books and stipulated units of systematic theology, with various disparate elective units along the way. The foundational units are intended to provide either a broad acquaintance with sufficient content to be useful in the event of discontinuation of study (for example, in a one-year course) or to provide a platform for more focused study as an extension and an intensification of that general base. Occasionally, there is scope for some kind of final term capstone unit, but this option is rare in practice, especially in undergraduate programs. While this approach to curriculum structure is common, there is little evidence that it is effective. Stated prerequisites of advanced units are rarely realistic or used as a base for development. The methodological skills of specialised disciplines are rarely taught in the early stage (if at all) and are often assumed to develop intuitively by the completion of the course. Scaffolded learning is often advocated but is rarely intentionally or consistently developed in the overall program. The result is all too often a smorgasbord of fragmented units loosely grouped in disciplines as 'majors' but rarely with any organic coherence or progressive

---

7   See Ball, 'The Role of Curriculum in Developing Character-Oriented Graduate Attributes', 251–264, for a fuller development.

mastery. It is clearly a content-based structure, with little apparent objective of learners' personal growth, yet even in the area of content mastery, it is less than convincing in the attainment of stated aims. Conversely, a curriculum that has the goal of developing independent and lifelong learners will be marked by several general characteristics, which need to be intentionally and consistently incorporated. These connected principles are:

- a clear sense of *order*, especially with first things first, with introductory units that establish skills and transitional frameworks for ongoing success
- a clear *progression*, with discernible and articulated links from introductory skills through to advanced skills and cognitive engagement
- an overall sense of *coherence*, with integration of disciplines, with connected knowledge, skills and values, and holistic and explicit connection with graduate attributes.

Within a usual range of individual tastes and interests, a positive perception of any two of these three characteristics will typically lead to course satisfaction, with the overall course viewed as 'making sense'; the absence of any two of them will typically lead to dissatisfaction, with limited attainment of desired graduate attributes.

> *Critical Reflection.* To what extent does your current curriculum design intentionally (as distinct from wishfully) consider the factors of learners' perceptions that help them 'make sense' of their overall learning program in relation to the realities of their life and personal relations? Where is there space to develop these elements?

All the above may seem to paint a rather bleak picture of the current state of curriculum. However, it is presented to underline that the commendable graduate outcomes that are often achieved are the result of good teachers and dedicated learners rather than the strategic outcome of curriculum design and management. Fortunately, that will always be the case. However, more effectual curriculum development can only enhance those good graduate outcomes.

Principles of Curriculum Design

We turn now to a general summary of some governing principles that view the growth of the learner as pivotal to curriculum design. These principles apply regardless of the content or disciplines involved in the program.

- The first principle of curriculum design is that all elements (that is, all units) should align with and *contribute to the overall mission and ethos of the institution.*

The governing body of the institution needs to define its distinctive *raison d'être* and to acknowledge the operational world view that shapes its educational enterprise. However, even the notion of a world view needs to be understood as having numerous nuances. For some, it will be viewed as a governing set of theological values and principles, intended to drive a particular stance and to illustrate a way of being in the world, essentially that which draws us into a commonness of being. For others, it is viewed as an expression of collectivity that embraces both commonness and diversity as it evolves and responds to various complexities of life.[8] A clear understanding of such a philosophical position will determine what courses are required to fulfil an institution's global mission. Within that set of courses, the overall learning goals and desired graduate attributes need to be explicit because these should overtly determine every element in the educational program.

Critical Reflection. What is the overall mission and ethos of your institution? What does your current course contribute to that mission?

- The second principle of curriculum design is that necessary *skills and values for successful study should be developed early* in the program.

A major complaint of first-year students, and I suspect a significant factor in first-year attrition rates, is the content overload without the provision of basic academic 'survival skills'. Many theological students enter the course with fervour and conviction, but not necessarily with academic preparation. In a first-year Church History class one year, I noted that students were struggling with the formal exercise of analysing a primary historical document, so I took 'time out' for an hour to teach a lesson on the necessary skills. At the end of the

---

8 See Belcher & Parr, '"Commonness", Diversity and Disequilibrium', 7–17, for an examination of the role of institutional world view and its educational practices and how an 'institutional narrative' both shapes the inherent practices of the institution and has a capacity to re-shape both learner and teacher.
    An example of grounding the curriculum in a cohesive whole-world perspective is provided in Eckel, 'Interdisciplinary Education within Biblical Theology', 384–395. This article presents a proposal for avoiding the oft criticised fragmented nature of curriculum by incorporating an interdisciplinary study across the curriculum within a pervasive biblical world view. It presents a contrast to the traditional model of chunks of discrete disciplines that seem not to speak to one another.

lesson, a vocal student spoke out, 'Now you have ruined document studies for all of us. No one has an excuse now for not getting 100%'. It was not rocket science, just a simple lesson in 'how to', employing general and transferable principles with clear illustrative demonstration, but the proof of it came in the ensuing years of study, when excellent mastery of the skills of historical analysis was evidenced by those students. As well, the distinctive nature of theological study is that it penetrates in a challenging way to the very soul of the student, and many a first-year student is troubled by the disruption to their spiritual security, which needs a 'safety net' for the critical processing of sacred beliefs. Assurance of a secure world view needs to be established early in the program.

> *Critical Reflection.* Does your first-year program focus on content surveys or skills and values development? What results of this approach have you observed? Can you suggest ways the first-year curriculum might be adjusted to improve the learners' 'survival skills' requisite for success?

- The third principle of curriculum design is that all units should *contribute to a coherent program* within the award.

This is the difficult one. Our received tradition has generally not focused on such overall coherence, yet it is an increasingly urgent need. The emphasis on content specialist teachers has led to a corresponding emphasis on majors, loosely defined as a set of units from within the same discipline, but without any necessary organic relationship either with one another or with subjects beyond that individual discipline. This relative isolation of units tends to generate an associated isolation of content-specific teachers, with the result that, too often, we operate as though we are the only one responsible for all the learning objectives for our students. A more efficient strategy (and a more exemplary model) is to have dialogue with colleagues in determining what subject matter and its placement, what developmental aspects and what learning outcomes and activities will complement the entire teaching philosophy and program of the institution. By limiting what we attempt individually and trusting colleagues to do their part as well, we are more likely to achieve greater efficiency and cohesion in outcomes.

> *Critical Reflection.* In what areas could you generate collegiate dialogue in curriculum matters? Can you think of some ways in which you may collaborate with a teacher from another teaching discipline

in enhancing congruent development of learning outcomes across your segments of the curriculum?

- The fourth principle is that all units should have an *explicit constructive alignment of learning outcomes, learning activities and assessment requirements* that are consistent with the overall curriculum objectives.

Good practice is to state clearly the alignment of all elements of any program. In designing course unit outlines, this will involve a succinct statement of how the activities actually achieve the learning outcomes. This should not be a simple form-filling exercise, but a thoughtful process that drives the activities of both teaching and learning within the unit.

> *Critical Reflection.* How convincingly do the students' learning and assessment activities in your teaching units relate to the attainment of the stated learning outcomes of those units? How does your teaching approach foster such outcomes?

- The fifth principle is that curriculum should *connect with the contemporary and anticipated experience of learners.*

'Experience' includes but is not limited to practical application. Rather, it encompasses the whole experiential journey of the learner: intellectual development, spiritual growth, practical skills, social setting, ministry context and so on. The important thing is that experiential connection focuses on the present and potential future living experience of the learner rather than the past lived experience of the teacher. Personal and testimonial anecdotes have their place, but they should not be seen as necessarily connecting to the learner's experience or needs. The personal experience to which I link my learning activity may well soon be totally irrelevant. The ministry experience of my past may not connect with the ministry needs of the learner's future. Sharing of a teacher's own personal experiences—successes, failures, and confusions—is generally highly regarded by students, but the personal rapport so gained should not necessarily be viewed as making dynamic experiential contributions to students' needs or development.

> *Critical Reflection.* What steps can you take to ensure living relevance of the units you teach, even before formal curriculum-wide reviews?

- The final principle is that curriculum should be *constantly reviewed for relevance*, currency and ongoing contribution to the overall program.

A curriculum that is set in concrete will soon weigh down the learning process. In a rapidly changing world, there is the constant danger of equally rapid obsolescence. Curriculum needs to be constantly updated to remain relevant to the community of learners, church, stakeholders and the academy.

> *Critical Reflection.* How and how frequently is curriculum reviewed in your institution? How do you personally contribute to any such review?

The above principles are general in nature with reference to any curriculum. Within the specific field of theological curriculum, some further nuances apply. In the 2012 publication *Transforming Theology*, four governing principles were extrapolated from the research input by numerous Australian theological institutions.[9] These principles summarised the prevailing practices and aspirations in theological curriculum in contemporary Australia. The principles are:

- the primacy of biblical and theological knowledge
- contemporary engagement of theology with society and culture
- holistic integration of learning and life
- intentionality and strategicality of a transformative agenda expressed in curriculum design and development.

In practice, the principles are ranked in descending order of current practice, with the final two being far more aspirational than demonstrable.

I warm to the words of Pope Francis in the Apostolic Constitution Veritatis Gaudium on Ecclesiastical Universities and Faculties, 2017.

> This provides a positive and timely chance to review, from this standpoint and in this spirit, the structure and method of the academic curricula proposed by the system of ecclesiastical studies, in their theological foundations, in their guiding principles and in their various levels of disciplinary, pedagogical and didactical organization. This can be accomplished in a demanding but highly productive effort to rethink and update the aims and integration of the different disciplines and the teaching imparted in ecclesiastical studies within this specific framework and intentionality.[10]

---

9 Ball, *Transforming Theology*, 124–127.
10 Holy See, *Francis Apostolic Constitution*, 6.

Table 2.3: Sample Statement of Graduate Attributes[11]

1. Statement of Graduate Attributes

A graduate of ABC College of Theology will have a broad and deep cognitive knowledge of the classical fields of theological thought and scholarship, will have the process skills to evaluate and to communicate such knowledge in a variety of social and ecclesiastical contexts and will demonstrate a personal integration of theological concepts within the conduct of vocation and life.

2. Characteristics

2.1 The acquisition of broad and deep cognitive knowledge is marked by the ability to:
- *collect information* (in various ways)
- *recall that information* on demand (by examination and other assigned tasks)
- *present that information* in an orderly and articulate manner (in various contexts).

2.2 The development of process skills involves both the evaluative skills of analysis and interpretation of material within specific disciplines and the vocational skills of communicating theological knowledge to others. These skills are marked by the capacity for:
- *critical analysis* (of documents, systems and situations)
- *evidence-based argument* (concerning ideas and practices)
- *cogent evaluation* (of philosophical and practical movements and structures)
- *experiential performance* of a variety of ministry or other service functions.

2.3 The personal integration of theological concepts is marked by the capacity for:
- *synthesis* of disparate and wide-ranging perspectives
- the *integration* of such perspectives into a holistic world view
- *the active implementation of such a conceptual integration.*

---

[11] Derived from Ball, *Transforming Theology*, 139.

Role of Curriculum in Developing Graduate Outcomes

It is no doubt clear from the foregoing sections that my overall goal is the development of learners so that they will graduate as autonomous and capable lifelong learners, in contexts that are not necessarily limited to the scope of content or skills encountered during the formal stage of an educational program. It is certainly true that curriculum considerations need to include an awareness of their determinative philosophical traditions, which in a sense are 'where we are coming from'. However, curriculum development also needs to have an eye to 'where we are headed to', that is, the graduate outcomes that are the product of curriculum. If we can establish a clear picture of what we want our graduates to look like—not in specific cloning detail but in general terms of qualities and attainments—then we have a pervasive goal that conditions our curriculum design and delivery: its content, structure, and sequence. Where we want our students to arrive will shape how we map their journey. Therefore, it is vital to establish such a picture so we can construct curricular components that will lead to the desired outcome.

Table 2.3 presents an example of how such a picture may be expressed. (Note: it is an example, not a template.) The elements in the table refer intentionally to the three focal domains of learning detailed in the philosophical approaches of Table 2.2 (knowledge, skills, holistic integration). The articulation of these characteristics suggests a scaffolded structural approach to curriculum design. Once we have such a design framework in view, we can start building the learning program and associated activities into a coherent curricular whole.

> *Critical Reflection.* With reference to the course you are most familiar with, how are the various graduate outcomes fostered by the curriculum design? What outcomes are given most weight?

Taking Table 2.3 as a sample, we can observe the impact on curriculum of the various emphases involved. If the dominant graduate outcome is special or new cognitive knowledge of the classical fields of thought and practice, then the curriculum will be framed to that end. Such a content-based approach aims at comprehension and depth of content, typically proceeding from introductory surveys of general themes or features to a more in-depth analysis of major content components, culminating in a defined specialisation. Such a curriculum has been criticised as fragmented or atomistic, with its increasingly narrow focus and lack of interdisciplinary cohesion. However, it produces a well-informed graduate with special knowledge of important content. It may ultimately mine a narrow shaft, but it mines that shaft deeply. Such a curriculum will feature much directed study and deep research, with early methodological training and progressively more complex analysis and reporting.

If the dominant graduate outcome is process skills, comprehensiveness of content is not in focus within the curriculum. The early stages will involve the development of transferable critical or practical methods of inquiry and analysis rather than surveys of content. Those skills are then refined and extended by application to specific representative cases, problems, and real-life issues, with a capstone study that demonstrates not so much specialist knowledge but rather comprehensive skills in processing. The skills-based curriculum incorporates limited content, on the assumption that if students learn well how to process materials, they will be able to apply those skills of analysis or practice to a wider and unpredictable frame of reference.

If the dominant graduate outcome is personal integration, the person becomes the centre of the curriculum. Such a curriculum will begin from where the student is and will feature early studies in world view discernment, connections with a student's prior and continuing experience and ongoing engagement with real-life events that are pertinent to the individual student's actual or aspirational objectives. Such a curriculum will incorporate opportunities for learner-driven experiential learning, with increasing autonomy as the course progresses. Ideally, it will culminate in a learner-designed project that will demonstrate the active implementation of appropriated knowledge and values.

> *Critical Reflection.* Using Table 2.3 (or an alternative model) as an example, what graduate attributes are most prominent in your institution's current overall curriculum? Are there ways in which you could integrate all desirable elements into your current curriculum?

B. CURRICULUM CONTENT AND DESIGN
Curriculum and Pedagogy in Theological Education

So far, we have considered the determinative influence of philosophical and educational traditions on curriculum, with curriculum simultaneously shaped by institutional tradition and mission and aimed at producing certain kinds of graduate outcomes. At this point, I want to stress that curriculum and pedagogy are not separate entities but are integrally linked. Simply put, curriculum is concerned with what we teach and how we shape it; pedagogy is concerned with how we teach. Such seemingly simple statements are subject to wide philosophical variations, but in all cases, approaches to curriculum are driven by similar philosophical approaches as pedagogy. In the treatment of curriculum and pedagogy in this and following sections, those close links will become apparent.

There are several ways educationists view the relationship of curriculum and pedagogy, often seen in terms of curriculum content and instructional methodology. Some hold to a dualistic model, in which the two dimensions are viewed as separate issues, even at times involving different strata of faculty involvement. Others bring content and technique closer to each other in an interlocking model, by depicting the interrelatedness of content and delivery, whereby the two have elements of independence but both are equally important. In this model, curriculum designers consider the way learners encounter content as a part of curriculum planning, although this typically occurs at the planning stage and is not universally carried through in delivery. A third model is a concentric one, in which delivery and content are connected throughout the course and the means of learning are not just vehicles of content transmission but are significant objectives of that learning, and so become an integral part of the curriculum. To adapt a phrase of Kenneth Coley, this approach leads a teacher to ask, 'As a teacher, what am I communicating (the what) to my students (the who) by my selection of the teaching techniques (the how) I choose to employ'.[12] It is the same educational philosophy that shapes both our pedagogical delivery methods and our curriculum selections and structures. In a sense, this involves backwards planning in that how we intend to teach will shape the way we design our programs. Such elements as teaching methods and intended learning and assessment activities are significant considerations in curriculum planning, all operating under the umbrella of desired learning outcomes. This is a fundamental platform for mathegenical teaching and it is the ethos that pervades all sections of this book. To advance our thinking in that direction, we will now examine how approaches to pedagogical purpose are integrally woven into cohesive curriculum design and delivery, with a focus on the significance of course levels, desired outcomes and the strategic development and location of appropriate learning activities within the curriculum.

---

12   Coley, 'How Would It Play in Peoria?', 415–417.

Course Levels and Curriculum

Once the mission statement is clear and the desired graduate outcomes are articulated (always the first steps in cohesive curriculum development), there is a need to determine the course/s required to match those two statements. There is a tendency for theological higher educational institutions to want to offer the entire traditional suite of undergraduate and postgraduate courses, but that can serve more as a badge of honour than as a pedagogically sound approach. Awards vary in levels and nature and the associated variable attributes need to be appreciated for cohesive operation. As we examine the pedagogical implications for various levels of curriculum awards, we can discern how pedagogy and curriculum come together.[13]

In Australian higher education, there are currently five broad categories of awards: certificate, diploma, bachelor, master, and doctor, with various substrata within those levels, as detailed in the Australian Qualifications Framework (AQF). The AQF is based on 'a taxonomic structure of levels and qualification types each of which is defined by a taxonomy of learning outcomes … designed to enable consistency in the way in which qualifications are described as well as clarity about the differences and relationships between qualification types'.[14] The framework details the nuanced nature of the various levels of awards and the expected standards and characteristics of awards. In doing so, it consistently exemplifies the principle of qualitative differentiation across award levels. Flowing out of the overall descriptors of the various awards, some summary inferences for curriculum design may be drawn. Table 2.4 depicts the significance of the general characteristics of course levels for determining the focus of curriculum development and learner performance.[15]

---

13 In this chapter, reference is made to the *Australian Qualifications Framework*, 2nd ed., 2013. At the time of writing, that framework is under review and there are mooted changes to the levels of awards. However, while various award permutations are being considered, the underlying principles set out in this chapter remain intact, even if award titles vary ultimately.
14 'AQF Levels Criteria and AQF Qualification Type Descriptors'.
15 In this chapter, we will not discuss doctorates because they are generally focused on individual research and are not so dependent on curriculum design.

Table 2.4: Significance of Course Levels

	Certificate	**Diploma**	**Bachelor**	**Master**
Characteristics	Locate relevant and accurate information	(Locate and) explain relevant and accurate information	(Locate, explain,) analyse and evaluate information	(Locate, explain, analyse, evaluate) synthesise and apply information
Curriculum Emphasis	Teacher-directed location of knowledge	Teacher-assisted location of knowledge	Development of learners' critical judgement	Development of learners' independent critical judgement in analysis and evaluation of disparate scholarly views
Learner Performance	Collect and report needed knowledge in a specified context	Report, explain and apply knowledge to defined context	Apply informed and evidence-based argument to complex documents or practice in wider vocational contexts	Synthesise concepts with creative application to professional or leadership contexts

General course level characteristics can be summarised as follows:

- *Certificate (AQF Levels 1–4): locate information.* The curriculum is constructed with an emphasis on teacher-directed location of needed knowledge. The emphasis is on a collection of content defined by the teacher that is known to be significant for specific outcomes. Learning focuses on familiarity with that content and understanding it in relation to its utility. This level will incorporate learning activities that are designed and clearly guided by the teacher. They will typically be grounded in activities that are pertinent to the living context of the learners, such as current or intended occupational practice or personal development within a social context. The focus is on the learner's known context and the development of skills of collecting and understanding relevant needed materials.
- *Diploma (AQF Levels 5–6): (locate and) explain information.* The curriculum is constructed with an emphasis on teacher-assisted location

of knowledge leading to learners' reporting, explaining and applying knowledge in a variety of defined contexts. The emphasis is on collecting, comprehending, ordering and presenting knowledge within determined contextual boundaries, commonly centred on guided reading and more descriptive tasks. This level will incorporate learning activities featuring more direct instruction that leads to guided application. Therefore, the focus is on the development of a learner's capacity to locate with increasingly reduced guidance the knowledge required in specific areas of operation and to marshal factual data in coherent and usable ways.

- *Bachelor (AQF Level 7): (locate, explain,) analyse, and evaluate information*. The curriculum is constructed to equip learners to exercise critical judgement with application to complex documents or practices in wider contexts. The emphasis is on analysis and application of such knowledge in a wider range of known contexts, commonly requiring a broader range of reading (primary/secondary, some engagement with current scholarship), less dependency on teacher guidance and evidence-based argument. While the introductory stages of a bachelor level will involve direct instruction in basic content and methods of inquiry, the emphasis comes more onto critical thinking expressed in analytical and cogent argument. Thus, it incorporates the location and ordering of content that typifies the diploma but adds that dimension of critical analysis (how come?) and argument (so what?) about issues arising from that material. The focus is on the development of the learner's capacity for independent critical judgement in the formation of a reasoned case. At this level, in practical areas, vocational performance is typically involved, either as an individual or in company.

- *Master (AQF Levels 8–9): (locate, explain, analyse, evaluate,) synthesise and apply information*. The curriculum is constructed to promote independent critical judgement in analysis and evaluation of disparate views and to synthesise concepts with application to professional or leadership contexts. The master level subsumes all the demands of the bachelor award, but the special focus comes onto more critical judgement in terms of independent evaluation and synthesising their own arrangement of a wide range of ideas, with creative application to a wider and not necessarily predictable range of contexts. This involves engaging with more complex, even contradictory, ideas grounded in wider and more contemporary scholarship, and an ability to process disparate scholarly opinion with critical empathy. It will feature increasing degrees of autonomy of learning, with greater involvement by the learner in identifying, shaping and conducting the learning activities. Ideally, the master course should lead to a defining study by way of a focused study unit incorporating a synthesis of concepts and applications. This may be a capstone unit that encapsulates the essence of the whole program, but equally it may be a learner-designed project of particular personal value to the learner. In this way, in collaboration with a facilitative teacher, the learner takes the highest possible responsibility for autonomous learning, which is the ultimate goal of mathegenical teaching and learning. At the Master of Arts level, which is commonly a more generic award, focused application to leadership, training or professional contexts is commonly involved in practical units. This will culminate in the production of a well-constructed integrated model of action suited to professional practice.

While a clear understanding of the differentiated characteristics of award levels is needed, implementation of these characteristics also requires a clear appreciation of the nuances of terminology used in communication, since common terms used at different levels have different meanings, which need to be clearly understood by teachers and learners alike. For example, three common terms used widely are 'analyse', 'apply', and 'evaluate'. These all have generally understood meanings:

- 'analyse': to break down into component parts
- 'apply': to show how a general idea can fit into a specific setting
- 'evaluate': to assess the worth of information or practice.

However, all have varying interpretations at different levels of operation (that is, courses) and these differences need to be understood in both pedagogy and curriculum development to ensure cohesion. Table 2.5 indicates the nuanced way these terms may be applied to different levels of awards. A clear understating of such terminological usage will guide both curriculum design and subsequent assessment activities.

From this brief discussion of the characteristics of award levels, and an understanding of the nuances of common terminology used in association with them, it is clear that the levels of award have a significant impact on curriculum design and, ultimately, on associated pedagogical practice. Curriculum design should proceed progressively from teacher direction and resource provision through various levels of increasing learner autonomy and initiative. The main implication of this is that one simple curriculum structure is not likely to serve all levels of award equally well, an observation that has large ramifications, especially for a smaller institution wanting to deliver a multiplicity of courses with limited personnel and resources. A consequently vital consideration in all matters of curriculum design and delivery is the need to ensure a constructive alignment of all elements of learning suited to and shaped by the differentiated learning objectives of the award. Table 2.6 indicates the ramifications of the elements of such an alignment across the whole gamut of curriculum and pedagogical considerations.

Table 2.5: Terminological Nuances

	General Sense	**Diploma**	**Bachelor**	**Master**
Analyse	Break down into component parts	Break down the overall information • to discern and select relevant and accurate information for a set task or operation	Break down the overall information • to gather relevant evidence to support an argument or to show connectedness	Break down the overall information • to test the validity of components within the range of scholarship and in relation to a wide and unpredictable set of contexts or issues
Apply	Show how a general idea can fit into a specific setting	Show how a general idea • can fit into a known and familiar context of information	Show how a general idea • can become operational in a variable range of vocational or professional performance	Show how a general idea • can be developed further to serve a wider range of unpredictable or complex situations arising from professional practice
Evaluate	Assess the worth of information or practice	Assess the worth of information • for its suitability for use in a known context or operation	Assess the worth of information • for its contribution to a cogent argument or informed position	Assess the worth of information • for its capacity to support or counter established thinking or practice or suggest new forms of thinking or practice

Table 2.6: Constructive Alignment

Curriculum	Selection and sequence of learning objectives and resources to foster objectives of course level
Pedagogy	Learning Activities and Assessment to match course level emphases and learner performance
Balance needed	Sacred content; needed skills; personal development to align with course objectives
Guiding motif	What do we want our graduates of a course to look like?

Critical Reflection. In the courses your institution delivers, how far is the curriculum tailored to align with such constructive concepts? To what degree is such an alignment practical in your context? What (if anything) needs to be done to achieve such conceptual alignment?

Unit Outcomes and Curriculum

At the unit/subject/module[16] level, curriculum and pedagogy most overtly intersect. The units are the coal face dimension of curriculum delivery. While the course descriptors shape the general course design, the specific learning outcomes of the individual units are the functional drivers of the curriculum, so the interaction of course and unit objectives needs to be clear in all curriculum design. In a content-based curriculum, provision needs to be made for broad surveys of knowledge, with opportunity to summarise and absorb such knowledge, but without the expectation of a high level of critical analysis. When diploma students are asked to analyse information, they will be expected to identify and collate accurate and relevant knowledge; when bachelor students are asked to analyse information, they will be expected not only to gather such knowledge, but also to appraise its validity in evidence-based argument. That sort of semantic nuancing of terms, as shown in Table 2.5 to be similar in form but different in context, needs to be a part of both curriculum (which provides space for attaining the outcome) and pedagogy (which provides the tools for attaining the outcome). Therefore, both the statement of individual unit learning

---

16 While various terms are used in program nomenclature, the generic term 'unit' is used here to denote a defined set of lessons within a specific teaching period, such as a semester-long unit in Theology.

outcomes and the language of key terms need to be explicitly shown to correlate with the course objectives. Keeping this correlation in view at all stages of documentation will help to establish coherence in the overall study program.

This strategic alignment of course objectives and learning outcomes should precede any decision on course content. With such a conscious alignment, we can then determine the most suitable content to include in a unit (which will always be a limited selection, regardless of any aim of comprehension) and the most suitable methods of learning to be employed. For example, if content comprehension is the objective, an early unit named *Introduction to the Bible* will focus on a broad spectrum of knowledge, with notes on the content, context and structure of as many of the biblical books that we can fit in. The statement of unit learning outcomes should focus on the identification and understanding of this comprehensive knowledge base, with less emphasis on more refined or higher order cognitive engagement. Conversely, an *Introduction to the Bible* that is skills-based will probably not mention most of the biblical books but will take representative samples of biblical text as a reference point for the tools of biblical study, a more hermeneutical approach. In this case, the unit learning outcomes will focus on the development and application of such skills without attempting comprehension of content knowledge. A person-centred curriculum will likely begin by exploring the learners' own biblical history and addressing emergent issues of concern, with typical samples of issues and text, leading towards skills of resolution and analysis. Hence, the unit learning outcomes should stress this sort of personal and philosophical development and social engagement, with less focus on specific textual knowledge or technical skills. The three approaches have different virtues and will have application at different stages of most courses, but the overall aim will shape the curriculum and determine the pedagogy. Thus, it is important that this sort of preliminary thought is given to curriculum and unit design within the overall program to achieve the overall course goals.

> *Critical Reflection.* In the discipline in which you are involved, how far do the learning/assessment activities incorporate a conscious awareness of the award level characteristics?

In light of the need for this course/unit correlation, a crucial element that affects every higher education teacher is the need to discern—and articulate—a meaningful differentiation in learning outcomes at different course levels, which is especially problematic when the unit content may look very similar at two levels (such as *Introduction to the Bible*). Knowing the distinction among course levels is essential, as appropriate discrimination in learning outcomes involves more than a semantic superficiality or simply a longer exercise. Learning at two levels involves learning activities at two levels. Tables 2.7 and 2.8 illustrate aspects of this sort of discrimination.

Table 2.7 is framed around the AQF (my *highlighting*). In this table, while intentionally generic to suit all areas of study, there is a visible gradation of all elements across the course levels and this sort of discrimination needs to be grasped in constructing appropriate learning activities. Personally, I do not like pseudo-discriminators such as 'analyse' and 'analyse critically' because, without nuanced definition, they fall into the category of semantic quibbling without precision. However, if the different qualities of the two terms are clearly explained in implementation, the escalation of cognitive demand becomes clear. The terms that I have highlighted are examples of where further such clear definition is needed to ground the learning activities at appropriate levels.

Table 2.8 illustrates a revision work in progress. It depicts how an unsatisfactory statement of non-differentiated learning outcomes for three levels of a comparable introductory unit has been revised, minimally as required by institutional mandate, to show some degree of differentiation. The revisions appear to be terminologically small but indicate an attempt at a more refined nuancing of cognitive level.

Table 2.7: Developing Learning Outcomes Across the Curriculum (AQF Level 5 -9)

	AQF Level 5 (Diploma)	**AQF Level 7 (Bachelor)**	**AQF Level 9 (Master)**
	AQF Learning Outcomes Summary Guidelines		
General	specialised knowledge and skills for *skilled/paraprofessional* work	broad and coherent knowledge and skills for *professional work*	*specialised* knowledge and skills for research, and/or *professional practice*
Knowledge	technical and theoretical *knowledge* in a specific area	*coherent* theoretical and technical *knowledge with depth* in one or more areas	*integrated* understanding of a *complex body of knowledge*
Skills	• *analyse* information • *solve* problems • *transmit* information	• *analyse and evaluate* information • analyse & generate solutions to *unpredictable and sometimes complex* problems • transmit knowledge	independently: • analyse critically, reflect on and *synthesise complex information*, problems, concepts and theories • *apply established theories* to a body of knowledge or practice • interpret and transmit knowledge, skills and ideas to *specialist and non-specialist* audiences
Application	defined responsibility within broad but *established parameters*	*self-directed* work within broad parameters to provide *specialist* functions	*autonomy, expert judgement, adaptability* and responsibility as a practitioner

Table 2.8: Differentiating Learning Outcomes: Introduction to Christian History

	Diploma	**Bachelor**	**Postgraduate**
Original	1) Demonstrate knowledge of a number of key events in the Church's past	1) Demonstrate knowledge of a number of key events in the Church's past	1) Demonstrate solid knowledge of a number of key events in the Church's past
	2) Understand a number of approaches to researching, constructing and interpreting the past	2) Understand a number of approaches to researching, constructing and interpreting the past	2) Understand and articulate a number of approaches to researching, constructing and interpreting the past
	3) Distinguish between primary and secondary source materials and use such sources appropriately	3) Distinguish between primary and secondary source materials and use such sources appropriately	3) Distinguish between primary and secondary source materials and use such sources critically and appropriately
	4) Show how historical knowledge provides a necessary context for theological studies	4) Show how historical knowledge provides a necessary context for theological studies	4) Show with precision how historical knowledge provides a necessary context for theological studies
	5) Construct and support a coherent historical argument in written form, according to the methodological conventions of the discipline	5) Construct and support a coherent historical argument in written form, according to the methodological conventions of the discipline	5) Construct and support a coherent and historical argument in written form that demonstrates capacity for critical thinking and analysis and utilises the methodological conventions of the discipline

	Diploma	**Bachelor**	**Postgraduate**
Revised	1) Identify the major events and people in the history of the Christian churches from their origins to the present	1) Trace the major developments in the history of the Christian churches from their origins to the present	1) Identify the major developments and critical turning points in the history of the Christian churches from their origins to the present
	2) Explain the main doctrinal and institutional issues which have marked the church's history	2) Explain the issues which have shaped the developments within the Christian churches throughout history	2) Explain the causes and outcomes of significant historical events and trends within the Christian churches throughout history
	3) Compare the contribution of key figures of the church's history	3) Analyse the contribution of selected people and movements to the development of the church's thought and structures	3) Analyse the problems, opportunities and attitudes of past Christians in their interaction with the societies in which they lived
	4) Utilise appropriate academic sources to inform their understanding of the church's history	4) Interpret individual primary historical documents in their social context	4) Evaluate the contribution of selected people and movements to the development of the church's thought and structures
	5) Apply their knowledge of the church's history to an account of a present-day contemporary church issue	5) Utilise appropriate methods of historical inquiry to construct a coherent historical argument in written form	5) Interpret primary and secondary historical documents in their social context in the development of a coherent historical argument in written form

Critical Reflection. Do the revisions in Table 2.8 go far enough to align adequately with the guidelines in Table 2.5?

Critical Reflection. Examine the course unit outline for a unit you actually or potentially teach (or have studied) which has different levels of offering. How closely do the stated learning outcomes align with the AQF Guidelines in Table 2.7 (or comparable accreditation guidelines)? Do they have a sufficient difference in kind across the different levels? If not, can you suggest ways in which this differentiation may be enhanced?

Learning Activities and Assessment

Here, I intentionally link learning activities with learning assessment. The purpose of designing effective learning activities is to provide learners with *opportunities for attaining* the learning outcomes. Similarly, the point of assessment is to provide opportunities for learners to *demonstrate the attainment* of learning outcomes. The two are inseparable, to the point of being virtually identical. As De Jongh has succinctly put it, 'The planning of assessment begins with the learning outcomes, which should be expressed in curriculum and study materials, then (in) choosing the appropriate type and form of assessment'.[17] The elements of 'good assessment' inhere in the same degree in considerations of 'good curriculum'. Hence, assessment construction should be envisaged as part of curriculum design, in conjunction with learning outcomes. The correlation between activities and assessment means that encountering the assessment item should never be the first time a learner has confronted the sort of activity involved. Designing suitable learning and assessment activities is to be done as part of the process of selecting pedagogical approaches and designing the overall curriculum. There are three aspects of activities to be considered: suitability for the award level; contribution to graduate outcomes; and appropriateness to the specific discipline involved.

As already noted, the diploma emphasis is on locating, understanding and ordering material, with sufficient direction provided to facilitate this. Activities should ensure relevant, sufficient and accessible resources are available to learners because the degree of teacher direction is significant at this level. Samples of the sort of tasks to be undertaken should be available; clear directions

---

17   De Jongh, 'Assessment of Learning in Curriculum Development', 183.

on methods to be used are needed; the scope of knowledge to be located and processed is to be clearly defined; the set parameters of application need to be spelt out. That is, learning activities should be guided rather than rely on learners' initiative and assessment instruments should reflect the learning activities in scope and form. Bachelor awards activities need to be more cognitively enhanced to focus on the development of those critical skills. Learning activities will include an expanded corpus of knowledge, less defined than in the diploma, with learners selecting from a wider body of available information to be critically analysed for its relevance to a developing argument. The 'how come' and 'so what' dimensions should feature prominently in these activities. Opportunities for exploration of information are appropriate and should be strategically incorporated into the curriculum design. At the postgraduate level, with its emphasis on more independent critical judgement, evaluation of a broad range of views and the synthesising of their own arrangement of ideas, learning activities should be progressively geared towards the learners' self-directed shaping of their own activities, determining their own context of application, based on an expanded critical mass, in engagement with an increasingly wide range of scholarship, presented in forms that align with scholarly conventions.

Learning activities also need to be geared towards the graduate outcomes and so require a variety of focus. It is not sufficient, for example, to rely heavily on formal written essays if performative skills or personal development are needed. Different learners have different dominant learning styles, personal contexts and 'life-after-study' aspirations, so learning activities should be designed to facilitate development across all the styles, contexts and aspirations. In the AQF Guidelines, unit learning outcomes focus on knowledge, skills and application, so learning activities and associated assessment activities should be designed to ensure all such desired outcomes are accommodated. Other frameworks will have different approaches and guidelines, but in all cases, variety and flexibility in activities are core to effectual learning and assessment.

Activities are to be tailored to meet the conventions of study in specific disciplines. Thinking theologically will have different conventions from thinking historically. So too the development of a biblical doctrine will have different parameters from constructing a pastoral ministry paradigm or constructing a case study. The specific discipline conventions need to be taught not assumed. That requires curricular attention as to where such introductory conventions will be taught and where they will be practised towards eventual mastery.

> *Critical Reflection.* In a unit you teach or are likely to teach, review the learning activities from the perspective of their suitability to course level, their contribution to graduate outcomes, and the development of discipline conventions.

So how does assessment fit into the overall learning activity? Simply put, it is a continuation of already experienced forms of learning, which has been constructively crafted to allow a summation of the attainment of learning outcomes. The Australian Tertiary Education Quality and Standards Agency (TEQSA) has issued guidelines, summed up as:

> *The expected learning outcomes for each course of study are ... consistent with the level of the qualification awarded.*
>
> *Methods of assessment are consistent with the learning outcomes being assessed, are capable of confirming that all specified learning outcomes are achieved and that grades awarded reflect the level of student attainment.*

At the risk of tedium, I return to that mantra: 'learning outcomes drive the unit'.

3 | CONSTRUCTING CURRICULUM

A. DESIGNING CURRICULUM: A TAXONOMICAL PLATFORM

To establish a base for the construction of a coherent curriculum, we begin with some basic principles of scaffolded curriculum design, drawing first on the classical work of Bloom, which is enhanced by later developments on similar lines. The links between such a curriculum design and effective pedagogy will emerge as various pedagogical approaches will be intentionally incorporated at various points throughout the following sections of this work.

A taxonomical approach to curriculum design undergirds the ideas proposed in this chapter. Simply put, a taxonomy is a systematic approach that categorises different attributes of development. In educational contexts, that becomes categorising attributes of learning, with consequent implications of a developmental approach to knowing and growing. Such an approach to curriculum design is expressed in a scaffolded structure, in which introductory stages of a course focus on lower-order thinking, which is followed by progressively advancing through the course to higher-order domains. Thus, there is a clear correlation between pedagogical principles and curriculum design principles.

Foundational Taxonomy: Bloom's Taxonomy

The classic statement of a taxonomical approach to learning is that developed by Benjamin Bloom, commonly referred to as 'Bloom's Taxonomy'. Indeed, Bloom's name has become virtually synonymous with taxonomical thinking. His original framework set out a taxonomy of three domains of thinking and learning: the cognitive domain (a knowledge-based domain, consisting of six levels); the affective domain (an attitude-based domain, consisting of five levels); and the psychomotor domain (a skills-based domain, consisting of six levels). However, his main development of that original framework was his comprehensive and most influential handbook published on the cognitive domain, which became the benchmark for all subsequent taxonomical work in this area.[1] Our starting point for scaffolded curriculum design emerges naturally from that taxonomy, following Bloom's emphasis on the cognitive domain as a base for any further development.

Bloom's system was created on the basis of a hierarchy of cognitive engagement, progressing through six levels of complexity starting from the base level of knowledge, which is fundamental to all levels of cognition, and scaling up to the highest point of critical educational engagement, which he termed 'evaluation'. The lowest three levels are knowledge, comprehension, and application. The highest three levels are analysis, synthesis, and evaluation. The taxonomy is hierarchical, that is, each level is subsumed and built upon by the higher levels. The value of this taxonomy lies in its guidance in establishing learning activities to achieve different levels of student engagement, which is an indispensable aid in matching activities with level of units and awards. This is core to pedagogical practice because teaching methods should not be employed on a 'one-size-fits-all' basis. Content may generally be similar in different contexts, but learning is concerned with not just content transmission, but with how that content is processed appropriately at different cognitive levels.

More recently, that schema has been revised in terminology and approach without changing the fundamental construct. In 2001, Anderson and others (former collaborators and students of Bloom) issued their revised Bloom's taxonomy, which changed the terminology to render more consistent the engagement with learner processes rather than learning product.[2] They amended the terms from nouns (products) to verbs (processes) and transposed the highest two levels to elevate creative synthesising to the peak of the cognitive processes. The revised six levels are expressed as remembering, understanding, applying, analysing, evaluating, and creating. The original and revised hierarchical approaches are represented in the comparative pyramids in Figure 3.1.

1 Bloom, *Taxonomy of Educational Objectives*.
2 Anderson & Krathwohl, *A Taxonomy for Learning, Teaching and Assessing*.

Figure 3.1: Bloom's Taxonomy and Bloom's Taxonomy Revised

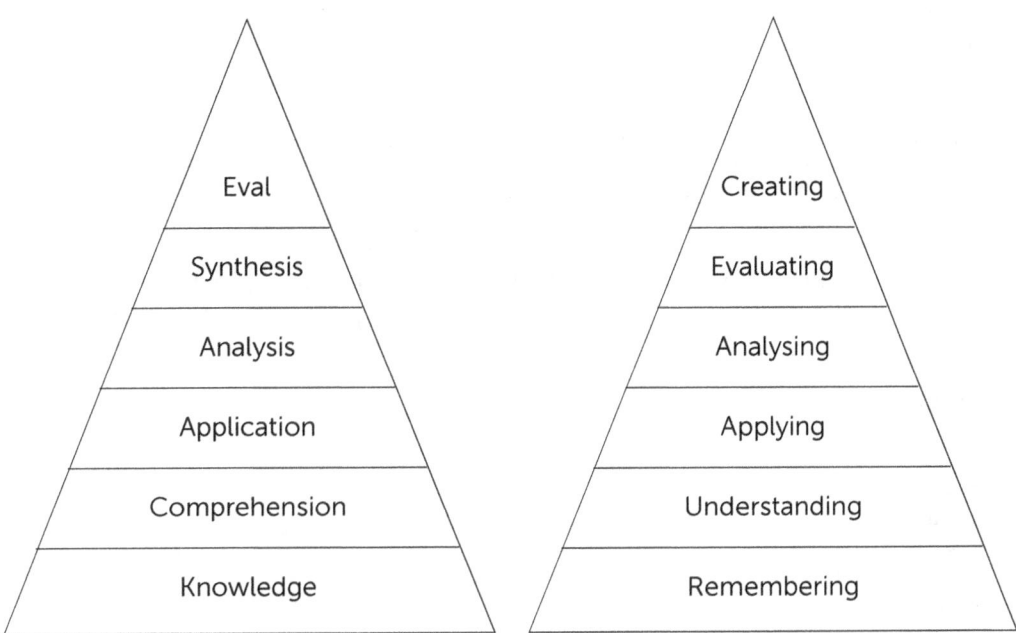

As they continued Bloom's original work, Anderson et al. expanded Bloom's fundamental approach to knowledge categorisation by suggesting four kinds of knowledge that need to be processed (see Figure 3.2). In their construction of the *Knowledge Domain*, they dissect the elements of knowing into a range of dimensions from the concrete (factual) to the abstract (metacognitive). Factual knowledge is the basic information that a learner needs to be familiar with to operate within a discipline. Conceptual knowledge is the awareness of the interrelationships among those basic elements that allow them to function together. Procedural knowledge relates to the ability to use methods of inquiry or technical skills of practice to complete a task. Metacognitive knowledge is the abstract awareness of one's own thought processes and the changes being experienced within those processes and the way it is incorporated into one's own sphere of functioning, or more simply, how one lives beside the new learning that is being acquired. In place of a simple cognitive hierarchy, this expanded matrix presents a two-dimensional framework that interrelates the various kinds of knowledge with the different cognitive processes that students use to gain and work with knowledge. The four kinds of knowledge dimensions are not, however, viewed as a linear progression. Rather, they provide a spectrum of ways of processing knowledge. It is helpful for designers of curriculum to be able to specify precisely what they are seeking to achieve by the use of selected content and the kind of cognitive processing that will be suited to the kind, level and stage of any particular course.

Figure 3.2: Knowledge and Cognitive Dimensions

The knowledge dimension	The Cognitive Process Dimension					
	1. Remember	2. Understand	3. Apply	4. Analyse	5. Evaluate	6. Create
A. Factual knowledge						
B. Conceptual knowledge						
C. Procedural knowledge						
D. Metacognitive knowledge						

Robert Marzano and John Kendall developed a different approach to correct what they deemed to be shortcomings of the Bloom/Anderson approach, but it also operates on a taxonomical base.[3] As with Anderson et al., this approach posits various elements of the knowledge domain, defined now as information, mental procedures, and psychomotor procedures. These fields provide the content of new learning. However, in place of the hierarchical cognitive ladder of Bloom, they present a construct of three systems of thinking, which relates more to the affective areas of learning. The three systems are defined as the self-system, which is the initial processing of the need and desirability to pursue the new knowledge being encountered; the metacognitive system, which sets learning goals and monitors progress; and the cognitive system, which processes all the necessary information by means of knowledge retrieval, comprehension, analysis, and knowledge utilisation. Framed more consciously around the ways learners respond to new knowledge, this approach highlights the need to engage

---

3   Marzano & Kendall, *The New Taxonomy of Educational Objectives*.

the learner in the process, with the learner's relationship to and acceptance of the relevance and value of new content being a prime consideration. It presents a variant perspective on a taxonomical approach to curriculum design.

Bloom's taxonomy stands as the watershed publication in taxonomical design and remains the most influential base for graduated learning approaches. Most exercises in course components' alignment stem from this taxonomy, which will be evident in the remainder of this book. However, regardless of whether we emphasise the cognitive or affective domains as the major guideline, the concept of a taxonomical design provides a useful set of building blocks for framing appropriate learning and assessment activities to match different learning objectives, which will be explored in greater detail in our pedagogy section. However, with this in mind, it is necessary that curriculum be designed to accommodate the inclusion in an ordered way of the complexities of knowledge and the range of learning styles and contexts that will employ a range of increasingly complex levels of cognitive engagement.

If we apply Bloom's taxonomy to curriculum design, we construct lower-level courses (for example, certificate and diploma) designed to focus on lower-order knowledge and understanding. Higher level courses, such as bachelor, would be structured to subsume such levels of cognitive operation but to progress to higher levels of application and analysis. The highest level courses (master or doctor) would go 'all the way to the top' by culminating in evaluation of complex materials with an active implementation or creative artefact (see Figure 3.3). Of course, there will always be overlap at the edges of the categories, and so within such generic terms, there is the need to define the terms relevant to the award level, as discussed in Chapter 2—empirical analysis of factual content at diploma level will differ in kind from the higher-order critical analysis of a bachelor learner's evidence-based argument. It is with such thinking in mind that curriculum designers should map out content, sequence, activities and resourcing for individual levels of course application, rather than depend on a one-size-fits-all approach of logistical convenience.

Figure 3.3: Bloom's Taxonomy and Course Levels

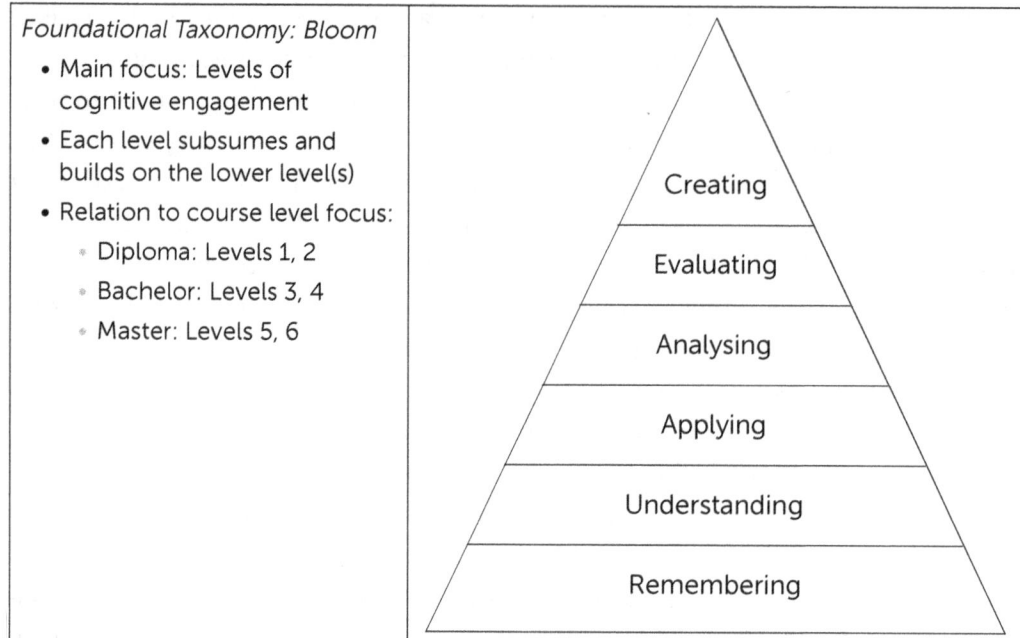

Critical Reflection. Reflect on the curriculum design encountered in your theological studies. In what ways and to what degree did it focus on the various concept process dimensions suggested in Anderson et al.'s knowledge–process intersection model above?

Curriculum–Pedagogy Nexus

As we have consistently maintained, there is a clear connection between curriculum and pedagogy. While the concepts of pedagogy will be explored in greater detail in the next section, we need to note here that close alignment of the principles of both curriculum and pedagogy.

One approach we will examine in more detail under pedagogy is that developed in Peter Mudge's adaptation of Jürgen Habermas's epistemology.[4] From a curriculum perspective, the interest is in how a scaffolded approach may incorporate the gradation of levels of such knowing. Mudge's interplay between epistemology (how we know) and education (how we learn), according

---

4   Mudge, 'Four Ways of Knowing'.

to the thought of Habermas, focuses on different ways of knowing, which can be utilised to maximise the efficiency of the ways we sequence units. He draws structural links between such cognitive conceptualisation and Bloom, by commencing at the lower-level instrumental–empirical–analytical way of knowing and moving progressively through historical hermeneutical way of knowing, emancipatory–critical and self-reflective way of knowing, and praxis and wisdom way(s) of knowing. At the various levels, the focus is on developing different qualities of knowing and the positional placement of learner and teacher (and curriculum designer) varies according to the type of knowing and learning envisaged. More empirical data-driven teaching will suit lower levels and introductory stages, while more critical reflective modes will feature more prominently in higher levels and at advanced stages. Mudge's approach is a useful adjunct to the taxonomical approach of Bloom.

A different approach to structuring learning is offered by the field of practical theology. Here, the guiding concept is that of ways of inquiry rather than cognitive processes. A leading exponent of practical theological method is Richard Osmer, whose approach will also be examined in greater detail under pedagogy.[5] Here, the focus is on the relevance to curriculum design, with particular but not exclusive reference to practical studies. Osmer's four-element model is not so much a hierarchical taxonomy, but a structured sequence of learning analysis, which is framed around four fundamental tasks of theological interpretation: the descriptive task (what is happening), the interpretive task (how did this come to be), the normative task (what should be happening), culminating in the pragmatic task (what do we do now). In terms of Bloom's taxonomy, the initial explorations involve the lower-order empirical knowledge gathering, which is followed by more complex analytical and evaluative processes, culminating in the higher-order creative strategising of active implementation. To facilitate such inquiry, curriculum design needs to accommodate the development of such inquiry skills and ethos, and these elements need to be structured progressively into a sequential curriculum.

Stephen Smith's approach to learning differs from the previous ones in that it focuses on complex living systems—that is, the learners and their preparedness to learn. Rather than starting from sacred content or important skills, Smith begins from what the learner wants to learn, needs to learn and is positioned to learn. This focus on the learner's situation highlights the sense-making dimension

---

5   See Osmer, *Practical Theology*.

of theological study, a notion that itself make sense of the purpose of theological education. In 'Moving from Instruction to Inquiry', Smith presents a model of sense-making in a complex living system (for which we may read, theological education), not as a mechanical 'how to' manual but as a device to aid inquiry.[6] This system is derived from the identification of 'four domains of knowledge within the complex living system, as well as a fifth area, a grey zone, where the unknowable seems to reside'. Smith's approach to categorising knowing differs from that of Mudge in that Smith works from the perspective of what is knowable rather than how we know. His domains are as follows. The *simple* domain contains knowledge with many knowns and is characterised by categorising, with an effective teaching approach framed around direct instruction to organise essential information. The *complicated* domain is where we know what we do not know and is characterised by analysing patterns, with an effective teaching approach framed around inquiry to engage with desired new knowledge. The *complex* domain contains many unknown unknowns and is characterised by experimentation, with an effective teaching approach of inquiry to open up to and explore the potential of new possibilities. The *chaotic* domain has many unknowables and is characterised by fast action, with an effective teaching approach of direct instruction to confirm the known and to provide certainty. The fifth domain, the grey area, includes an unknown number of unknowables, but with a transcendent awareness of something bigger than we are, which holds assumptions lightly, and develops within a learning culture of intuition and discernment, which lives comfortably with the uncertainty of not knowing. Awareness of such reaches of knowability influences curriculum in both ethos and structure. When we construct curriculum, we need to allow space and to establish order within the learning program for the extent of certainty and uncertainty to be explored and, when possible, to be established. To confront early-stage learners who are seeking confirmation of faith and growth in known areas with the complex and the chaotic, with a potentially overwhelming and indeterminate number of unknowns and unknowables, is to court educational and personal disaster. As well as issues of content selection and sequencing, the issue of personal preparedness to tackle the varying demands of learning needs to be considered, not only in terms of student welfare and pedagogical engagement, but also in the design of the curriculum itself. Too often, the plaint is heard that the excessive overload of unexpected and

---

6   Smith, 'Moving from Instruction to Inquiry', 35–51.

personally confronting and challenging content is the major problematic concern for first-year theological students. They need to be given the space to make sense of their learning.

Table 3.1 summarises the essential features of the various approaches to structuring learning that we have discussed above.

Table 3.1: Approaches to Learning

Mudge	Osmer	Smith
Epistemological approach Basis: 'how we know' • empirical • hermeneutical • self-reflective • praxis and wisdom	Pragmatic approach Basis: 'strategic tasks' • descriptive • interpretive • normative • strategic	Sense-making approach Basis: 'what is knowable' • simple domain • complicated domain • complex domain • chaotic domain • 'transcendent' zone

In summary, we can suggest that all taxonomical approaches to curriculum design have merit. What is important is the need to decide the basic taxonomical approach that will shape the curriculum, which may incorporate elements of various approaches but always in a coherent way. Whatever approach is chosen, that approach needs to have a clear rationale that is articulated, implemented and communicated.

> *Critical Reflection.* Select one of the approaches discussed above (Mudge, Osmer, Smith). How would you incorporate the principles involved in designing a sequence of units in your discipline or overall award structure?

Scaffolding the Curriculum

Thus far, we have focused on the cognitive domain of Bloom's taxonomy and variant expressions and expansions of those cognitive understandings. That is intentional, since this is the area in which most formal educational planning is based and so it remains the fundamental building block of scaffolded curriculum design. However, a taxonomical curriculum design is not limited to the cognitive domain but also extends to include the affective (attitudinal) and psychomotor (skills) domains. So, as we focus on developing a scaffolding approach to curriculum design, we will seek to align the several domains of learning into a cohesive framework.

I find it interesting to compare and combine the approaches of Mudge, Osmer and Smith. In varying ways, they all align conceptually with Bloom's taxonomy, with their gradation of complexity of knowing and learning. Mudge examines ways of knowing, from simple to complex operations. Osmer proposes a sequence of learning, from simple description to complex creative strategising. Finally, Smith seeks to make sense of domains of increasingly complex and therefore less dogmatically knowable knowledge. The common thread in all these approaches is the movement from simplicity to complexity and therein lies the fundamental principle of scaffolded curriculum design.

At every level of course development, the principle of simple → complex → coherent sense-making needs to be interpreted. First, the principle applies at the overall award level, at which the coherence of the entire program is noted simply and conceptually at the beginning of the program, all ensuing and increasingly complex component parts are viewed to fit into that initial concept, and the final stages encapsulate the sense of the overall ethos. Second, the principle applies at the unit level, at which the learning objectives are explicitly derived from the overall course ethos and in turn drive the learning activities of the unit. The early stages of the unit need to be an initiation into the components of the unit, which will be analysed in greater complexity as the unit advances, until the final stages bring it all together in a meaningful way—I have found it unsatisfactory and quite exasperating to leave the final lesson in a term-long unit as simply the last in a list of new topics, without having drawn the whole unit together into the required meaningful whole. Finally, the principle applies at the individual lesson level, with a strategy of introducing a simple guiding idea followed by analysis and development of component parts, which are put back together at the end of the lesson in a way that adds meaning for the learner. This principle of sense-making is relevant at both the curriculum design and the pedagogical delivery levels of all programs and their component parts because both combine to produce the overall learning intention of the course. When this sort of planning is conducted at all points of curriculum design, the development of the learners' capacity to learn is consistently progressed.

The initial stages of learning in a new and challenging field need to take cognisance of the disorienting dilemma that consistently confronts theological learners. The first thing they need to establish is a safety net for the challenges ahead, that is, an intellectual and spiritual safety net that will allow them to explore, question, make mistakes, and remain in wonder, without loss of personal security. This requires a clear and confident world view so they are established in their own sense of identity and their place in creation, which will give them a safe framework within which to process the unknown elements that lie ahead—and to make sense of them all in terms of that secure world view.

When the development of the learners is in focus, it is necessary to incorporate the situation of the learners into curriculum considerations. Theological learners all come from a base of wanting to grow in their personal knowledge and appreciation of theological and/or ministerial concepts and practices and they have put their trust in a theological institution to lead them to that goal. The first stage of an effective scaffolded curriculum design needs to establish a learning base. This cannot be done by generic assumptions as to where a learner may be (let alone a class of learners). So, the curriculum needs to inject and craft opportunities for learners to communicate what they already know, express what they know they do not know and project what they think they want to know. This needs to be augmented by input to lead them into an understanding of what they will need to know to achieve their goal, whatever that goal may be. Good curriculum design begins with the learners having established a cohesive rationale for their own learning program. It progresses as all ensuing components fit into that sense-making rationale. This primary stage includes both cognitive and attitudinal development, with any systematic content being a servant to that initiation rather than an end in itself.

However, as well as the 'why am I doing this?', there is a need in the early stages for the psychomotor (skills) issue of 'how can I do this?' to be addressed. Again, this involves both levels of 'how have I already learned to do this?' and 'what new skills do I need and how can I develop them?'. Adult learners will have an already-formed approach to thinking and 'doing things', which may need to be affirmed and consolidated or corrected and remediated. Either way, the promotion and constructive development of new and developing skills are a necessary part of curriculum design. As with content, these skills need to be developed from simple beginnings to increasingly complex operations.

So far, I have focused on the early stages of a course. That is justified, since much attrition occurs in those stages, a sure sign of educational problems. It is my firm conviction that this first-year syndrome is caused largely by a crowded and daunting curriculum rather than by intellectual difficulty or lack of other support structures. If beginning students can know why they want and need to do the course, if they are confident that they have or will develop the skills necessary to master the course, and if they are secure in their role as students, they are likely not only to persevere, but also to thrive. Curriculum design has an important role to play in creating the environment and structures for such thriving.

> *Critical Reflection.* If we are to locate the learner at the outset of study, and if we are to set the learners up for success in their learning with the provision of necessary safety nets, how would you design a first semester curriculum base? How would your design improve on current curriculum design?

But first year is (generally) not the endgame of a curriculum. On the basis of such a personalised approach to beginnings, progress can be made to enhance and to systematise knowledge and analysis of content and to develop and refine critical skills of performance. However, all should be done in continuation of, not disregard for, what has preceded it. Consistent reference to established world view will ensure and consolidate learners' security. The performative skills development commenced in the early stage will have consistent and increasingly complex opportunities for application, and increasingly complex concepts and practices will be engaged. Learners will have increasing control over what they learn and will clarify their personal focus within the broad ambit of theological study. Whereas first-year syndrome is typified by novelty, excitement and trepidation, and final-year syndrome is typified by impatience and expectation of completion, second-year syndrome is commonly expressed as frustration, loss of zeal and direction, and general boredom with 'business as usual'. In the middle stages of a curriculum, freshness of perspective is necessary, with new encounters of concepts, issues or skills. At various points throughout the long haul of an extended program, learners need opportunities to appreciate and to express the new perspectives they have established thus far, the new sense they have been able to make of things and a sense of personal growth with anticipation of 'more to come'. Effective curriculum design will factor such opportunities strategically into the program.

Finally, the end stages of a curriculum should provide the structures of an articulated 'making sense of it all'. This will ideally involve greater autonomy in content and approach by individual learners, as they give expression to what graduate attributes they have developed in a personal application of their learning to their particular context. This will involve the highest levels of learning domains that have emerged during their course and will typically provide some form of 'capstone' experience, even if it does not include a formal unit by that name. It should be an opportunity to overcome any (unwanted) atomistic discipline-based fragmentation of learning in a way that will give evidence of a rounded formative educative experience. The final stages need not be marked by longer and more intensive assignments. Rather, at this point, higher levels of complexity should feature, as all the elements of cognitive, affective, and psychomotor domains coalesce. At this stage, learners will demonstrate the highest level of their capacity for effectual learning, which should show promise of an ongoing capacity for independent initiative in learning in diverse, as yet unknown, and more complex contexts.

> *Critical Reflection.* What are some elements you would include in your curriculum (at the level of either a discipline or an award) to inject (a) freshness and growth in the middle stages and (b) cohesive 'making sense of it all' in the final stages?

A Planning Cycle

Given that learning in a theological context has so many nuances of cognitive, affective, vocational, relational, attitudinal and spiritual complexities, these need to be kept in a consistent balance throughout the planning and implementation stages of curriculum development. Hence, curriculum design should not be a haphazard or piecemeal activity. It needs to be carried out as an ordered system.

Figure 3.4 was created on the basis of a helpful cycle of curriculum planning provided by Alan Harkness. It suggests a coherent sequence of the elements of curriculum design and the processes involved in developing a structurally designed program. It harmonises with the general tenor of the content of this chapter. Such a cycle views curriculum as being constantly under review, with periodic points of formal revision as it is adapted in light of both assessed effectiveness and emerging needs. The seven steps are both sequential and cyclic. Once the planning review is 'complete', it resumes a new period of monitoring and review. Curriculum is never static, but it should always be systematic and strategic.

Figure 3.4: The Curriculum Cycle[7]

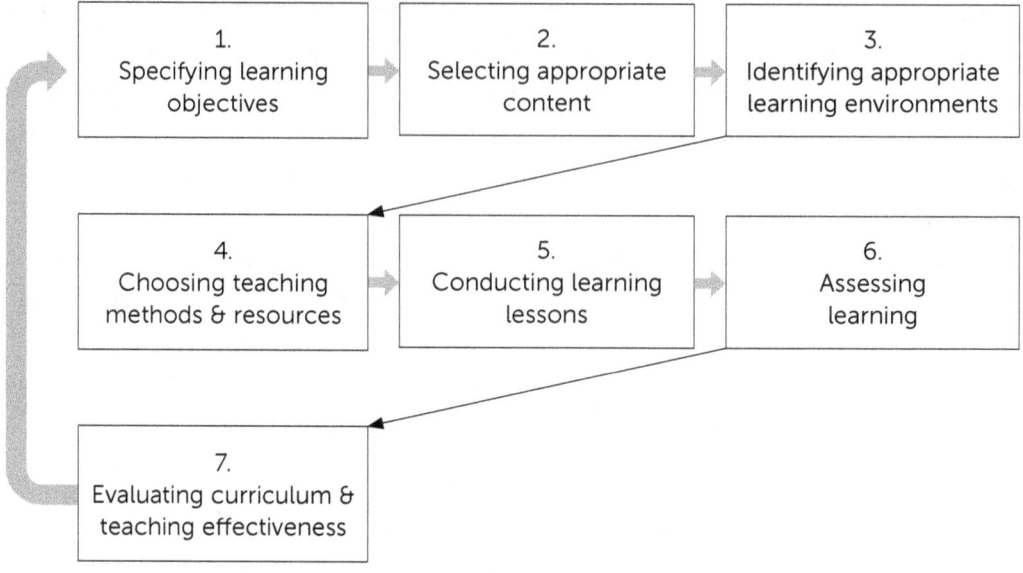

B. CONSTRUCTING CURRICULUM: CONTENT, SKILLS, VALUES

This section examines the role and nature of the essential elements of all theological curriculum: content, skills and values. It concludes with recommendations for desired levels of curriculum construction that may be applied regardless of the course content. In doing so, it encourages a seemingly radical but realistically attainable overhaul of traditional curriculum structure and sequencing. The ultimate quest is for a holistically integrated curriculum.

Curriculum Disposition

The first decision to be made in designing any curriculum is to define the designer's disposition to the overall task because such a starting point will very much shape the entire construction process. In this regard, the recommendations of the Transforming Theology project proposed a student-centred curriculum in

---

7   Based on Harkness, 'The Role of Academic Leadership', 143.

which, rather than introducing students to the world of theology, theology was injected into the lives of the students. The ethos of these recommendations reflected a contest of recent decades between advocates of a (traditional) content-centred curriculum and advocates of a (progressive) student-centred curriculum. As author of that book, I located myself in the student-centred camp. I maintained that position in a paper in 2014, in which I asserted: 'I am (now) more committed than ever before to a philosophy of student-centred learning and teaching' in contrast to my long tradition of 'a thorough-going delivery of content-centred curricula'.[8] Since that time, however, as I have continued my work on curriculum development, I have come to a more mediating position of a holistically integrated curriculum, which is what I seek to promote in the following paragraphs.

As noted previously, the strengths of a content-centred curriculum are grounded in the faithful transmission of sacred content and immersion in the classical fields of theological knowledge and disciplines, which remain a core requisite. Yet, its implied claims to comprehensive and foundational coverage are unrealistic. On the other hand, the strengths of a learner-centred curriculum are grounded in the theological formation of the person as the main objective, acknowledging all the individual differences in each learner's background, experience, capacity, aspiration and future roles. However, ideal individualised learning is largely impractical and lacks confidence in its overall adequacy. Consequently, an emphasis on either approach will entail positive strengths with collateral weaknesses. Advocates of both approaches have valid causes and make valid criticisms. My ideal of a holistically integrated curriculum is a quest for the combined strengths of both camps and the conquering of the noted shortcomings of both causes.

Curriculum Components: Content, Skills, and Values

When it comes to the basic building components of curriculum, there are as many myths as there are constructive guidelines. As we examine now the components of content, skills and values that need to be incorporated into curriculum, I will begin by refuting a myth and then proceed to offer proposals for inclusions.

---

8   Ball, 'Where are we going?', 12.

Table 3.2: Typical Traditional Course Structure[9]

Year	Biblical Studies	Christian Thought	Christian Practice	Electives
1	Introductory Biblical Languages Introduction to Old Testament Introduction to New Testament Hermeneutics	Foundational Theology Introductory Church History	Introduction to Ministry Introduction to (Christian Education, Communication, Missions, Youth)	Christian World view Spiritual Formation Field Placement
2	Advanced Greek/Hebrew Old and New Testament Exegesis	Systematic Theology Ethics Philosophy Church History Unit	Core Pastoral Unit Supervised Field Education	Bible, Theology, Pastoral Units
3	Old and New Testament Exegesis	Systematic Theology Philosophy	Core Pastoral Unit Supervised Field Education	Bible, Theology, Pastoral Units Independent Studies
4	Old or New Testament Exegesis	Systematic Theology	Internship	Research Project

(a) Content

Perhaps the most problematic myth about theological content is the claim of *comprehensiveness,* which incorporates two dimensions. First, it is self-evident that no curriculum can possibly contain all the content that is involved in the world of theological thought and ministerial practice. Second, no standard curriculum can possibly meet equally the range of needs of all students. Yet these two misconceptions, explicitly stated or implicitly pervasive, have long dominated standard theological curricula. Historically, the most prevalent theological course in Australia is the Bachelor of Theology, which has served as a platform for variant streams of undergraduate and postgraduate parallels. It has traditionally had a strong emphasis on a first year of study devoted to introductory units in various sub-disciplines and a heavy concentration of biblical and theological studies throughout the course, with a relatively lesser emphasis on practical units and even less on personal development units (although the more recent Bachelor of Ministry and its parallel awards, with similar basic structures,

---

9   Derived from Ball, *Transforming Theology*, 41. The fourth year shown is not common, but where it is employed, it serves mainly as an intensification of the focus of the third year.

have a heavier presence of skills-based units). Table 3.2 is generally indicative of the typical traditional structure of most bachelor degrees in Theology.

In practice, content selection always commands the most attention in constructing a curriculum. However, there are various operational predispositions, aligned with educational objectives, that come into play in the selection process. The various criteria of selection can be summarised as:

- what the learner should know, which has a societal base, aimed at equipping the learner to fulfil societal expectations
- what the learner needs to know, which has a formative or vocational outcome in view
- what the learner wants to know, which has an inquiry-based personal developmental approach
- what the learner can get to know, which I suggest is a fundamentally mathegenical quest.

The first two of the above approaches have a teacher-oriented focus in the determination of what is needful for the learner—every learner—to master. This will result in a firmly set and organised construction that can be consistently delivered and readily mapped. The third approach will by its nature be far looser in construction because it will operate on a more general base with greater flexibility and inbuilt points of divergence to accommodate emergent individual contexts. The fourth approach provides a clear framework for growth, encompassing both necessary structure and desired flexibility, in charting a course in which individual learners may develop their potential to learn in whatever direction and to whatever extent they may be capable of attaining. This approach focuses not so much on an individual's vocational need or personal aspiration, but on developing potential to learn.

Regardless of which approach guides the selection of content, the futile quest for comprehensiveness of content needs to be replaced with *judicious and sufficient representativeness* of content. The biblical canon is basic to the Christian faith and must take a significant place in curriculum. But what selection of biblical text is sufficient to be legitimately representative? That is a fundamental question that needs to be addressed and its answer will depend on the needs and philosophy of a particular institution: what a theologically articulate graduate must know of the biblical canon versus what a theological learner needs to engage to develop a mastery of biblical learning. My guideline is always: what does a graduate of this college need to master a biblical text, any text, including the texts not specifically incorporated in the syllabus? Simply offering a vast array of biblical books for exegesis may look comprehensive in a syllabus document, but the reality is that no one student can take all those units, so why offer so many? I am convinced that it is far wiser to limit the amount of text coverage—in both a unit and a course—to allow a greater depth of mastery of both conceptual analysis and technical interpretation, which combines the need for content (sacred text), skill (of interpretation), and values (of personal appropriation). So too with all elements of the curriculum content. What will our graduates need to know of systematic theology, of the church's historical traditions, of ministerial duties, of ethical processes, and of other life situations? A Catholic college will need far more on Vatican studies while a Coptic college will place high value on the wisdom of the Desert Fathers. A candidate for accredited Catholic ministry will need a heavy focus on Holy Sacraments, while a Reformed candidate will focus more on Preaching the Word. Social issues of today may well have a short lifespan, so the processes of resolving issues may be more permanently relevant than the content of those issues themselves. In general, the mission of the college and the desired graduate attributes will drive the representative selection of content in all awards. The selection of content will always be very limited, so that limitation needs to be as productive of effective learning as possible.

As well as content selection, there is the consideration of content sequencing within a curriculum. The issue of sequencing will be taken up in greater detail below, but at all times there needs to be an appropriate introductory level of content (rather than an overload), followed by a cohesive and developmental selection of content located at pertinent points in the curriculum, and culminating in a coherent application of integrated learning.

> *Critical Reflection.* Does the content coverage in your discipline within a specific award (for example, Bachelor of Theology or Bachelor of Ministry) meet the criterion of 'judicious and sufficient representativeness'?

(b) Skills

The skills myth that needs to be rejected is that of *currency*. Society has always been in a state of flux, probably never more so than in our contemporary world. The skills needed for critical analysis or ministry performance are constantly changing and a curriculum that develops fixed skills and methods of operation is unwise and likely to have a very short shelf life—or at least a very short useful life. Skills come in two sets of functioning. One set is the process skills of critical analysis—of texts, concepts, movements, and practice. The other set is the performative skills of vocational practice—of preaching, leadership, counselling, and interpersonal relationships. There is an irony in the curricular engagement with these two sets of skills. There is a tendency to demand the former set of critical skills, yet we do not devote much curriculum space to their development, despite their capacity to be transferable to variable contexts and developing life circumstances. Conversely, we spend much more structured time and space in the curriculum on the performative skills, despite the fact that the pace of change is so outrageously rapid that today's cutting-edge methods are likely to be tomorrow's obsolescence. In a contemporary curriculum design, there needs to be structured space for the development of critical skills and the management of fundamental principles of performance coupled with a capacity for methodological agility in such skills.

So, how do we factor into curriculum these essential skills? First, I advocate the strategic inclusion of introductory units that focus on critical process skills development, preferably with an interdisciplinary perspective. In this way, students are immediately aware that theological education is not just about *what* we think but about *how* we think. The development of the particular hermeneutical skills in any discipline will provide basic tools for the deep processing of the content to be encountered. 'Losing valuable time' to early skills development at the cost of 'valuable content time' is a wise investment that will pay dividends in the later and more efficient encounter with content. However, such early skills development will need ongoing consolidation and, therefore, should be both assumed and progressed in later units of study. To expect students to be efficient exegetes or theologates or historians without first equipping them with the necessary critical tools is a serious flaw in curriculum design.

Similarly, performative skills need progressive development and practice. In a large class setting, it is common to provide beginning students with a set of basic methodological principles and ask them to present a written statement of implementation, but with limited opportunity for practical experience. It is also common to include current and successful practitioners in the instruction and oversight of students' performance, often in a workplace setting. While all such approaches are valid, there are some words of caution needed. Theoretical awareness of principles is a very limited basis for skills development, so space for active experience within the curriculum is needed, in which a student may develop by means of trial and error, but the error should not be counterproductive. This is where that safety net of world view and understanding the processes come into play. While a successful practitioner is valued, such a practitioner may unconsciously tend to present 'this is my way and it is the way to succeed', without the critical understanding of the inherent ephemerality or non-transferability of many methods. Students need to learn to hold lightly to pet methods and to be prepared to leap with agility in the performative domains of their life and ministry. That will need progressive development at pertinent points in the curriculum.

As an illustration of this sort of developmental thinking, an introductory unit on theological study has been designed by a course manager Stephen Parker. The following unit details indicate the essence of that unit.[10]

Unit: Introduction to Theological Study

Discipline: Pastoral Theology

Goal: To help beginning students to develop the skills, knowledge, and character that will assist them as they prepare for practical Christian ministry.

Objectives:

1. To improve the performance of students by helping them to begin developing the skills, knowledge, and character that will assist them in the rest of their studies.
2. To improve the specific skills required for academic success.
3. To help students increasingly to acquire the Christ-like character that is crucial for Christian ministry and helpful for academic study.
4. To scaffold basic knowledge in a cross-disciplinary way, to allow students to develop a broad but coherent base of knowledge and skills that will equip them for both their remaining studies and future ministry.
5. To help students' self-location academically, helping them to identify their academic skill set and provide helpful pathways for their improvement where relevant.
6. To help students' self-location with respect to their overall reasons for studying by helping them to explore their motivations, goals, and plausible outcomes from their study.

---

10 The details presented here are extracted from a planning paper presented by Stephen Parker to the Course Committee of Australian College of Ministries, Sydney, 2021. They are included here by permission of Dr Parker.

Outline

Topic	Sub-discipline	Focus	Links	Key skills
The how and why of ministry training	Pastoral Theology	- Academic skills: 'Why are you studying?' - The nature of Pastoral Theology	Session 8 Vocation Session 10 Lifelong learning	Academic skills generally
The God of Love	Theology	- Theological idea that God is loving as foundation for identity, theology, mission, and spiritual formation. - The nature of Theology	Session 10 Mission	Comprehension of the love of God
Identity and Spiritual Formation	Christian Spirituality	- Identity - Spiritual Disciplines - The nature of Spiritual Formation	Session 1 Why studying? Session 2 Love Session 8 Vocation John's identity as 'beloved'	Exploring our unique purpose
The Biblical Text	Biblical Studies	- How to read and interpret the Bible - Importance of context, need for humility before text and textual analysis	Session 5 Humility Session 10 History	Basic biblical interpretation
Humility and Critical Thinking	Pastoral Theology	- The Bible on humility - Connections between humility, critical thinking, and theological analysis - Osmer's tool for theological analysis	Session 3 Identity Session 10 Lifelong learning John's identity as disciple/learner	Applying Osmer to a theological issue
Empathy and Pastoral Reflection	Pastoral Theology	- The Bible on empathy - Pastoral reflection, empathy, and humility - Adding 'reaction' and 'empathy' to Osmer for Theological Reflection Tool	Session 5 Humility	Applying expanded Osmer/TRT to a pastoral situation

Topic	Sub-discipline	Focus	Links	Key skills
Listening	Pastoral Counselling	- Personal value derived from Image of God - Need to listen well - Listening, loving, mission - Skills for listening - Listening as a tool for spiritual formation, mission, counselling and conflict resolution	Session 3 Spiritual Formation Session 5 Humility Session 6 Empathy Session 9 Mission	Developing listening skills
Vocation	Pastoral Theology	- Vocational identity. - Balance and boundaries - Sabbath and rest	Session 1 Why studying? Session 3 Identity	Reflection on vocational clarity
Mission and History	Mission and Christian History	- Document analysis - Nature of historical literature as distinct from biblical literature - Significance of history for pastoral reflection on ministry	Session 2 Love Session 7 Listening	Document analysis
Lifelong learning	Pastoral Theology	- Importance of lifelong learning	All previous sessions	Developing plans for future learning

Reflection by designer on process: Interestingly, in compiling the readings and other resources for students to learn from, it became tempting to shift the focus of the unit to a content-based learning environment. What will be crucial with these units is to write carefully crafted introductions to each session that will keep the focus of the students and the unit itself on skill and character development as much as informational acquisition.

Critical Reflection. What is the balance of critical process skills and performative skills in your area of involvement? Where is there space across the curriculum for the progressive development of these skills?

(c) Values

Values are the slippery cousins in this family of curriculum components. Often, this is an area left largely to the informal hidden curriculum, which certainly has a significant part to play, but remains at best intangible and often unreliable, and at times it may even be in contradiction to what the institution purports to teach. The hidden curriculum may be beneficial in enriching the personal and spiritual life of the learner or it may be malevolent in embedding unhealthy values as a norm of life. In either case, the hidden curriculum is well understood as 'the unwritten, unofficial, and unintended values and dispositions that those involved in the educative process learn'.[11] A key word in that definition is 'unintended', which in terms of designing a cohesive institutional curriculum, is fraught with uncertainties and potential corruptions. The formal curriculum needs to be aware of, consistent with, and contributing to the culture of the prevailing hidden curriculum of the institution. Hence the formal curriculum needs to incorporate elements that remove disharmony and restore harmony with the hidden curriculum. A key consideration in this aspect is to ensure congruency between the content and stated goal of our teaching and the processes by which we teach. That is, the content we present and the skills we promote need to be dynamic demonstrations of the values we espouse.

While the power of the hidden curriculum is pervasive, the dominant myth that I want to dispel immediately is that of the sufficiency of learning *values by osmosis*. It may happen—it may not. It involves the informal curriculum, but it should also involve the formal curriculum. Our responsibility as curriculum designers is not to hope it happens but to construct formal protocols and processes that encourage it to happen, to provide opportunities and activities that will facilitate the development of learners' appropriation of values and personhood.

As with the previous components, the groundwork needs to be laid early and built on progressively. An early awareness of the desired personal graduate attributes will be grounded in a coherent world view articulation. What sort of person the institution wants its graduates to become will determine the shape of this institutional world view. The student needs to understand from the outset that the development of values is to do with the concepts that become a part of a person's identity and thereby shape the whole of one's life. It relates to a way of *becoming*, not just knowing or doing. Progressively throughout the curriculum, learning practices that promote personal integration need to include

---

11 Jusu, 'The Impact of Hidden Curriculum', 255.

regular strategic opportunities for critical reflection, review, and modification of held positions. Such opportunities may involve the need for the 'deformation' of some prior positions, since many learners will have barriers of fear, prejudice or false humility that resist integration in learning, and such distorting perspectives need to be processed and repaired through learning. The reflective review may be done at an individual student's level, by means of personal journaling; it may occur in a peer situation in seminars or discussion groups; it may be facilitated by intentionally designed assignments processed by the teacher. Such formal work allows for intense theological synthesis, which is especially relevant to the later stages of a course.

> *Critical Reflection.* How do/can you manage the process of 'de-formation' and 're-formation' of students' conceptual frames of reference? Can you identify points in your teaching program where such processing would be particularly pertinent?

Two particular items warrant attention: the role of peer learning and the distinctive case of online learning. Peer learning is surprisingly under-utilised, considering the frequency with which team functioning is required by theological graduates. Perhaps this is an outcome of a keenly individualistic assessment mentality built on competitiveness. It is also the area most commonly noted in student and stakeholder reviews as a weakness of theological education. Yet the promotion of peer collaboration is an effective means of facilitating holistic integration. It is an area of relational development in which relational integrity as well as conceptual integration may be promoted. Peer learning ranges from group discussion and presentations to more extended projects (in virtually any field) and to individual tutoring of students by students. Progressive responsibility for not only one's own learning but also for that of one's peers may not be traditional, but it does sit well with concepts of integrated service within a social setting.

The realm of online learning seems the most problematic for the development of personal values. The inherent sense of remoteness and isolation militates against group cohesiveness, which is the natural arena for the development of values. The main obstacle is this sense of 'absence of presence', so that is the element that needs to be redressed within the curriculum (as well as in pedagogical methods). A conceptual framework of a community of inquiry focuses on cognitive presence, social presence and teaching presence. Such a community needs the strategic incorporation of academic leaders, teaching faculty, general staff, and students who together contribute to the creation of an atmosphere in which teaching and learning become 'part of the formation of life for ministry'.[12] The institutional starting point for such an online community of learning is the establishment of teacher presence. This involves curriculum design, which selects and meaningfully integrates learning and assessment activities, the creation of opportunities for discourse to develop an effective group consciousness for the purpose of sharing meaning and understanding, and direct instruction, where a teacher provides scholarly leadership in terms of expert input and timely and extensive constructive feedback.[13] In our contemporary digital world, rather than fretting over the perceived shortcomings of online learning, we need to be moving strategically towards harnessing its potential for enhancement of the learning process, be that in totally online or blended delivery. As the teacher presence is vital to classroom teaching, so too it is vital in the online platforms. No matter how logistically attractive it may be to consider online teaching as less labour intensive, and thus more economically efficient, than classroom teaching, such a view is a fallacy: the requirement of a community of learning with teachers and learners in collegiate functioning is imperative in all forms of delivery.[14]

> *Critical Reflection.* Examine a typical offering of units in your discipline through a typical course of study taken by a student in a major degree (for example, Bachelor of Theology or Bachelor of Ministry). To what degree does this suite of units accommodate the contribution of content, skills, and values that are important to your institutional tradition?

Curriculum Structure and Sequencing

Cohesion and integration are the hallmarks of a curriculum structure that produces the desired graduate outcomes of effective learning. In addressing the

---

12 For more on general principles and specific suggestions for the implementation of a meaningful community of inquiry, see Deininger, 'Developing a Learning Community'.
13 For a case study of how teaching presence was increased in a graduate unit, and for some suggestions for implementation in other online courses, see Budhai & Williams, 'Teaching Presence in Online Courses', 76–84.
14 For more on the nexus between modern technology and learning design in an online and blended context, and for further thoughts on implementation, see McEwen, 'Blended Learning', 201–223. This chapter complements the thoughts in the article cited in the previous footnote.

notion of integrated curriculum design, Vera Brock advocates the desirability and necessity of a holistic curriculum that balances knowledge, living, and doing. But such an outcome should be more than merely aspirational; it needs conscious and careful planning and implementation. Brock notes that 'writing a curriculum is a challenging creative activity', as 'a curriculum that is well planned is similar to a house that has been well planned. Everything flows with clear explanations for why it is as it is'.[15] A former principal of mine would regularly remind both his staff and his students, 'This college has a proud history of over 100 years; but longevity of existence is not a justification for continued existence'. I add, as for the college, so too for our curriculum. With these thoughts in mind, where do we start the curriculum construction process?

In the relatively recent period of the need for official accreditation of theological programs by external agencies, an ethos of benchmarking of curriculum has become dominant. The admirable goal of this is to ensure comparability of educational standards, but in the process, it has tended towards mandating a uniformity of courses, in both content and structure, which militates against any radical variation in programs. Against this backdrop, I suggest that a pressing need in current theological curriculum design is to change the starting point from 'what have we (and others) always done?' (a benchmark compliance approach) to 'what do we need to do?' (a benchmark setting approach). An integrative curriculum structure that espouses mathegenical principles will be strategically concerned with levels and progression of learning rather than comprehensiveness of content or comparability of structures. This does not dispense with the required content, but it bases its course framework on the *learners' level of operation rather than on discrete sets of content*. This concept of Levels of Learning provides a fruitful structural base for curriculum that harmoniously and concurrently combines the virtues of knowledge mastery, skills development, and values formation. The following proposal is one suggestion for consideration.[16]

Level 1: Establishing a Hermeneutical Skills and World View Base

Level 1 introductory units will dominate the early stages of a course, notionally between one semester and one year in most courses. The focus of units at this level is the creation of a platform for integrative learning. These units will:

---

15   Brock, 'Integrated Curriculum Design', 281–315.
16   This proposal is based on the model first suggested in Ball, *Transforming Theology*, 142–144.

- introduce academic and research skills
- initiate process and performance skills
- establish a philosophical frame of reference for the whole course.

They will draw on a range of content from the traditional bases of theological learning, but not in a compartmentalised way. Rather, they will use such content in ways that show their complementary interconnectedness and their effective use in theological inquiry and personal application. Students will be encouraged to see the Bible, theology, and philosophy in a holistic light which will guide the whole course of study and personal development. Many colleges currently include a small number of such units, but their delivery is generally piecemeal, and they are typically delivered as extracurricular topics because there is no room for them in the crowded award structure. However, these elements are not extracurricular but essential curriculum. Currently, it is common for first level units to offer a smorgasbord of content, which typically involves an overwhelming body of material in total, with little space for deep processing. In an integrative curriculum structure, the pace of Level 1 needs to be slowed down to allow an effective learning base to be firmly established.

Level 2: Application and Development of Level 1 base

Level 2 units will comprise the bulk of the course, occupying notionally around two-thirds of the award. The focus of these units is:

- the development of mastery of the skills of inquiry initiated in the Level 1 units, with
- regular and consistent provision for experiential learning, and
- critical reflection on and development of personally held views.

The bulk of the theological content of the course will be transmitted in these units as students progress in their analysis and processing of core content and their development of skills related to personal contexts and vocational areas. There will be a continuation of the prevailing motif of the interconnectedness of all units, in their historical development, their conceptual consonance, and their practical and personal application. A curriculum designed with these components in mind will have ramifications for the methods of pedagogical delivery, which will be addressed in more detail in the following section of this book.

Level 3: Integrative Synthesis of Studies

Level 3 units will provide the final stage of the course, with 'integration' being

the guiding motif. The focus of these units is:
- the students' individual self-location
- expression of world view in theory and/or practice.

These units provide the learners with an increased responsibility for shaping and conducting their own learning as the culmination of their study. These units will not involve the formal transmission of additional content but will require the student to execute interdisciplinary studies to link various strands of study already undertaken or to extend those learnings to an identified area of individual relevance. Such inductive studies as synthesising personal biblical, theological, or historical surveys (as distinct from having had these overviews given to them in first year), the creation of an individual ministry or other vocational philosophy, and the integration of any such concepts within an articulate theological framework are aimed at developing a well-formed and integrated graduate. Capstone studies to personalise and apply studies, individually designed research studies to promote individual further in-depth inquiry, and action projects to apply learning to a practical situation typify such units.

The structure proposed above is but one example of a curriculum built on mathegenical principles. Its primary objective is to maximise the learner's capacity to learn efficiently, independently, and expansively, with reference to syllabus materials and beyond. Such a curriculum design structure facilitates the progressive and consistent development of such desired graduate attributes. However, two associated questions immediately arise. First, if we include these sorts of personal developmental units, does that mean we will need to double the length of the course? Alternatively, if we add these units without extending the time for the course, does that mean we will need to dispense with important content? One answer suffices: neither of these negative implications needs to follow because there is no need to abandon sacred content or to take extra years. What is required is a thoroughgoing review of why and, especially, how we do what we do. What is needed is not an expansion of the curriculum but a smartening and refining of it. Since the quest for comprehensiveness of content is arguably as futile as it is flawed, and since the popularity of modern techniques will inevitably fade into obsolescence, it makes good sense to ensure a mastery of the skills of learning and personal development, so that a lifetime of effectual learning and development may be generated rather than seeking merely to transmit an inevitably limited corpus of knowledge or to train in a transitory set of vocational skills.

4 | CURRICULUM REVIEW AND DEVELOPMENT

This final chapter of Part 2 examines the important aspect of curriculum review and development, as introduced in the statement of Principles of Curriculum Design in Chapter 2, which stated that 'curriculum should be constantly reviewed for relevance, currency and ongoing contribution to the overall program'. That statement was expanded to note that 'a curriculum that is set in concrete will soon weigh down the learning process' and that 'curriculum needs to be constantly updated to remain relevant to the community of learners, church, stakeholders, and the academy'. If our curriculum aims to produce effectual learner-graduates, then it needs to maintain currency for learning in settings that are continuously evolving. No matter how successful a curriculum design may be now, it will always have opportunities for development and enhancement as new influences and contexts arise. Formal comprehensive curriculum reviews are large and daunting undertakings, but they are ideally facilitated by a system of continuous review so that the global review flows out of a developing culture rather than being viewed as a point-in-time venture. This chapter examines elements such as the frequency of and personnel involved in reviews and offers suggestions for the process of strategic review.

A. FREQUENCY OF REVIEW

There is no one optimal time period for a curriculum review, other than to note that any curriculum that has not been seriously reviewed for five to seven years is well past due! In saying that, I repeat—curriculum review is not a moment-in-time event but is, or at least should be, a continuous dynamic process. There will be a time, typically around three to five years, when a comprehensive review of all programs is warranted, but much curriculum review will take place along the way, as various factors emerge.

Factors that commonly generate such ad hoc responses usually relate to the need for currency (such as with new legislative or regulatory requirements), necessity (such as changing stakeholder requests, student enrolments), or pragmatics (such as staffing availability, administrative elements). However, these aspects are largely externally driven and essentially forced on institutions, which need to respond appropriately, typically by way of amending official documentation or reducing or expanding unit offerings or combinations. This does not really cut to the core of a learner-oriented curriculum. From a learning perspective, more vital elements for continuous review are the efficacy of the curriculum for achieving its aspirations among graduates (its outcomes) and the identification of opportunities for enhancement (of content and/or processes).

Rupen Das has framed a review process based on gathering feedback from constituents in the areas of course activity (what the students have done), course outputs (successful graduations and employment), and course outcomes (post-graduation impact of learning). While there is much more to curriculum review than merely receiving feedback, his recommendations provide a workable idea of the frequency of review. Table 4.1 is a summary structure composed on the basis of his scheme.

The optimal time for the various elements of review is as close as possible to the actual time of delivery of units under review or, in the case of a new award, after the first cohort has passed through it. Ideally, every unit and course offering should be critically reviewed with a view to active enrichment to be implemented. Such continuous inputs are not typically radical overhauls but more commonly involve nuancing of functioning. At the more formal review stage, the accumulation of such nuanced developments should serve as a clear guide to whatever major revisions are needed and are likely to enhance the overall learning. While such ongoing curriculum refinement will be continuous, it is wise for all institutional academic leadership to conduct a formal review and projection of curriculum at least annually. By such regular critical reflection on what has been done, what has and has not gone well, how it was received, and what plans may be implemented in the next period, a curriculum retains freshness and vitality. This regularity provides an enhanced capacity for agile and quick response as necessary and prevents insidious curricular morbidity.

Table 4.1: Frequency of Review Feedback[1]

ACTIVITY			
Content	Participants	Methodology	Frequency
1. Feedback on a unit by student and faculty	Faculty and students	Course evaluation	At the end of every unit delivery
OUTPUT			
Content	Participants	Methodology	Frequency
1. Output from the educational program	Students	Fulfil graduation requirements	Once a year
2. Graduate profile	Students	Self-assessment	
OUTCOME			
Content	Participants	Methodology	Frequency
Self-Assessment What (from their learning) are they using? Not using? Wish they had learned? etc	Graduates	Questionnaire Interview	Every 2–3 years
Community Assessment Assess the graduate in each of the above areas	The employing body of the graduate/s	Focus groups	

Critical Reflection. When was the last time your institution's curriculum was comprehensively reviewed? What elements of curriculum have been progressively reviewed? How satisfactory has this approach been?

B. REVIEW PERSONNEL

Who should be involved in curriculum review? Short answer: everyone. Real answer: shaped by the institutional leadership. As with all organisational development, leadership should lead, but that leadership should embrace all

---

[1] Based on Das, *Connecting Curriculum with Context*, 48–49.

parties of interest as meaningfully as possible in any given context.

Effective management of the review process will involve one leader (for example, chief academic officer, principal, academic dean) who will have overall management of the process, working in liaison with a small core group (for example, department heads, curriculum committee), with reporting accountability to an overseeing and authoritative body (for example, academic board, council). Such management provides a coherent framework of critical review, creative input, and regulatory checks and balances, on the basis of good governance. What is not healthy management is any system that has individuals working in isolation without clear guidelines and without recourse to the input of others. Too often, I have seen such formal reviews fall largely on the shoulders of one diligent senior faculty member, who ultimately presents a worthy review report and recommendations, but the overall process results in little real action, as the ownership of the process has been severely limited. The people who will be needed to implement the improvements also need to be meaningfully involved in the formulation of those improvements if they are to gain any traction in practice. A coherent curriculum will require coherence in review, not 'lone wolf' operations.

Participants in the review process should be drawn from a wide and representative range of personnel. While curriculum reviews are often concentrated in teaching faculty, that is an essential but too narrow a scope for genuine review. Curriculum needs to be informed by various intelligences, and the process of gathering such intelligence requires engagement with various stakeholders. This will include the college's institutional masters (local church, denominational leaders, private owners, and sponsors), whose interests need to be known and honoured, even if they do not always sit comfortably with the inclinations of faculty. The academic board will represent these views to some extent, but the board's closeness to the college may blur some issues, so a wider range of institutional personnel helps to provide a more 'arm's length' perspective. Regular employers of graduates also need input because their perspective will be shaped by their experience of graduates, whose work beyond the college (and beyond the observation of faculty) will determine the wider standing of the college and the utility of its curriculum. These perspectives are vital in assessing the value and relevance of the curriculum.

A major stakeholder is always the student body, past, present, and prospective. Faculty may tend to dismiss student input, especially from present or prospective groups, as being uninformed in matters of curriculum and higher education. However, a curriculum that claims to have learners as a central part of its purpose but does not legitimately respect their input is a self-contradiction. Graduates of the college, both recent and long-term, have experience-based reflection to bring to bear on the curriculum in ways that no other group can. Current students are real-time users, and their voice is current and relevant, even if unsophisticated in educational formalities. Prospective students, either serious inquirers or remotely connected, are like any potential buyers of a product, who present as a virtual focus group on what is marketable in a curriculum. A curriculum review needs to take seriously those trends and issues, of both positive affirmation and negative criticism, which arise from student course evaluations and other student forums.

The teaching faculty also needs to have input into and to share a sense of ownership of the review process. A curriculum designed without such involvement will have minimal commitment to it in implementation. A key function of the leadership of review is to ensure the early 'buy-in' of teachers so they feel informed and important to the process and have genuine input into development and decisions. A key guideline for leaders seeking to create participant buy-in is to listen more than talk, to ask more than tell. Teachers are the coal-face deliverers of curriculum who are best placed to give expert intelligence on the dynamics of any curriculum proposal.

> *Critical Reflection.* Who is involved in (formal or informal) curriculum review in your institution? Who is the main 'driver' of that curriculum review? What are the governance mechanisms for review? Is this process satisfactory?

C. REVIEW PROCESS

In a helpful chapter in Deininger and Eguizabal's *Leadership in Theological Education*, Steve Hardy suggests four general questions that need to be addressed in a review process:

- What are you doing well? Keep it! Celebrate it! Strengthen it!
- What is weak and needs to be fixed?
- What is weak and should be dropped?

- What is missing and should be added?[2]

I would add four more, which are aligned with Hardy's questions but provide a more specific focus:
- What aspects have produced the sort of autonomous learners we seek?
- What aspects have prevented autonomous learning?
- How can we strive for best practice?
- What resources do we have? Do we need? Are attainable? Are beyond reach?

It is common that much curriculum review data will emerge from faculty and student engagement, but there is also the need to obtain feedback from other major stakeholder groups, especially graduates and wider community agencies who employ or otherwise engage with graduates. There are various processes by which the data required to address curriculum issues may be gathered. Bernhard Ott lists five common forms of such data gathering from beyond the campus community:

- individual interviews (formal or informal) with people from the various stakeholders;
- group interviews or observation of group discussions;
- surveys using questionnaires (open questions, rating scales, multiple-choice questions);
- observation of real-life praxis;
- evaluation of indirect sources such as job descriptions, performance reviews, etc.[3]

In combination with student evaluations and faculty critical reviews, such stakeholder input plays a significant complementary role.

These are the sorts of inquiry lines that drive the review process. Answers will come from the variety of stakeholders engaged. Where are we satisfying the demands of our institutional masters, of graduates' future employers? We need to understand not only what works, but why it is working well and ensure we do not jeopardise that strength by any amendments we may make. What issues have arisen from graduates' observations of the curriculum's fitness for their purposes? Are there new and previously unknown or unanticipated issues

---

2 Hardy, 'Steps for Curriculum Design', 69.
3 Ott, *Understanding and Developing Theological Education*, 287.

emerging from the prospective personnel and from a growing awareness of significant changes in societal and cultural perspectives and demands? When we look at our graduating cohort of students, can we identify the growth in their learning capacity that puts them in good stead for whatever they will encounter? Have our strategies for developing that capacity worked?

As well as such marketing perspectives, we need to engage with the academy and educational enterprises. What does the most current and relevant research in education in general and theological education in particular have to offer as guiding insights? What principles have been developed to enrich various teaching modes and community engagement? What new opportunities does technological progress provide for curricular enhancement? How do we optimise our resources to empower learning and generate flexible learning activities? While the marketing issues may be reasonably addressed with point-in-time conversations, these sorts of academic and educational issues require progressive engagement with the academy, which is largely the responsibility of the faculty, especially the senior faculty, who will drive a culture of scholarly development within the learning community. A program of continuing professional teaching development among faculty will have periodic input by faculty members on their own pedagogical learnings and innovations as well as input on educational principles and practices gleaned from the scholarly literature. Such collaborative practice creates an ethos of productive curriculum enrichment.

> *Critical Reflection.* Of all the possible stakeholder consultants, which group (or groups) does your institution value most highly – in principle and in practice?
>
> Is your curriculum review process adequately informed by current research and scholarship?
>
> How could these two elements (stakeholder engagement, scholarly information) be enhanced?

D. TYPES OF CURRICULUM REVIEW

The term 'curriculum review' needs to be understood at different levels. It may of course refer to the comprehensive review of an institution's overall offerings, such as at those crucial reporting periods for formal accreditation. However, much of the continuous review happens at lower levels of individual courses and units to check on the adequacy and quality of aspects of those elements, which can lead to varying degrees of enhancement along the way.

At the level of comprehensive curriculum review, there are a number of stages that need to be included to ensure that meaningful revision and development actually occur, rather than its being an official task that satisfies accreditation bodies but has minimal if any impact on the learning processes. Too many review reports become inert collectors of dust instead of being dynamic spurs for invigoration. If the following stages are actively implemented, active outcomes are more likely to ensue:

- Review the institutional mission statement and global objectives to ensure currency and relevance. What was appropriate ten years ago may need updating or even jettisoning. Being clear as to what we now want to achieve is the first step in meaningful development. An openness to all new input and a willingness to forgo traditional 'sacred cows' where necessary are important aspects of a revisionist ethos.
- Review current courses to check their worth in achieving the global objectives. Are they still necessary? Are they still relevant'? Do we need more or fewer courses? What new things do we now need to address in award offerings?
- Collect quantitative data on course implementation, completions, evaluations, outcomes.
- Gather input from all major stakeholder groups: faculty, students, graduates, employers, and other community agencies. This sort of wide-ranging data collection is often laborious and seemingly less useful in some ways, but it is vital to the successful development and implementation of any improvement that may be envisaged.
- Analyse and draw recommendations from the findings to emerge from the collected data, first at a leadership level and then, most significantly, with the meaningful involvement of all faculty in formulating recommendations, since they will be the ones charged with implementation of the curriculum. Without this level of engagement at this stage, the prospects for active implementation are poor.
- Devise a realistic plan for revision and implementation, including specific time frames and resourcing proposals.

At the level of an individual award, especially a relatively new award, it is helpful to conduct an analytical review of some specific element of the award as a measure of its educational adequacy in delivery. In particular, it is a good idea to check whether the stated learning outcomes are actually suited to the level of the award and whether the learning activities employed are constructively aligned with such learning objectives. This area of the constructive alignment of desired outcomes and learning activities has a constant need for monitoring, as it is in such a congruence that strategic deep learning occurs. In conducting such a review, it is advisable to begin from a set of evaluative criteria and apply those criteria analytically across the award so that a balanced review emerges.

As an example of such a review, I offer here the result of a recent analytical review of a newly created graduate certificate in theological education. The compactness of the award (consisting of four clearly defined units, delivered across the two AQF postgraduate Levels 8 and 9) made this a straightforward case for analysis, but its principles are indicative of the process involved. The specific aim of the review was to analyse the correlation of learning outcomes (LO) with learning activities (LA) that were employed. The evaluative matrix used was Heer's development of the Anderson et al.'s knowledge–cognitive process paradigm associated with their revised Bloom's taxonomy. The report in its entirety presented analytical findings of the various units across the award and drew a summary evaluation, as encapsulated in the concluding table and comment. Such a mapping exercise has provided a valuable insight into not only this award but also other more wide-ranging review undertakings.[4]

---

[4] The report was compiled in 2019 by my colleague Edwina Blair, the Biblical Studies Coordinator at Australian College of Ministries, Sydney, who was also a graduate from the first cohort of the award. I reproduce her table here with her permission.

Comparison of Learning Outcomes, Curriculum Design, and Learning Activities in Grad Cert Units According to the Highest Levels of the Heer's Knowledge-Process Intersection Model

Model Descriptors	D8501 Principles of Theological Education		D9601 Theological Pedagogy		D9602 Theological Curriculum	
	Curriculum Design	Learning Activities	Curriculum Design	Learning Activities	Curriculum Design	Learning Activities
Create			LO5: Create effective programs/materials	Teaching portfolio	LO5: Construct elements of curriculum LO4: produce LO and LA.	Curriculum design analysis; Curriculum design project
Reflect	LO1: Articulate a personal statement...	Individual short answers	LO4: Evaluate strengths and weaknesses of personal teaching styles	Individual short answers Teaching evaluation	LO2: Identify needs in own tradition & context	Individual short answers
Design	LO3 & LO5: Establish general principles & basic design principles	Group project Essay	Also LO5	Teaching portfolio	LO5: Construct elements of curriculum LO4: produce LO and LA.	Curriculum design project
Deconstruct	LO4: Evaluate learning and teaching methods...	Individual short answers	LO2: Identify methods LO3: Match different learning styles	Individual short answers	LO3: Evaluate components	Individual short answers; Curriculum design analysis
Judge	LO2: Assess effectiveness	Individual short answers; Group discussions	LO1: Analyse teaching styles	Individual short answers; Group discussions	LO1: Analyse principles	Individual short answers; Group discussions
Assemble		Reading Face-to-face facilitations		Reading Face-to-face facilitations		Reading; Zoom facilitations

Conclusion: From this analysis it can be seen that that the curriculum design and learning activities in the three Graduate Certificate units do focus on the higher order components of Heer's Model, and that there is a distinction between D8501, at AQF 8, and D9601 and D9602, at AQF 9, predominantly in the area of creating. It is assumed that the final unit of the Graduate Certificate, a Focused Study / Project, will also be located in this highest art of the model, utilising create, reflect and design tasks, in keeping with this model.

The third level of review is that of a single unit of course delivery. A similar process to that of an award review is applicable, but at this level, more focus comes onto the pedagogical aspects of the unit. Once again, I present here a sample of such a review as an illustration of the process. The unit is an introductory online undergraduate unit in Old Testament, which has the following five LOs:

LO1	Demonstrate a general understanding of the overall structure and contents of the Old Testament
LO2	Identify the literary shape, themes, social and historical background of the individual books of the Old Testament
LO3	Employ critical methodologies in the interpretation of Old Testament texts
LO4	Access secondary literature
LO5	Convey the relevance of the Old Testament to Christian life and the contemporary world

The associated student activities included a series of required but non-assessed LA, designated readings (R), instructional videos (V), student placements (SP), and a set of three assessment items (AF forum discussions, AB book report, AE exam). The analytical paradigm employed is that of the knowledge–cognitive process intersection of Anderson et al. As with the previous sample, I reproduce here the summary table and extracts from the final recommendations.[5]

---

5   Blair, 'Analysing Alignment in a Biblical Studies Unit' (forthcoming). This is the second sample analysis provided by my colleague Edwina Blair. I am indebted to Edwina for sharing her insights and for her permission to reproduce her table and comments here.

Introduction to the Old Testament Taxonomy Table						
The Knowledge Dimension	The Cognitive Process Dimension					
	1. Remember	2. Understand	3. Apply	4. Analyse	5. Evaluate	6. Create
A. Factual Knowledge						
B. Conceptual Knowledge		LO1, LO2 R 1, 2, 4, 6, 8, 9, 10 V 1, 2, 4, 6, 8, 9, 10 AF3a, AF3b, AB1, AB2, AB3, C1b AE1c, AE2a, AE2b	LO3, LO4, LO5 R 3,5,7 V 3, 5, 7 A1a, A2, AF3c, AF4a, AF4b AF5a, AF5b, AB4, AE2c	LA2, LA3a, LA3b, LA4a AF1b, AE1a	LA4b	
C. Procedural Knowledge	SP1					
D. Meta-cognitive Knowledge				LA1, LA5 SP2		

6. Recommendations

6.1 Improving the Pedagogical Rigour of B7120

In terms of improvement of B7120, this analysis has provided a visual representation of those areas of weak alignment and misalignment. The weak alignment that exists due to instructional and assessment elements being disconnected from learning objectives can now be targeted specifically.

The areas of misalignment can also be rectified. While the relevance and interconnectedness of the student placement aspect in this has already been mentioned, this is an issue for the entire curriculum rather than B7120 specifically. That is not the case, however, for the isolated misaligned learning activities in B5 and

D4. As previously noted, these non-assessable instructional activities were designed to be done by the student who does not attend a facilitation. The student is therefore more isolated and learning independently and therefore it is even more necessary to ensure these activities are well aligned to the wider unit.

6.2 Improving the Pedagogical Rigour Beyond B7120

The application of this type of analysis in the wider biblical discipline and beyond is significant and has the potential to improve pedagogical rigour by increasing the alignment in any unit to which it is applied. However, in order for this to be undertaken, further steps are required.

6.2.1 Creating a complete Biblical Studies Specific version of the Taxonomy Table (details follow …)

6.2.2. Collaborate with others (details follow …).

While the process is similar to the previous illustration, in this example, the review highlights the weaknesses of the unit in its limited range of knowledge inclusion and its high degree of misalignment of learning outcomes and learning activities. Thus, it clarifies where revisions are necessary and, importantly, how they may be implemented. These two examples show how the application of a tool such as Anderson et al.'s matrix can bring a methodological consistency and operational efficiency to a process of ongoing review and development.

E. A FINAL WORD

In closing this part of the discussion, I note that I have tended to align my approach throughout this study of theological curriculum to the practical theological inquiry model of Richard Osmer. At various points, I have sought to *describe* what is the current state of theological curriculum and the issues and approaches that currently dominate, including some critical analysis of their strengths and weaknesses. There has been engagement in the *interpretive* task of explaining how this state has come into being, with an emphasis on the institutional philosophies and traditions that have driven theological education. The *normative* dimension of what curriculum should look like has had recourse to current thinking and scholarship around curriculum principles and design.

Finally, I reached to the *pragmatic* task of recommending a strategy of action in some proposals for curriculum structure, sequence, and review to try to bring 'what is' into a closer alignment with 'what should be' and ultimately 'what may be'. I suggest that this approach could work well as a guiding pattern for ongoing curriculum review.

PART 3
PERSPECTIVES ON PEDAGOGY

5 | INFLUENCES AND GENERAL PRINCIPLES OF THEOLOGICAL PEDAGOGY

Pedagogy is the study of how we teach learners, that is, how we implement the process of teaching. While we tend to think immediately of practical teaching methods, we need to realise that such pragmatic methods do not exist in isolation. We have already suggested close links between curriculum design and delivery methods, but there is more than that. There are pervasive influences that affect our choice of such methods that need to be understood and critically addressed. There are also certain general principles that govern our implementation of teaching methods which involve all agents of teaching delivery: institutions, teachers, students, processes. In short, we need to grasp the fundamental notion that pedagogy is not so much about the mechanical practices or methods of teaching, but rather it is about what facilitates effective learning. This chapter examines the sorts of influences that surround our teaching practices, engages with some basic principles grounded in a psychology of learning, and reviews the characteristics of the teachers, learners, and processes involved in a variety of approaches to learning.

Influences on Pedagogy

The first influence that has a major bearing on our teaching methods is that of *tradition*, both of the teacher and of the institution. Teachers have their own personal traditions that have shaped their professional development. They are typically products of a teaching approach that has been successful for them, so they tend to resort to how they were taught by their good teachers. This is particularly so in the early formative stages of their teaching career, but once the mould has been cast, it becomes progressively harder to break, and so a pedagogical conservatism can develop to the point of stagnation. Good teaching models are good to emulate, but enslavement to them is not so good.

As well as such personal background and habits, the teaching tradition of the institution may well be set, and teachers are expected to conform. Much of the contextual tradition of a college operates in the political sphere rather than the pedagogical, so it is important to distinguish the two areas. As Brookfield says, 'The first rule of political survival is to know what you are dealing with'.[1] The institution has been established with a purpose; it has a clear mandate expressed in its mission statement, so all employed faculty have a responsibility to honour and to work towards the attainment of that mission statement. Many theological faculty view their roles as being leaders in the preservation or development of the institution's essential doctrines and practices, which often leads to a tension between those two at times conflicting prongs. The constant dilemma is: when does fidelity to tradition breed stagnation and when does critical innovation extend to betrayal of the tradition? Knowing and appreciating the institutional mission statement should always be a prime factor in introducing pedagogical innovation, not only from a pragmatic consideration of being more readily acceptable, but also from the philosophical perspective of modelling an integration of policy and practice.

In a major American research project on the education of clergy, Charles Foster and associates provided an intensive analysis of teaching practices in a wide range of theological institutions. Their book *Educating Clergy* identified four basic patterns of pedagogical intentions across various schools: a pedagogy of *interpretation*; a pedagogy of *formation*; a pedagogy of *contextualisation*; and a pedagogy of *performance*.[2] As a prelude to their analysis, they introduced the notion of 'pedagogical imaginations' reflected in the methods employed in teaching. Where an institution locates its main pedagogical intention will greatly influence not only the course content, but also the very teaching and learning methods employed in the educative process. Then, the first of their pedagogies is concerned with texts and concepts and their full and methodologically sound understanding. The second is to do with the dispositions and habits needed for gathering the community in prayer and worship and to facilitate discussion and expression of feelings. The third is to do with locating and communicating their

---

1 Brookfield, *The Skillful Teacher*, 254.
2 Foster et al., *Educating Clergy*, 67–69.

knowledge in relation to the world around them, in its complex situations and crises. The fourth is to do with the skilful conduct of leadership roles in worship, preaching, rituals, management, counselling, and a host of other traditional roles within churches. True, educating clergy is not the entirety of theological education, but its prominence in the overall educative program is significant for the overall enterprise. Simply naming such an array of pedagogical facets indicates something of the complexity of the teaching role. How we approach each of these four 'apprenticeships' is a fundamental factor in the effectiveness of what we teach and, importantly, in the development of the people whom we teach.

These contextual traditions have a direct bearing on pedagogical practice. When a college is administered by an ecclesiastical body, that administration can easily progress to control, even of teaching methods. If a church establishes a college to preserve its heritage of solid dogmatics, for example, it may well require formal scholarly presentations by its teachers, with no sympathy for methods that may tend to challenge its doctrinal *status quo*. Thus, the emphasis will be on direct instruction rather than critical inquiry and discovery. When inquiry methods are employed, they will typically be within defined and acceptable parameters rather than entering the murky waters of critical challenge of establishment positions. Conversely, if a church seeks to challenge traditional ecclesial expressions in a contemporary society, its teachers may be required to be more actively engaged with community in their methods. Such an ecclesiastical tradition of challenge will manifest itself in dialogical teaching methods focused on argument, debate, evaluation, and creativity rather than direct content delivery and absorption. Of course, even such 'progressive' traditions can themselves become concretised into a new form of dogma that seeks its own preservation, so caution needs to be exercised to maintain critical vigour. Whatever the prevailing contextual tradition, it needs to be recognised, respected, and accommodated as far as political context demands, but it should not be used as a rationalisation of pedagogical limitation or inertia.

> *Critical Reflection.* What traditional expectations or restraints operate in your institution with regard to teaching styles? How much pedagogical freedom to innovate do you have?

The second major influence on teaching methods is the college's main client—the *student body*. The social, ethnic, cultural, educational, and religious backdrop of the group is a constant presence that will often set parameters of pedagogy within which the teacher must operate. Certain cultural and educational backgrounds based on reception of wise knowledge, for example, will demand that the teacher provides all the content they need so they can return it as assessed proof of learning. I have worked with a lecturer who was dismissed when student pressure was brought to bear for failing to do this, as his insistence on a problem-solving approach was quite beyond the class's capacity to appropriate, with a consequently high level of frustration and low level of learning. Other backgrounds will require a greater sense of individual initiative to question and to experiment, and so the boredom of a scholarly lecture presentation will not be long tolerated. A traditional Asian culture that highly regards the wisdom of a teacher may learn best from methods of direct instruction, while a more self-assertive youthful Australian group may need constant opportunity to question and to challenge in order to make sense of their learning. It is important that a teacher learns to read the tenor of the class accurately so teaching methods can be effectively developed.

There are many strategies for tuning in to the attitudes and general ethos of the student body involved, but they all focus on the basic idea of asking the students. This may be done in simple one-minute papers in which the class is asked to write down in one sentence a key point of the lesson at the end of the session, or where they would want to go from there to the next thing to learn, or what they found most (or least) helpful in the previous lesson. Regular learning audits, in which students are asked to write simple statements of what they now know or can do that was not the case a week ago, help both teacher and student to be aware of what learning has—or has not—occurred. The many faces of social media can be exploited to gauge student interest and responses to learning activities. Brookfield offers a detailed explanation of what he calls a critical incident questionnaire, which is an anonymous five-minute one-page response formed around five key questions:

- At what moment in class this week did you feel most engaged with what was happening?
- At what moment in class this week were you most distanced from what was happening?
- What action that anyone (teacher or student) took this week did you find most affirming or helpful?
- What action that anyone took this week did you find most puzzling or confusing?
- What about the class this week surprised you the most?[3]

---

3   Brookfield, *The Skillful Teacher*, 34.

An occasional use of such a response will provide valuable insights for the teacher and opportunity for ongoing dialogue with the class. In all these methods, the simple key to learning how students are engaging with the methods of teaching is to ask them.

> *Critical Reflection.* Describe the main demographic of your student body (either as a college or in a specific unit). What implications for (your) pedagogy might arise from a consideration of this profile?

The third influential factor is *resources*. While there are vast differences across theological colleges and universities in terms of physical resources available, I want to stress that the major pedagogical resource is the teacher. A simple learning audit of the class will reveal some ways to enhance pedagogy: it is up to the teacher to respond creatively to such audits. A radical change in teaching can be effected with simple processes. Many years ago, I had a college class of twenty-five students, many of whom had English as a second language, who politely let me know via a learning audit that I spoke too fast for their notetaking and that they wanted more visual aids to complement my wordy presentations. In response, I simply switched my mode to emailing them a six-to-ten-page lecture note the week before class and made the class time a period of processing rather than delivering the content—with significant PowerPoint and in-class internet activity as essential 'value added' components. The whole teaching–learning dynamic was radically enhanced, which was demonstrated in all future learning and assessment activities. This primitive sort of flipped learning was highly successful, but it required no particular resources to implement—other than my learning the new skill of PowerPoint production. Historically, 'resources' were largely conceived of as hard copy library books and scholarly journals. Today, however, we add things like online resources, internet search engines, workplace settings, social media, global travel, and much, much more. So, resources are helpful, but in general, we have sufficient resources if teachers themselves are sufficiently resourceful.

> *Critical Reflection.* What resources could/would you use to enhance your teaching methods? What resources do you predominantly use? What resources do you need to acquire or develop?

Understanding the Teachers: What They Value and What They Seek to Teach

Having noted these significant influential factors around teaching, the next agency in education is the character of the teacher involved in the process. Stephen Brookfield's seminal work on college teaching, *The Skillful Teacher*, presents an impressive array of pedagogical concepts and practices that are applicable to virtually all teaching disciplines, including theological education (though that is not a specific focus of his work). It begins by listing four core assumptions of skilful teaching: (1) that skilful teaching is whatever helps students learn; (2) that skilful teachers adopt a critically reflective stance towards their practice; (3) that teachers need a constant awareness of how students are experiencing their learning and perceiving teachers' actions; and (4) that college students of any age should be treated as adults.[4] Such qualities are basic to the enhancement of all teaching methods and so warrant repeating at the outset of this chapter.

> *Critical Reflection.* Recount a situation or incident in your teaching that involved you in doing something methodologically abnormal simply in an attempt to help (some) students learn? How did it turn out? Would you repeat the experiment?

As noted above, the teacher is never separated from the institution's character and purpose. The overarching pedagogical intention of the institution, that is, what the institution as a whole considers its main educative purpose, will largely shape not only the content of its programs, but also the methods of teaching that content, and the methods employed need to be understood as an expression of that purpose. A primary focus on interpretation of classical texts and the perpetuation of historical wisdom, for example, will employ teaching methods geared to the development of cognitive intellectualism, while a focus on the formation of spiritual or vocational identity will engage learners in a normative understanding of vocational role and the exploration of personal character expectations. An intentional focus on societal contextualisation will be characterised by methods of engagement of a specific context or agency, while the intention to produce competent 'work-ready' performers will emphasise the

---

4   Brookfield, *The Skillful Teacher*, 15–26.

performing skills for ministry or other associated vocational practice.[5]

Bernhard Ott has added to such insights in his review of the various models of theological institutions that have emerged, which he categorises as Bible schools, universities, seminaries, and alternative extension approaches. He shows how Bible schools have been largely praxis oriented in their explicit missionary purpose and focus on community life, yet at the same time the pedagogy of the Bible school has assumed an uncritical primacy of scriptural theory. Thus, the educational approach is not academic and analytical but is designed to be spiritually affirming and personally motivational. The university approach is clearly more academic in purpose and style. It is conducted as a scientific discipline within the context of a modern university charter, which embraces the critical exploration and advancement of knowledge for its own sake as well as a purpose-driven external outcome of professional preparation, such as in positions of leadership or associated vocational and cultural utility in society. The third model of the (essentially American evangelical) seminary system is viewed as a resolution of the tension between Bible school and university as it seeks to combine personal spirituality, missionary motivation, and praxis orientation, within the ambit of academic work. In his final 'alternative' category, Ott examines examples of such tailored approaches as clinical pastoral education and theological education by extension (with its associated online education). Such specialised approaches have emerged largely from the pedagogical paradigms of the twentieth century and are consequently shaped largely by the operational principles and new opportunities associated with such paradigms. In particular, two driving features of such alternatives are their openness and wide access and the opportunity of integration of workplace learning as a complement to theoretical input.[6] In providing such a review of different institutional models, Ott emphasises the pedagogical significance of the institutional culture, in that it provides teachers and students with a common core on which to build. It provides a coherent framework (which can be either conducive or restrictive) for the setting of its educational goals, and it provides a clear and comprehensible picture of itself to the wider community in its public profile.[7]

While most theological teaching institutions will seek to achieve a balance of the various 'apprenticeships'—the cognitive intellectual apprenticeship, the

---

5   Foster et al., *Educating Clergy*, 20–39.
6   Ott, *Understanding and Developing Theological Education*, 117–136.
7   Ott, *Understanding and Developing Theological Education*, 420–427.

skills apprenticeship, and the normative or identity formation apprenticeship—it is generally true that one such will be a prevailing influence. As such, an individual institution will find itself aligned quite naturally with one of the various models reviewed above. Such shaping influences will be pervasive throughout the teaching methodology, the creative imagination, of the institution. While compliance with the institutional pedagogical intention will drive elements such as content selection and curriculum design, that intention is revealed most clearly in those teaching methods most commonly employed within an institution. When the overt intention of the institution and the ethos of teaching methods align, there is a coherence in the overall educational program; where they are misaligned, there is a strong potential for discord and fragmentation in purpose and outcomes.

> *Critical Reflection.* With which of the models presented by Ott does your institution most naturally align? What sort of formative 'imagination' characterises your institution? What could that imagination become? What are the pedagogical implications of this for your teaching?

The Learner in Context: Developmental, Motivational, Social Factors

Before examining some representative teaching methods, we need also to understand the context of the learners. It is well established that human development has identifiable stages and we do well to have a basic understanding of key developmental markers. Names such as Erikson and Maslow are associated with such developmental stages and needs with regard to psychology and motivation. Further, the social and cultural context of the learners is an ever-present reality that needs to be acknowledged and utilised for effective learning to occur.

Erik Erikson's work, while not always fashionable in critical theory, remains a classic starting point. His theory consists of eight stages of development through which, it is argued, people typically pass from birth to late adulthood at approximate ages. Erikson described particular challenges (or crises) that should be mastered at each stage for healthy development to occur, with failure to master these challenges potentially leading to later difficulties in adulthood. The challenges and outcomes are typically experienced at all ages and stages of development, but the crises and tensions to be encountered, with psychological conflicts to be resolved, most significantly dominate the eight progressive stages in Erikson's schema in a range of psychological tensions that need resolution for healthy development. These conflicts are designated as trust v. mistrust; autonomy v. shame/doubt; initiative v. guilt; industry v. inferiority; identity v. confusion; intimacy v. isolation; generativity v. stagnation; and integrity v. despair. The stages in Erikson's scale are commonly linked with age groups (with young adulthood being 18–40, adulthood 40–65, old age 65–death) but such age indicators are not at all fixed. However, they do suggest a sequence that is quite common. The important thing for us to note is that, if a person has not dealt satisfactorily with the challenge of a particular stage, then successful management of a subsequent stage will be impeded. Theological students are essentially adults, and so will commonly be expected to fall into the later stages of Erikson's schema. Young adults are commonly more focused on establishing and consolidating their identity, roles in society, and personal relationships, so effective teaching methods will promote development in such areas. Conversely, older adults who have established mature roles and relationships will tend to respond positively to more creative outworking into a wider network as they consolidate their contribution to the world around them. If we want our students to be adult, we need to understand what that expectation entails and teach accordingly.

Ellery Pullman analyses Erikson's theory in more detail as applied to education, with a more nuanced expansion to ten stages of development, but with similar overall concepts. However, he extends the overall discussion of developmental analysis to delve beyond such a psychodynamic approach to consider other perspectives of cognitive, intellectual–ethical, and social learning theories.[8] Cognitive theories stem from the classic work of Jean Piaget, who identified four stages of types of sequential cognitive growth, commencing with the sensorimotor stage (from birth to 24 months), which focuses on the establishment of object permanence; progressing through the preoperational stage (2–7 years), which focuses on the development of symbolic thought and the concrete operational stage (7–11 years), which focuses on the development of logical thought; and culminating in the formal operational stage (adolescence to adulthood) with its focus on scientific reasoning. In healthy development, no stage can be missed, but there are individual differences in the rate at which progress occurs through

---

8   Pullman, 'Life Span Development', 63–72.

stages, and some individuals may never attain the later stages.

Piaget's interest was primarily with children, which explains the wide age range and largely undeveloped analysis of adulthood. However, his construct of 'schemas' is helpful even at the adult stage of learning. Piaget's schemas are the basic building block of intelligent behaviour—a way of organising knowledge. From such innate schemas as the sucking impulse of a neonate, intellectual growth develops as a process of adaptation or adjustment to the world. Such adaptation happens through assimilation (fitting new information into existing cognitive schemas), accommodation (revising existing cognitive schemas, perceptions, and understanding so that new information can be incorporated), and equilibration (the resolution of disequilibrium occasioned by discomforting new information). It is these notions of learning by means of assimilation, accommodation, and equilibrium that are most helpful to our understanding of adult cognitive operations.

Intellectual–ethical theory can be understood as a progression from Piaget's concept of concrete and formal operations. Here, Pullman analyses the work of William Perry related to college students, which brings us closer to our target study. Perry's scheme of cognitive and ethical development concludes that later adolescents and early adults move progressively from a general mode of dualism (viewing the world in polar ethical terms of right and wrong) to multiplicity (when they begin to see the possibility of several 'rights'), on to relativism (when they identify with and can relate to various sources of authority and values), and finally to commitment (when they make value choices from among identified alternatives and commit themselves to those choices). Such development in ethical thinking is clearly discernible in theology students, who often begin with simplistic ethical beliefs grounded in basic Christian tenets and teachings, are then exposed to a variety of critical views and alternatives, which at first disturb but then may lead to critical confusion, followed by the need to accommodate and (ideally) resolve the ethical and cognitive dilemmas inherent in such a journey of critical exposure.

An extension of such cognitive-ethical development is the behaviouristic nature of social learning theory, that is, that behaviour involves the interaction of people, with many different environmental conditions affecting a person's role and learning within a given context. Key elements in this theory are the concepts of imitation, modelling, and observational learning that account for many learned behavioural patterns. Albert Bandura, a leader in this field, has identified a number of common themes that can be helpfully engaged in effective social learning: (1) an individual is continuously engaged in two-way interaction with the self and the environment; (2) we can learn through observation without any immediate external reinforcement; (3) our cognitive expectations and perceptions affect what we do, and our awareness of the consequences of such behaviour influences our choices of behaviour; (4) we are active processors of information and not merely passive absorbers of external influences.[9] The apparently incidental influence of imitation, modelling, and ethical observation are indeed significant forces in the educative program, of which teachers need to be constantly aware and which they can in fact strategically utilise to enhance learning through imitation and modelling, since students are more likely to imitate a model they admire and perceive as being similar to themselves than someone who is not highly regarded.

Abraham Maslow conceptualised a hierarchy of needs as a motivational theory comprising a five-tier model of human needs, often depicted as hierarchical levels within a pyramid.[10] The hierarchy begins at the lowest level of basic human needs (physiological and safety needs), then progresses upwards to the more complex psychological needs (of social belongingness and esteem born of a sense of accomplishment), and finishes at the uppermost level of self-fulfilment needs (that is, self-actualisation, when one reaches full potential including creative activities). Recognition of the stage of need in a learner at any given stage of a program will help teachers to devise teaching approaches that are motivational and thereby conducive to effective learning. Maslow (1943, 1954) stated that people are motivated to achieve certain needs and that some needs take precedence over others. Our most basic need is for physical survival and this will be the first thing that motivates our behaviour. Once that level is fulfilled, the next level is what motivates us, and so on. Again, the stages are not mutually exclusive or indeed simply a matter of increasing maturity. Often, a person may be at a high level of motivation in one context, but at a very low level in another context. A highly achieving scientist or social leader will not be focused on achievement if he is lost in the bush for several days or has suffered personal loss or recent bereavement. So too with learners: the lower level needs must be reasonably met before the higher levels may be mastered.

While these psychological and motivational theorists have naturally focused

---

9   Bandura. *Social Learning Theory*.
10 See, for example, 'Simply Psychology' https://www.simplypsychology.org/maslow.html#gsc.tab=0 [accessed 24 March 2021].

on the various psychological models, there is an increasingly urgent need for theological educators to develop a far more informed and nuanced contemporary social awareness in relation to their students. Traditionally, 'generation' was applied to a rather standard time frame of about thirty years, in which generalised social markers could be reasonably identified. In the rapid societal developments of contemporary history, there seems to be a new 'generation' every decade or so—Gen X, Gen Y, Millennials, and so on—with each narrowly defined group having distinctive social markers. However, within this almost chaotic social stratification, there is one identifiable commonality: the reality of the digital age in which all contemporary theological education is now located. We now acknowledge that today's theological students are more likely to be 'digital natives' (those born into the world of digital technology, which is thereby the only world they have known) than 'digital immigrants' (those born into a non-digital world, but who have moved into that world to improve their roles in life).

During the past forty years or so, the digital native population has increasingly become the major population base of higher education students, while many theological teachers tend to be older and therefore more likely to be digital immigrants as they strive to adapt to the new shapes of the learners' world, a world in which the 'virtual' is in fact their 'reality'. In short, members of the student population of theological higher education are typically members of the 'iGeneration'. That does not mean that they will all be technological virtuosos, any more than earlier students who were taught formal English grammar rules were universally expert writers of English essays. However, there are some reasonable generalisations that we can note. The iGeneration tends to be seeking instant attainment, rather than the long haul. Its members know how to access (and check) masses of information independently, even if they are not skilled in evaluating that information. Much recent literature has emerged on the characteristics of modern young adult learners, with which we need to have more than a passing awareness.

It is interesting to observe the trajectory of the critical literature in this field. As with any new and confronting paradigm shift, an initial reaction to the technological tsunami of contemporary times was one of resistance, warnings, and even alarmism. Then there was a cautious if sometimes begrudging acceptance of and various approaches to managing this phenomenon, in increasingly sophisticated ways. Next came an embrace of its potentialities and possibilities, on both pragmatic and philosophical grounds. Finally, there is the realisation of not only the necessity but also the positive power of engaging such media in the furtherance of legitimate theological education. The successive critical questioning responses have tended along the following lines: 1. We just cannot do theological education online! (Rejection). 2. Can we really do theological education online? (Scepticism). 3. How can we do theological education online? (Inquiry). 4. How can we do theological education well/better/best online? (Exploration). 5. How can we harness the rich power of technological advances to enhance authentic theological education? (Enrichment).

Valid warnings about the problems of online learning have been sounded by Peter Bolt. Bolt's essay 'Deep Learning from a Shallow Surface? Encouraging Good Research in the Internet Age' focuses on the challenges and pitfalls of technology in the quest for deep learning. Bolt presents a catalogue of challenges to the quality of information encountered on the internet and the reliability of conversations that inhabit online forums. While acknowledging the internet's infinite quantitative dimensions and the popularity of peer group engagement in online forums, he warns that there is no corresponding guarantee of quality assurance or peer group methodological expertise, which can ultimately lead to little more than 'the confidence of the dumb'. Despite the 'encouragement' indicated in the title, the essay in general presents a rather dire warning about the perils of generally poorly managed online theological teaching.[11]

Charles De Jongh also expresses genuine concerns about the relative shallowness of online learning in his essay 'Challenges to Learning in the Age of the Internet'.[12] Like Bolt, De Jongh examines the challenges raised by the digital age to teaching theology in a technological age, an issue which he claims was largely ignored in the excitement of all the technological possibilities that suddenly emerged. His treatment of the negative impacts of online learning is expressed in terms of five contrasting challenges, or tensions, in an analysis that shows the manifold problems that need to be overcome. Those tensions are:

- *Distraction vs attention* ('The medium has become the distraction').
- *More ≠ more* ('Access demands that students need tools to access that material. However ironically, the use of the tools—the key one being search engines—undermines access to the vast quantity of material available, which ultimately undermines the quality of the material accessed').
- *Breadth v. focus* ('While students have access to a far greater breadth of material, that breadth is significantly undermined by their inability to mean-

---

11 Bolt, 'Deep Learning from a Shallow Surface?', 352–372.
12 De Jongh, 'Challenges to Learning in the Age of the Internet', 113–126.

ingfully focus on—and thus absorb and understand—the given material').
- *Surface v. depth* ('They are increasingly unable to plumb the depths of the material and find themselves "trapped" on the surface (and) risk losing (their) means and ability to go beneath the surface, to think deeply').
- *Information ≠ understanding* ('Perhaps future generations will no longer have the attention span or cognitive skills to follow the narrative of a story').

So, for De Jongh, the dominant negative impacts of the digital age include the rise in superficial reading, an inability to concentrate for extended periods, a decrease in the ability to develop sustained linear argument, and the loss of attention. Clearly, Bolt and De Jongh—both very experienced and effective theological teachers—are more alarmed than amazed by the powers of the Internet in theological education.

A degree of balance to these concerns is offered by James Dalziel, a former professor of online learning.[13] He is especially clear on countering the common assumption held by teachers inexperienced in online learning that the online educational experience is less than the face-to-face equivalent. While acknowledging that video conferencing lacks some of the non-verbal cues that strengthen physically present discussions, for example, he also points out the greater depth of discussion enabled by asynchronic discussion forums, in which far more critical consideration can undergird the individual contributions. He summarily 'take[s] issue with those who suggest that online is always worse and face-to-face is always better'.[14]

Kara Martin is another who moves beyond the warnings of Bolt and De Jongh to demonstrate some significant insights into the 'now and coming' generation.[15] She analyses important ramifications for theological education of this generation, delivered in the context of a case study of a particular program designed specifically for such a clientele. Martin begins from the axiom that the iGeneration is a reality, which needs to be acknowledged and engaged in learning and teaching—and not only in online learning. The program she developed at her college was specifically tailored to a digital learning environment, with the emphasis on its portability, accessibility, and engagement. A guiding motif was that the learner has control of the learning experience, in terms of when and

---

13 Dalziel, 'Graduate Attributes and Theological Education', 90–104.
14 Dalziel, 'Graduate Attributes and Theological Education', 96.
15 Martin, 'Theology of the iGeneration', 147–157.

where it occurs, how deeply it is studied, and the pace at which it is completed. For Martin, the salient learning characteristics of contemporary adult learners, which need to inform the very content and approach to all courses, include learners sourcing their own information, learners controlling their learning, and learners engaging with technology. She lists seven identifying characteristics of the iGeneration:

- Multitasking.
- Using multiple inputs.
- Sourcing own information.
- Controlling their learning time and depth.
- Preferring short spurts of information.
- Desiring to combine learning with other pursuits.
- Preferring formative to summative assessment.

Many of these categories overlap with the areas of concern raised by Bolt and De Jongh, but Martin views them not as problems to be overcome, but as opportunities to be seized. Her essay prompts serious thought concerning the methods we use in facilitating the learning process.

An interesting perspective is offered by Emily Southwell. She is one of the emerging young academics who are changing the profile of theological teachers from the stereotype of pedagogically conservative older teachers to younger more innovative digital natives. Having recently completed online undergraduate and postgraduate studies, she confidently acknowledges that, during her higher education studies, she has never been to a brick-and-mortar library to find books, as all her resourcing has been online. As such, she provides a strong foil to those sceptical concerns noted above. In a recent paper, she developed a proposal for the integration of information literacy in higher education programs.[16] Prompted by the largely negative criticism that paints online learning as inferior to print-based and physical campus-based learning, and based on the most recent research, the proposal first highlights the unique benefits available in online research, with an emphasis on its convenience and the issue of equity in affordability of access. Then it critically analyses the concerns raised by various authors surrounding the assumed inferiority of online reading in comparison with print mediums to provide a balanced critique of the opportunities and challenges that permeate the discussion. In doing so, it dispels the implicit assumptions about the comparative

---

16   Southwell, 'A proposal'.

effectiveness of face-to-face learning, whose common shortcomings in practice are typically treated with silence by critics of online learning. In particular, the proposal cogently addresses the identified difficulties around online reading including reading retention, hypertext and distraction, and an excess of information that is not easily accessible via search engines. The proposal shows clearly how good teaching by teachers who teach good researching practices to learners can successfully manage such issues, in the same way as they do in print-based learning. The practical proposal itself proffers a program for furthering information literacy among higher education students to equip them to take full advantage of all online research has to offer. This paper is indicative of the way forward in online learning.

In considering all such developmental and generational markers, we need to ensure we do not fall into stereotyping our learners. However, the classical studies and detailed concepts offered by such people as Erikson, Maslow, and others provide valuable insights into the nature of the people we are trying to grow into their full potential in Christ: their ultimate Christ-actualisation. Then, to remain relevant and effective in a contemporary setting, we need to engage with the realities of the social and cultural elements that shape our learners' worlds, which requires a constant awareness of the most recent literature and currency in latest societal and technological developments.

> *Critical Reflection.* Consider a class that you know quite well. Can you at least tentatively identify various of Erikson's stages within certain members of that class? (Note: in any group discussion, you should not identify any individuals.) Suggest one teaching method that you could use that would be appropriate to motivate such people.
>
> *Critical Reflection.* Privately review your own situation in terms of Maslow's hierarchy. Can you identify areas in your own life where you would locate yourself at different levels of need within that hierarchy? Can you relate this to any student you know (again, not to be identified)? How could this help to enhance your teaching of that student? How may you meet the range of learners' needs within a class when there are so many individual variables?
>
> *Critical Reflection.* Where do you locate yourself on the spectrum of Rejection to Enrichment in terms of your attitude to technologically assisted learning? How much time, and what sort of methods, do you use in teaching effective study/research skills to your learners – in face-

to-face and/or online classes? Are there differences in how you approach those two formats?

Understanding the Learners: What They Value and What They Fear

'If the learners are not learning, the teacher is not teaching' is a truism that cannot be rationalised away. We do well to understand that the most important agent in the educative process is the learner, without whom no educational institution has a need (or right) to exist. In the preceding section, we examined the context of learners in terms of their general developmental, motivational, and social factors. In this section, we seek to understand the internal values and fears that characterise most student bodies as they embrace their studies. It is these values and fears that shape the perspectives of students towards both their teachers and consequently towards their studies. We do well to understand what learners want to see in the ways in which teachers teach.

Again, Brookfield provides a useful starting point for this understanding. He crystallises a number of salient personal qualities of a teacher that have a direct bearing on how successful their teaching strategies will be. Above all, he encapsulates the most valued characteristics of teachers as perceived by students in the words 'credibility' and 'authenticity'. Students do not demand scholarly perfection, but they will not respect teachers who lack professional credibility—in knowledge and conduct—and personal authenticity—in lifestyle and relationships. Without the legitimate exercise of such qualities, it hardly matters what methods are employed because the teacher who has lost credibility has inevitably lost effectiveness. That explains why Brookfield begins his discussion with the heading 'An Authoritative Ally: Credibility and Authenticity', which he then expands into common indicators of credibility (expertise; experience; and rationale) and common indicators of authenticity (congruence of words and actions; full disclosure; demonstrating responsiveness; and disclosing personhood). The idea of a credible and creditable teacher is of the utmost importance to a theological student.[17]

But students often bring with them a range of inherent fears when they engage in tertiary study, which are only exacerbated by the intensely personal

---

17 Brookfield. *The Skillful Teacher*, 41–53.

and often challenging nature of theological study in particular. Such personal emotional backdrops can affect study as much as personal values. While such fears are rarely if ever mentioned in any assessment tasks, they penetrate often into the learning process, and can often be exacerbated by the methods of teaching adopted by their mentors. The kaleidoscope of such emotional canvases is vast, but several common ones can be identified and, perhaps not surprisingly, they often mirror the fears of teachers themselves in their own role. The first of these is *self-doubt*. Often, students will have doubts as to their ability or even their right to be undertaking their study. When confronted by an overload of new and challenging material, ideas, and practices, they can tend to panic and have overwhelming self-doubt about their academic ability, a sense of 'what have I got myself into?'. This sense of being out of their depth, misplaced in the whole study enterprise, can be disastrous, especially in the early stages of study. However, even those who fare well academically can have encroaching self-doubt. Students will often compare themselves with their perceptions of their peers and can often develop a default sense of either inferiority or superiority. While the attainment of academic success is universally associated with positive progress in educational programs, in theological programs, the quest for such success can ironically generate internal conflict about personal motivation and the spiritual rightness of seeking such success. Teachers will also often have such self-doubt but tend to suppress it by assiduous work and preparation, at times to the point of overloading the students even more. The issues of self-doubt need to be considered in the way in which we teach and mentor students. Our approach to pedagogy has a clear role to play in avoiding casualties.

A second common fear among theological students at any stage of their course is that of *cultural disorientation*, a sense that they are being punished by their cultural associates for being changed by their learning, especially if they are the first in their family or church to enter such learning. When confronted by a more analytical and critical treatment of previously held sacrosanct tenets of faith, students are shaken out of their comfort zone and their growth involves a number of inevitable growing pains. Growing away from the ways of thinking and expressing things as they had done more simply in the places where they had come from, they often experience a sense of 'growing apart' from their associates. Thus, students can feel a sense of growing cultural isolation from their accustomed cultural group, with a sense of estrangement and even alienation, and a fear that they have betrayed their roots. This becomes particularly acute when members of that former cultural group—family, friends, church associates, even current classmates—increasingly criticise the growing differences. The sense of cultural loss without a compensatory sense of belonging can be devastating.

Understanding the emotive context of students' lives will allow the teacher to tailor teaching methods more effectively. Not all learners feel confident or secure in their studies, regardless of motivation for commencing. As theological teachers, we need to take care that we do not add to such pervasive underlying emotions by a careless assumption of student wellbeing. Even those who study with a genuine sense of conviction and vocation can still experience emotional discomfort at stages in their studies. The 'authoritative ally' needs to be a constantly reliable ally as students confront and hopefully overcome their doubts and differences. Teaching methods need to be attuned to these common fears and teachers need to ensure that an intellectual and emotional safety net forms part of their overall teaching strategy.

> *Critical Reflection.* With reference to a specific teaching context, how could you tailor your teaching to fill the role of Authoritative Ally to your students?

Understanding the Process: How Learners Learn

We come now to the all-important topic of how learners learn. In doing so, the general psychological profile aids discussed above will be fleshed out further to analyse various learning styles that we may accommodate within our teaching.

We have already encountered Bloom's taxonomical approach to curriculum design. In implementing a curriculum scaffolded on taxonomic lines, it is appropriate to design learning activities (and corresponding assessment activities) along corresponding lines. That is, the concept of a hierarchical understanding of cognitive processes applies equally to pedagogical methods, as there is (or at least should be) a symbiotic relationship between curriculum and pedagogy: curriculum policy shapes pedagogical practices; pedagogical practices deliver curriculum objectives—as the curriculum has been conceived, so too the learning methods should deliver. Such a symbiotic relationship between curriculum and pedagogy lies at the core of coherently constructive alignment in educational method.

To apply this sort of thinking to pedagogical methods, we can usefully return to that intersection of the knowledge dimension (the kind of knowledge to be learned) and the conceptual process dimension (the process involved in that learning) that we introduced in our consideration of curriculum. Table 5.1 is an example of how this sort of intersection can guide the teacher in establishing a coherent congruency across curriculum, lesson objectives, and learning activities. The chart serves to illustrate the idea of creating hierarchical learning approaches, as the intersection of the six cognitive process dimensions (defined as remember, understand, apply, analyse, evaluate, and create) with the four knowledge dimensions (defined as factual, conceptual, procedural, and metacognitive) forms a grid with twenty-four separate cells. While the terms used in those twenty-four cells may be open to discussion, their value lies in the fact that they provide a sharp focus for the appropriate level at which the kind of knowledge and the type of cognitive process cohere at a point in a learning program.

Table 5.1: Knowledge–Cognitive Process Intersection

The Knowledge Dimension	The Cognitive Process Dimension					
	Remember	Understand	Apply	Analyse	Evaluate	Create
Factual Knowledge	List details	Summarise main points	Sort into categories	Deconstruct argument	Rank in priority	Integrate knowledge
Conceptual knowledge	Describe main features	Explain	Experiment with ideas	Explain issues	Assess validity	Form a coherent statement
Procedural knowledge	Describe operation	Predict outcome	Calculate results	Identify key differences	Confirm a process	Construct a personal plan or statement
Meta-cognitive knowledge	Suggest use	Demonstrate use	Construct a plan	Reach a position	Design a strategy	Implement action

In keeping with the ethos of the above table, Mary Forehand gives some simple indicative examples of how the focus on a particular process suggests types of corresponding learning activities:

    Remember: Describe where …
    Understand: Summarise …
    Apply: Construct a theory ….

>   Analyse: Differentiate between …
>   Evaluate: Assess whether (this) is valid …
>   Create: Compose a …[18]

Having chosen curriculum content at a level suited to an award, the teacher can then strategically develop the learners' appropriate learning processes that will promote effectual developmental learning mastery.

A variant approach to categorising how we learn has been explored by Peter Mudge in his adaptation of the epistemological work of Jürgen Habermas (see Chapter 3). Mudge offers an interplay between epistemology (how we know) and education (how we learn). Instead of a taxonomy of cognitive levels of learning, he summarises four distinct styles of knowing, which he describes as analytical, hermeneutical, self-reflective, and wisdom ways of knowing. His summary suggests the sorts of areas of learning suited to each way of knowing and links each style with a step in Bloom's taxonomy. His schema identifies the principal focus of each way of learning and notes its relation to the relevant Bloom taxonomical level. The main points are as follows.

Instrumental-Empirical-Analytical Way of Knowing
- Focus: Technical control and mastery; knowledge generated via science and analysis; the technical interest of prediction and control of objectified processes in the form of instrumental action.
- Relevant Bloom level: Level 1—Remembering/factual, lower-order thinking.

Historical Hermeneutical Way of Knowing
- Focus: Understanding meanings and interpretations (hermeneutics); focused on the practical interest of intersubjective understanding associated with life in the context of the human social world.
- Relevant Bloom level: Level 2—Understanding/conception, middle-order thinking.

Emancipatory-Critical Self-reflective Way of Knowing
- Focus: Critical or self-reflective way of knowing for the purpose of emancipation; becoming free from the constraints of ideologies, world views, and value systems; developing interpretive and critical moments of communicative action.

---

18 Forehand, 'Bloom's Taxonomy: Original and Revised', 1–9.

- Relevant Bloom level: Levels 4/5—Metacognitive, higher-order thinking.

Praxis and Wisdom Way of Knowing (Part 1—Praxis)
- Focus: Praxis (continual cycle of action/reflection) way of knowing for the purpose of Wisdom beyond Knowledge and Information; Stretching or extending current ways of knowing.
- Relevant Bloom level: Level 3—Procedural, middle-order thinking.

Praxis and Wisdom Way of Knowing (Part 2—Praxis as Wisdom)
- Focus: Praxis (continual cycle of action/reflection) way of knowing for the purpose of wisdom beyond knowledge and information; Stretching or extending current ways of knowing.
- Relevant Bloom level: Level 6—Metacognitive, higher-order thinking.

Thus, Mudge provides a stimulating interplay of epistemology and educational enterprise, which provides a useful adjunct to the taxonomical approach of Bloom.[19]

Understanding the Methods: How Teachers Teach So That Learners Learn

To develop specific and effective teaching methods, teachers need to incorporate several elements so that their teaching may be sufficiently versatile to accommodate a range of learning styles, stages, and settings. First, they need an awareness of what sort of learning theory best suits their class situation. A behavioural theory of learning generally utilises methods of behaviour modification by means of positive and negative reinforcement as methods of developing desired learning and responses. This typically involves regular cycles of praise and punishment, by way of comment, feedback, and critique, both within the class setting and in individual correspondence. While such a Skinnerian approach to teaching is commonly associated with primary stages of learning development, the elements of regular constructive and corrective feedback are relevant to all levels of learning, provided that such comment is focused on student action not personal qualities. At a tertiary level, such feedback is

---

19 Mudge, 'Four Ways of Knowing'.

valuable if it is essentially formative rather than summative. If students are to grow as learners, then teacher input needs to be focused on clear and meaningful 'ways forward', not just summary judgements on quality already attained.

It is useful to supplement such behavioural approaches to learner development with the insights from cognitive theories of learning, such as those pioneered by Piaget and Bruner. This adds the level of structured learning based on staged cognitive complexity. At an early stage of study in a new field (such as theology), there needs to be a focus on understanding the fundamental precepts and disciplinary processes of the field of study, with progressive increase in discovery, exploration, and problem-solving. At all points, students need to appreciate the sense of what they are learning, so that the gap between where they are and where they are being led is not too great and the pathway to reach that goal needs to be clear, logical, and attainable, rather than remote and unrealistic. However, when more than desired responses or cognitive mastery is in view, the tenets of humanistic theories of learning become operational in focusing on the development of personal emotions, values, and commitments. Teaching methods that seek these outcomes will entail exploration, discovery, mystery, challenge, and real-life issues, with the learners taking a more active role and greater personal responsibility in shaping and charting the course of their learning. There is not one optimal theory of learning that theological teachers should employ. Rather, it is in the cohesive balance of the best insights from all such theories that integrated learning is most likely to evolve.[20]

As well as such a variety of learning theories, there needs to be a practical engagement with a variety of learning styles. A traditional view of learning is that all students learn in the same (linear) way: teacher presents information; students take notes and memorise information; teacher and students interact with questions and answers; students return the information to prove their learning of the content. However, instead of relying on such a simplistic linear approach, Marianne LeFever explores learning styles, which are defined as the ways a student views or perceives things best and *then processes or uses what has been said*. The emphasis here is not so much on how teachers lead students into new knowledge, but on how learners perceive and use new information.

---

20 For a useful introduction to the variety of learning styles with direct reference to Christian education, see 'Rick' Yount, 'Learning Theory for Christian Teachers', 101–110. In this chapter, Yount details the historical development, elucidates the essential operational principles and practices of the various learning theories, and helpfully suggests how the strengths of each camp can be legitimately applied to Christian teaching, with balancing warnings about common abuses of such methods.

LeFever details four steps of a natural learning process and identifies different kinds of learners with each step in the process. By structuring lessons to follow this cycle, the teacher allows every learner to have an opportunity to shine, as their preferred learning style will allow them to participate and even take a leadership role at different stages of the learning process. The first step in this natural process accommodates *collaborative learners*, who readily connect new learning with past experiences and help the class to answer the question 'Why do I need to know this?' Once that is established, the second type of learners come into their own as the *analytical learners*, who prefer to delve into what new things need to be learned or what new perspective needs to be revealed, and who need to have that something new in each lesson to keep them engaged. They address the question 'What do I need to know?' This is the point where many Western learners thrive, but it is also the point where many stop. Step three engages the *common-sense learners*, who want to know if what they have learned makes sense, if it is applicable in some way: 'How does this work?' The fourth group are the *dynamic learners*, who will lead the class into discovering new and creative ways of using what they have learned in the classroom, to be implemented in the world beyond the classroom: 'What can this become?' While no one learner will fit easily into all preferred learning styles, all learning types can engage meaningfully at some stage. Thus, LeFever presents a thorough and practical discussion of how these learning styles can be utilised for more effective teaching, in association with the various visual, auditory, and tactile/kinetic modalities.[21]

> *Critical Reflection.* Which learning theory are you most comfortable with? Are there ways in which you could profitably use other theories to enhance your teaching?
>
> *Critical Reflection.* What is your personal preferred learning style? How far does this influence your preferred teaching methods? (How) can you expand this to accommodate a variety of learning styles?

It is worth examining some overarching pedagogical values that pertain specifically to theological education and that can reinforce the authenticity of both teacher and learner in promoting an openness to growing in learning. Ian Payne has provided a provocative set of headings that bear reflection, as he

---

21 LeFever, 'Learning Styles', 130–139.

develops and applies a trinitarian theology of knowing. His model focuses on three components when approaching a topic for study: a commitment to learn of the topic; an involvement in that learning; and an openness to the outcomes of that learning. Theological education thereby becomes relational, with a balance of faith, reason, and missional action. He warns against the false assumptions of theological neutrality or singular and absolute certainty. Instead, he advocates the conscious nexus of committed faith and sound reason in confronting new knowledge, and an openness to critical reflection upon that knowledge, even if it involves discomforting outcomes. Ultimately, authentic new knowing will issue in authentic active display.[22] From such a combination of committed faith, dynamic engagement in the process, and active behavioural outcomes will flow a range of teaching methods that will drive challenge, exploration, discovery, and the personal appropriation and integration of theological learning. That is, learners will learn to become more effectual learners.

Teaching for Learning: Some General Approaches

This final section will bring this chapter to a close by presenting a brief general summary of the principles involved in various teaching approaches. These approaches to learning and teaching arise from our basic educational philosophy that the driving force in effective theological teaching is the desire to provide opportunities and structuring approaches that allow learners to become better learners. Some basic approaches that are geared to this end can be divided into three typical categories. No one category is 'best' as all have their place. However, across a teaching program, there would optimally be evidence of all three categories.

Lecture, in its many forms, is the classic form of direct instruction that is probably the most common form of teaching method in current use (evidenced in the common appellation of the tertiary teacher). The lecture format is most appropriate when a set amount of information needs to be conveyed accurately in a uniform way to a body of learners at the same time. Topics such as legal requirements and rules, required conventions and systems, operational needs, introduction of unknown and not readily accessible information or protocols are best delivered by lecture. While it is easy (and sadly common) to label such

---

22 Payne, 'A Theology for Advanced Theological Studies', 167–183.

one-way delivery as a tedious process, that is not necessarily (and indeed should never actually be) the case. A lecture need not be the stereotypical dry delivery and may well be engaging, interactive, and dialogical. Even in this format, the teacher is not always the sole—or even the best—source of delivery. Many forms of lecture delivery are available, with variety and clarity in presentation and involved personnel being just as much a part of good lecturing as they are in any other format. The key distinctive of a lecture is its capacity to deliver a large and universally required body of information to a large number in a set time frame. When learners are aware of the purpose and need for the information, they are most likely to receive it positively and thus grow in their learning. Well constructed, the lecture is a most efficient way of conveying bulk information when uniformity of reception is a priority.

Exploration changes the dynamic of learning to a more active experience. There are all kinds of exploration possible at both individual and group levels. Essentially, exploration requires the teacher to set the parameters of a task and the learners to explore individually or in groups. This may take the form of student presentations, research, project, field exercises—the scope is limitless. The fundamental principle is that what learners explore extensively for themselves will be more deeply learned than content that is delivered to them as passive recipients. Exploration is by nature more time-consuming than a lecture for the acquisition of the same amount of information and it requires more vigilant and agile supervision in the process. However, its key value lies not only in the quantitative acquisition of knowledge but rather in the qualitative dimension of the process of having acquired that information. True, there is an inherent satisfaction in having formed one's own pathway to locating what was needed—a sort of treasure-hunt type satisfaction. However, in terms of developing an independent capacity to learn, it is the process of exploration itself that adds immeasurable value to the quest for learners learning how to learn. Such deep learning will greatly enhance the likelihood of personal integration of such learned knowledge.

Discovery learning ascends to yet another level of learner initiative and, when properly managed, is likely to provide the highest level of learner motivation. Here, the learner is involved in setting and designing the tasks, which may be individually tailored for different individuals or groups. The learner(s) may construct the scope and methods of inquiry and presentation. The teacher will constantly facilitate the discovery by the provision of guidance when requested (or at times when needed), resources, and occasions for reporting, feedback, and evaluation of milestones. This is the process of scientific empirical investigation, which begins from a sense of purpose, but with a lot of unknowns, and reaches towards some as yet undefined known. It is an approach that fosters transformative experiences in the midst of rapidly changing technologies. As Smith and Healey discuss in their essay 'On the Frontiers of Change', it is an approach that can effectively 'cut through the noise' of sophisticated technology by being flexible, contextual, and experiential, with a constant drive for improved theory and practice'.[23] It requires sustained critical analysis and rigour and, especially in theological educational programs, it involves a more person-centred holistic and transformational development of learners. The fundamental principle is that when adult learners take responsibility for their own learning in terms of purpose, reach, and method, they are far more likely to become that independently capable graduate that the programs seek to produce.

While there is no hard and fast rule for when the various styles should be employed throughout a course, it is common for lectures to dominate in the early stages, with a progressive decrease in later stages and a corresponding increase in the other styles. Constantly working towards student independent management of learning is a holistic principle that should characterise all teaching of adult learners. Such a gradation of learning approaches is an essential plank in the overall architecture of learners progressing as learners.[24]

> *Critical Reflection.* Review the most recent lecture you have delivered (or received). How much of it was the delivery of essential information that needed to be received uniformly? What part of it, if any, could have been learned by student exploration or discovery? Which format is the most suitable to your class context and why?

---

23 Smith & Healey, 'On the Frontiers of Change', 147–166.
24 As some useful practical pointers on the construction of a variety of methods, many university schools have provided sets of Tip Sheets. A typical example is the set of Teaching Tips posted by The University of Queensland, which contains a series of two-page summaries for each method, with a brief description of the method, along with a rationale and ways of implementation. They cover such topics as blended learning, case-based learning, flipped classroom, minute paper, problem-based learning, and project-based learning. Many universities have similar website publications, which could prove useful sources for exploration and experimentation.

6 | FOCUS ON TEACHER OR LEARNER— PEDAGOGY OR ANDRAGOGY?

There is a relationship between pedagogical philosophy and pedagogical methods, not always explicit, but always operational. As noted in the *Introduction* to this book, there has been in recent decades a demarcation between the methods of pedagogy and those of andragogy. Proponents of both approaches present an array of teaching methods that align with the undergirding principles of their respective positions. In this chapter, I want to outline broadly the distinctive pedagogical approaches and practices that align with those fundamental principles and follow that with some ideas on practical implementation of these methods in higher education.

A. PEDAGOGICAL METHODS: FOCUS ON TEACHER

The first set of methods I call simply 'pedagogical methods'. While the term 'pedagogical' is commonly used generically to apply to any form of teaching methods, I use it here in its etymologically more specific sense of 'leading children'. (No doubt, this developed from the stereotypical notion that it is only children who need to be formally taught.) However, I use the term with some distinctive nuances attached in terms of specific methods that are suitable to the philosophy that formal teaching is to do with instruction, that is, *imparting knowledge and wisdom by an expert teacher to a receptive learner*. The emphasis in this philosophy is on the teacher, whose expertise is the focus of teaching valued and essential content. In this content-based approach, a learner 'sits under' the teaching of the master and teaching methods reflect this philosophy or, as Foster and others put it, 'students participate in a teacher's practice as apprentices to a master craftsperson'.[1] Such an approach to teaching stems from a desire to ground students in a particular tradition or to lead them into a strong sense of biblical or theological orthodoxy. It focuses on Foster's 'cognitive apprenticeship', in which students develop the ability to read accurately and with appropriate methods the classical texts of the tradition. Drawing on the resources of the inherited religious and academic traditions, it generates a model of student development. Such an approach is both traditional and important, when properly employed.

There are times when important information needs to be conveyed to a class of learners in a uniform way at a given time and place and this is most efficiently done by means of direct instruction. The sort of learning required is substantially technical or legal content, for which precise and consistent details are compulsory learning, or the conventional methodology of specific disciplines, which need to be introduced as a basis of effective study. The main methods used are the lecture and set reading tasks and the presentation and practice of 'rules of engagement' applicable to a field of operation. In such methods, the responsibility rests with the teacher to select and order the content in a logical and clearly delivered form and to provide a clear model for students to employ. The strengths of this method are its assurance that the content received by the learner is accurate and relevant and that learners are provided with a confident base of study technique. Its shortcomings rest in its reliance on the knowledge of the teacher as sufficient and accurate in its selection and presentation for the purposes of the wide range of students and the vulnerability of a limited methodological formula that may inhibit the possibilities of understanding and exploration. The focus of this methodological approach is clearly on the teacher, with the learner being more or less a passive and willing recipient, being shaped by the master craftsperson. The following extract is obviously from a stern advocate of such an approach:

> Never mind what is Sanctifying Grace, Quigley. That's none of your business. You're here to learn the catechism and do what you're told. You're not here to be asking questions. There are too many people wandering the world asking questions and that's what has us in the state we're in and if I find any boy in this class asking questions I won't be responsible for what happens.[2]

---

1 Foster et al., *Educating Clergy*, 28.
2 Frank McCourt, *Angela's Ashes: A Memoir of a Childhood*, 130. Cited in Astley, *Ordinary Theology*, 13.

Ideas for Implementation

The key elements of such pedagogical methods are the *teacher's preparation, information, and presentation*: preparation of subject content and of teacher; information about content and students; and presentation of material with active engagement. Our task now is to explore methods that can make such a delivery suited to a contemporary context in ways that genuinely lead learners into an engagement with and ownership of the knowledge and wisdom that is imparted by an expert teacher. This section is intentionally pragmatic in its goal, but hopefully it will also contain an element of challenge to expand our teaching repertoire.

Content preparation is generally done well by highly qualified teachers. They know their subject well and can often talk about it at length with minimal prompting. However, when a teacher relies on such personal knowledge, two things need to be constantly guarded against. The enormous amount of time that goes into initial preparation of a series of lectures can lead to a static approach to content awareness. Lectures we received from our teachers may well be a good starting point, but they should never be viewed as the end point. There is a constant need for a teacher to refresh knowledge and to reflect critically on knowledge previously delivered. Is there something in that material that was irrelevant? Is there more knowledge that has emerged since last preparation? Are there now recognised gaps that need to be rectified? Reflective vigilance with regard to their personal knowledge base is a necessity for all teachers.

The second major concern for teachers is the appropriate selection and ordering of content to be included, since this is to become the authoritative corpus on which learners will rely. Not all learning groups will necessarily require the same content, so the utilitarian value of the content needs to be considered, not just the teacher's interest and enthusiasm for the material. While both these latter aspects are excellent qualities, they may not always align with student need. I was once teaching an advanced class in Greek exegesis and was expounding the arcane knowledge that I had discovered about a unique word in the text, when one student politely raised a comment that engendered the following brief exchange: 'You know how you are always teaching us that parsing and analysis of Greek terms should be done with a "so what" in mind as to its relevance for interpretation?' 'Yes.' 'Well, so what with this verb?' 'Nothing really, I just found it fascinating.' I was thereby a little embarrassed at my personal waywardness, but I was pleased to experience firsthand that the class had learned the lesson of process so well. While that provided a moment of general class hilarity at my expense, it has remained with me as a reminder that, in all our knowledge impartation, we need to ensure that we address the important rather than the merely interesting. Our key question is always: why does this group of learners need to receive this specific information? On any given topic, a diploma class may need procedural drills that have been successfully developed; a master class may need a range of alternative viewpoints to evaluate relative merits. Judicious selection of content to match the students' needs and award levels is a vital element of good lecturing. Effective teaching starts from the learning objectives of the course and unit and selects and arranges content accordingly.

> *Critical Reflection.* Review a unit you are familiar with. Is its content (a) comprehensive, (b) current, and (c) necessary for learners' development at their level of study?

Then there is also the personal preparation of the teacher. Theological teachers are in some ways peculiar beings, given their sense of a high calling to teaching as their ministry. However, in other ways, they are the same as any other teacher: human, busy, prone to take short cuts when pressed, and skating by on natural talent. There is a vast literature dealing with personal wellbeing in all forms of ministry, and it goes beyond the scope of this pedagogical exploration. However, I take the time here to stress the need for a theological teacher to be ever mindful of the vocation and to maintain a composite sense of privilege and responsibility that demands commitment in every semester, to every student, at every stage of the task.

Information about the subject matter is a natural product of a teacher's own completed and ongoing education. However, information about students is a constant work in progress. It is imperative that teachers develop an understanding of a variety of learning styles, as discussed previously. In the early stages of any teaching unit, there need to be opportunities to determine the range of learning styles that are active within the class. If diagnostic exercises are not practical, then a range of learning styles needs to be incorporated across the learning activities of the unit. As well as such general knowledge about learners, specific knowledge of actual learners is valuable. The use of previous class evaluations of teaching will, over an extended period, provide insights into students' perceptions of teacher performance, which can be taken as both affirmation and constructive criticism, both of which serve to enhance good teaching.

Progressive insights into current students' perceptions, interests, and engagement can be gleaned from various in-class activities, such as those suggested by Brookfield in a previous chapter (see Chapter 5). A constant awareness of how students are relating to the content of a unit will help the teacher to confirm, adapt, or remediate the delivery of that content to optimise its value. Different classroom contexts will involve a variety of approaches to such student awareness and response. In a physical weekly class setting, immediate adaptation is possible. In an online course dependent on static content over a cycle of some years, regular reviews are needed with the built-in opportunity for content revision at various points in the cycle. In all cases, information about students' needs and perceptions are a significant guide to methodological development.

> *Critical Reflection.* Where in your teaching program are there opportunities for you to gain insights into your students' learning styles and perceptions?

A focal element in this chapter is that of presentation methods. As previously noted, the most common form of direct instruction is the lecture. There are two basic dimensions to consider here: when to use direct instructional lectures and how to conduct such lectures. As a general rule, direct instructional methods should be used predominantly in early units or through the first year of study, when the learner needs to be made aware of the areas of new knowledge to be encountered and introduced to the basic disciplines associated with different domains of study. That is, the beginning student who has not yet learned what is commonly known needs significant direct information on content and procedures, which is the strength of the lecture format. As learning progresses, such direct instruction can be adjusted to allow more student directed inquiry and discovery.

Formal lectures sadly have a bad reputation as sessions of tedium and disengagement. That need not—in fact, must not—be so. What makes a lecture engaging, gripping, or inspiring? My fundamental suggestion is to avoid uninterrupted teacher talk. While core information may be needed, it does not have to be delivered as a monologue. A lecture will engage if it is dynamic, that is, it provokes activity by the learners as participants. A lecture will invariably involve much teacher talk (even in text-based online materials prepared by a teacher); however, it can still contain significant student-centred involvement. A topic may be introduced as a question, even a provocation, with breakout discussion periods, spontaneous mini-role plays, scenarios to explore, readings to be discussed, questions to be answered, or applications to be constructed. At tertiary level, *a lecture should critically re-orient students in some way by stimulating critical thinking.* 'This is the way we must do this' can be engaging with the prompting of a devil's advocacy approach, or a following 'So how will you do it in your context?'. The teacher needs to introduce periods of silence—both the teacher's silence and the students' silence—to allow creative and critical engagement. Lecture and discussion are not mutually exclusive teaching approaches; in fact, they make very good bedfellows. A lecturer should be not a demagogue but a director, leading the learners into a personal grasping of the material that is so important.

Numerous works are available to give insights into a vast array of suitable teaching approaches to generate dynamic lectures, but there are some fundamental principles that undergird most of them. First, a series of lectures should employ a variety of communication processes. Students may well have questions, but they often also have answers and the engagement in dialogue within a lecture space can be most rewarding and developmental. Provocative questions challenging conventional wisdom can be respectfully discussed. In the era of digital technology and social media, the internet is a constant third party to every lesson, so that medium can be advantageously exploited to increase the scope of immediately available knowledge or attitudes—smart classrooms are now commonly available, so we need to use them smartly, even if that requires some retraining for teachers. Even such simple mechanical details as where and how the teacher takes a position will influence the reception of the content. If a teacher sits statically at a desk in front of the room or stands behind a fixed lectern to deliver material, then an air of remoteness is established. Conversely, a dynamic atmosphere is generated when the teacher is mobile and visits all points of the room during conversational engagements. To place oneself in close physical proximity to individual students is a commonly used form of class control in primary school rooms, but it is also a positive form of bridging the gap of remoteness from students at every level.

Second, a lecture needs to be clearly organised in a way that students may follow the thread at all points, with a sense that they know where they are up to and are not feeling lost at any stage. The 'whole to part to whole' approach is effective. That is, an opening statement of what the topic is and how we will approach it sets up an organisational trail to be followed and provides a point of constant reference throughout the delivery. The subsequent dissection of the parts should be logically and overtly connected, so there is a sense to it all along the path. Finally, the opening question or point at issue needs to be cogently wrapped up in terms of the preceding analysis, so that students are left with a sense of reasonable closure—even if that is just a pointer to the next episode to come. Such organisation may be effectively supported by scaffolded or skeletal notes that give a summary of the elements and progression of a lecture and by oral clues that indicate stages of progress in the overall lecture, points of development or departure, and emphasis of essential items. Learners have a sense of intellectual comfort and receptivity if a lecture is clear and easy to follow, even if the content may be complex and challenging. The absence of such a learning 'comfort zone' will certainly militate against learning effectiveness. Attention to such details of delivery have the added bonus of modelling exemplary learning behaviours as students imbibe processes of clarity of organisation, developmental argument, and logical progression to a conclusion as means to enhance critical thinking.

Of course, many teachers (of whom I am one) will bemoan their lack of personal creative talent. Thus, they will experience a degree of 'creative inertia' at times, when the constant questing after creativity can be draining and self-defeating, and at its worst can reduce to novelty without an effectual cause or outcome. We need to realise at the outset that creative teaching is not so much a matter of mastering special techniques but rather its processes are essentially interpersonal and intentional: *its goal is not to demonstrate creativity in the teacher but to develop creativity in the learner*. A particular teaching method is not in itself creative, but it becomes creative when used in such a way as to elicit creative thinking and activity within a learner. It is an invitation to learners to make sense of things in their own way. The teacher's main role in this area is to establish an atmosphere and an opportunity for such creative expression to be produced. Even in methods of direct instruction, such creativity can—and arguably should—be fostered. Shelly Cunningham suggests a number of means that are conducive to establishing a suitably creative environment:

- Provide an initial experience to pique the interest of the learner: media, role-play, demonstrations that prompt a problem, an issue, an investigation.
- Provide manipulative situations and materials to begin the exploration: games, media, files, sourcebooks.
- Provide information sources for students' questions: external sources, field trips, speakers, peers.
- Provide materials and equipment that will spark student experimentation and production.

- Provide time and opportunity for students to manipulate, experiment, fail, succeed.
- Provide guidance, reassurance, reinforcement for students' ideas and hypotheses.
- Reward and encourage acceptable solutions and strategies.[3]

Critical Reflection. How do you facilitate critical thinking in your teaching style? How do you know if this is effective?

B. ANDRAGOGICAL METHODS: FOCUS ON LEARNER

The second set of matching philosophical and methodological approaches is what I call 'andragogical methods'. The term has become fashionable since it was coined by Malcolm Knowles, who wrote:

> [T]here is an urgent need for all programmes of higher education ... to be geared to developing the skills of autonomous learning .... To reorient higher education ... in this direction is a tremendous challenge. It is a concept that is foreign to most educators. It has not been part of their training .... It requires a redefinition of their role away from that of transmitter and controller of instruction to that of facilitator and resource person to self-directed learners. It is frightening. They do not know how to do it.[4]

In short, andragogical methods relate to 'leading adults'; that is, they begin from the assumption that (college) *students are adult learners and should be treated that way.* While that seems obvious, the tenet bears within it a number of important assumptions by implication. First, if a learner is an adult, then there has been a significant 'life before study' experience, whatever that may entail. The notion that every student is a blank page, that all students are starting at the same page (and that page is 'zero'), is unrealistic. If we accept that a learner is an adult, then we need to employ methods that engage with the adult life experience that the learner is bringing to the learning table. Often, theological education is viewed as a side-step from 'normal life' into a separate world of new beginnings, whereas, in fact, all theological students bring with them a set of already formed

---

3   Cunningham, 'Creative Teaching Methods', 140–146.
4   Knowles, 'Preface,' in Boud, *Developing Student Autonomy*, 8.

perspectives on many aspects of life, which include theological understandings, no matter how poorly articulated they may be. An andragogical approach to teaching recognises that the term of theological study is a part of a continuing life, not an isolated detour. Second, adults are to be treated as responsible people, which includes taking (and being given) responsibility for their own learning. This does not mean the teacher's abrogation of such responsibility, but it changes the approach from the teacher's sole prerogative to determine the learning to the teacher's role in assisting the learner to take such responsibility. It is obvious that not all adult learners will be equally capable of such independent self-determination and that all will need substantial and variable guidance. So, this approach is inherently risk-taking, as is much of adult life.

The two prongs of this andragogical methodological approach relate to being *respected as an ad*ult and being *expected to act as an adult.* Learners are engaged in shaping the learning and in 'making sense' of the learning in relation to their own lived experience (past, present, and potential future). Learners will be led to examine their existing positions and practices and to modify them to align with new concepts or to accommodate the new concepts to fit into their held positions, rather than adopting new components as additives. Real-life scenarios are vital, in terms of observation, exploration and analysis, all with the safety net of the classroom (however constructed). If the adult learner is to make sense of new learning, then that learning needs to connect in real and recognisable terms to the learner's life situation by way of affirming, correcting, or evolving. This methodological approach is strongly learner-centred in its focus on the learner's experience, with the learner being an active participant and the teacher being a trusted guide.

> *Critical Reflection.* As a learner, did you experience teaching methods that would be classed as pedagogical or andragogical? What impact on your learning did this have? As a teacher, do you employ mainly pedagogical or andragogical methods?

Ideas for Implementation

The key elements of andragogical methods are the *teacher-provided opportunities for learners' connection with, explanation of, and application to experience.* Thus, they will feature connection with the lived reality of learners, explanation of how things make sense in the context of that reality, and practical application to the contexts of the learners.

To relate to students as adult learners requires both a mindset and a method. The Transforming Theology research project encapsulated the mindset of learners in this regard. It depicted adult education as a stage in a lifelong journey, not a detached 'time out' in isolation from the reality of a student's life. Thus, the educational program needs to begin by recognising the pre-existent life experience of the learner in order to position the learner to review critically the frames of reference already established by that prior experience. To be meaningful, an encounter with new knowledge will necessitate either assimilation of that new knowledge into the existing frameworks or accommodation by revising existing frameworks in light of the new knowledge encountered. In other words, learning development does not consist in memorisation or absorption of discrete and unrelated facts, but it is a process of bringing new knowledge into dynamic connection with ongoing life experience. The crux of andragogical learning methods is the goal of encouraging a holistic development of a critically reviewed and shaped world view that is more inclusive of others' philosophies and lifestyles, and which serves as a platform for future experience.[5]

Experiential grounding of knowledge and its application is central to adult learning. For an adult, new knowledge is valued only insofar as it is perceived as relevant to life. Dogma in an experiential vacuum may be recalled for an examination or an assignment, but it is soon cast aside as having no further point. Though life application/illustration is often claimed and attempted in formal courses, too often, the 'application to life' has been reduced to a factitious addendum to an essay or a project. A common alternative to this has been anecdotal narrative of the teacher's 'real-life' experience which, while interesting and even inspirational at times, remains remote from the learner's personal experience. As one recent ministry graduate put it, 'The lecturer's experience of yesterday is not likely to be our experience of tomorrow'. That is even more the case when that yesterday's experience is itself a long time past. Today's experience and tomorrow's probabilities are the things of importance to adult learners. So, how do we connect with the lived experience of the learner, especially if we are teaching in the distancing mode of online education?

The extreme diversity of contemporary theological classes makes it at once more difficult and more vital to incorporate the learners' personal stories as an

---

5   Ball, *Transforming Theology*, 50–65.

explicit part of the educational process. That is, there is the need for the explication of the life experience that brought the student to theology. This can be done in various ways, such as personal inventory and journals; by a 'syllabus of questions', in which topics are generated in conjunction with students; by initial discussions of graduate attributes and how students plan to attain them, with follow-up discussions at later stages; by intentional creation of introductory learning tasks which strategically link to prior experience and present aspirations; or by field placements which have been sought and initiated by students themselves, although it must be added that such field experience needs sound educational and supervisory structures to facilitate development. The key thing is that the motivation of the students to be in the classroom or other learning format needs to be honoured.

The introduction of new knowledge typically involves content description and associated explanation, of both its complexity and its significance. The process of explanation in adult learning is a two-way activity. The teacher presents explanations in a general, systematic, or historical way and the learner wrestles with the new knowledge to render that explanation specific and personal, which in turn adds to the corporate sense-making package. One very versatile approach to such dialogical development can be borrowed from the dynamics of practical theology, whether understood as a discrete academic discipline or as a useful tool to be employed broadly. A key value of practical theology is its provision of a cohesive and interdependent interplay of theology-informed practice and practice-informed theology, expressed in terms of a real-world setting, which lends itself particularly well to adult learning in biblical and doctrinal study as well as in applied ministry areas. The practical theologian Richard Osmer provides a useful processing format, on the basis of four fundamental exploratory questions, which he terms descriptive empirical, interpretive, normative, and pragmatic. The questions are addressed sequentially, with each step in the sequence being informed by the previous step and thereby providing a more solid practical base for subsequent steps. The questioning sequence is as follows:

- First: what is going on? This is the descriptive task of gathering empirical data of the current *status quo*, whether that be conceptual or observational.
- Then: why is this going on? This is the interpretive historical task of understanding how this status developed.
- Then: what ought to be going on? This is the normative task of analysing the status from the perspective of theological or ethical norms.

- Finally: how might we respond? This is the pragmatic task of determining strategies of action.⁶

The process is not a closed system that arrives at a definitive end. Rather, its pragmatic outcomes will, eventually, prompt ongoing analysis and development. By adopting such a process, the teacher and the learner are mutually informing and being informed, as both learn new ways of making sense of things.

A good account of how this approach can be applied to a specific area of learning is provided by Steve Taylor and Rosemary Dewerse, who have constructed an educational strategy for leadership formation. The first step in the overall strategy is the listening stage of learning—what is going on: what are the needs of leaders in the churches. The interpretive analysis of this empirical data then seeks to understand why the current state has arisen, with a particular focus on the social construction of theological learning communities. Third, the normative task of discerning what should be the case based on theological and biblical precepts is concerned with interpreting the shape of good practice in leadership formation. Finally, there is the pragmatic response to the foregoing analysis that created an active strategy of what the authors term 'unbounding learning communities'. This paper is well worth close reading, both for what it says about the specific task, but more significantly here for how it illustrates a dynamic application of practical theology in adult theological learning within a formal postgraduate unit.⁷

> *Critical Reflection.* Could Osmer's practical theology principles be applied to your field of teaching? If so, how? If not, why not?

In terms of more specific teaching methods, Smith and O'Flynn have suggested sixteen learning approaches that assist learners to make sense of their new knowledge:

1. Orienting inquiry around the question, 'How do I improve my practice?'
2. Helping the learner to remain curious.
3. Asking provocative questions.
4. Encouraging learners to incorporate different ways of knowing into their inquiries.
5. Using intuition.

---

6 Osmer, *Practical Theology*.
7 Taylor & Dewerse, 'Unbounding Learning Communities', 420–434.

6. Gathering stories for mutual sense-making.
7. Creating metaphors to learn and adapt.
8. Developing heuristic models.
9. Initiating co-operative inquiry.
10. Experimenting to nudge change.
11. Learning while taking action.
12. Emphasising holistic learning.
13. Researching the action.
14. Inquiring appreciatively.
15. Building a lifelong pattern of reflective practice.
16. Creating immersion experiences.[8]

All of these suggestions are student centred and inquiry based, which has come to be associated closely with andragogical methods. That is, the adult learner is always going to be at the centre of the sense-making process. As the learner's motivation for study needs to be understood, so too the learner's contribution to sense-making needs to be both expected and honoured.

It follows from the preceding sections that adult learners, having learned to make sense of new knowledge, need to ground that new understanding in the practicalities of their life, either as it exists now or as it is in clear prospect. Remote generalities of 'how could this apply in real life' are too vague to be valuable. The learner needs to be given—and to take—responsibility for shaping how the grounding will take place because that will give an ownership that an externally prescribed task can rarely achieve. Within a set of known educational parameters, the more the opportunity for a learner to shape personal learning tasks, the more will be the sense made of it all, and the more lasting will be the educative value of the undertaking. Bonnie J. Miller-McLemore is another leading author in the field of practical theology, who presents a cogent treatment of how the tools of practical theology can be used in the pursuit of effective theological learning linked with dynamic ministry. Her work focuses on the need to complete the hermeneutical circle by way of not just reading theology but also by enacting theology. Theological learners, she says, 'need more than the capacity to "*think* theologically" … but also the capacity to "*practice* theology" by putting theology into action through one's body on the ground'.[9] The ethos of meaningful application to enacted outcomes is a core plank in andragogical learning.

---

8 Smith & O'Flynn, 'Responding to Complexity', 123–127.
9 Miller-McLemore, 'Practical Theology and Pedagogy', 173.

Of course, there is often a resistance, on the part of both teacher and learner, to this sort of approach, but such resistance needs to be managed and overcome—in both parties—for adult learners to be able to commit to their learning. Much of the common resistance by students to such self-directed learning stems from a lack of self-confidence as they embark on a new journey of discovery, equipped only with a sense of their own academic inadequacy and a fear of the unknown that they may not be able to control. A diploma student who had transferred from another Bible college to my institution discontinued his study with us because, as he related to me, 'The other college taught us what we should know; this college makes us ask more questions and all I want are the right answers'. At least one of those two colleges had failed that student, as neither had accurately gauged his aspiration or need. In higher theological education, it is necessary for the teacher to build an atmosphere in which experimentation is rewarded and self-confidence is developed. Too much responsibility imposed prematurely can be overwhelming, but too little responsibility taken can be unproductive.[10]

Regardless of any resistance emanating from teacher, learner, or traditional task construction, a salient point is noted by Brookfield concerning the design of learning and assessment projects: '*Any assignments that ask students to take responsibility for at least part of their learning can add to a learner's repertoire of skills*' (my italics).[11] Common methods of achieving this are often associated with field placements or work integrated learning, but in such approaches, care is needed to ensure that learners are indeed learning by doing and not just 'doing stuff' with the tacit (but false) assumption that all activity is learning activity – at least, it is not all good learning activity. There are in fact two dimensions of work-based activity: the physical activity itself that focuses on learning how to produce an external object or to perform a skill and what Pietsch calls 'expansive learning activities', which focus on the internal development of the participants engaged in the activity so that they become better equipped to engage in other activities beyond and even quite different from the present activity.[12] Such expansive learning is a crucial part of personal

---

10   The issues of student responsibility and resistance are well treated by Brookfield in Chapters 15–17 of *The Skillful Teacher*, 199–238. In these chapters, he offers strategies for building student confidence to take responsibility for the design, conduct and outcomes of their learning and identifies the grounds of student resistance to learning, some of which are inherent in the learners, but some of which are also generated by the teacher.
11   Brookfield, *The Skillful Teacher*, 209.
12   Pietsch, 'Educating for the Kingdom', 337–338.

growth. In all cases, work-based learning activities and associated expansive activities need to be constructed to align with clearly articulated, attainable, and demonstrable learning objectives.

There are other forms of activity that can be based in the classroom or in the field. Case studies provide opportunities for students to view how new knowledge has been operative in real situations, and they have an inbuilt 'safety net' for such student exploration. More directly and intensely engaging are action research projects based on situations or settings in which the student is personally involved, although they come with a higher degree of vulnerability because of the student's closeness to the subject. Scenario learning and role plays also provide active expressions of the operation of knowledge and, appropriately crafted and managed, can lead students into a greater awareness of theories in practice as they both perform and critique such action. It is worth noting that such active learning need not be limited to 'practical subjects', but they can equally well be applied to the traditional 'academic subjects' such as biblical, theological, and historical studies, as they have been in the anachronistically imaginative dramatic scenarios and role plays created by Tim Cooper in the study of the history of the early church.[13] The incorporation of a range of such applied practical and active learning tasks accommodates a range of individual learning styles and assists the learners to make sense of their new knowledge in personally meaningful ways.

> *Critical Reflection.* To what extent do your assessment profiles facilitate students' taking responsibility for their learning? Can you cite a case where this has been particularly successful? Are there strategies by which you could enhance this aspect in your teaching?

---

13 Cooper, 'Examples of Online Exercises', 209–210.

7 | FOCUS ON LEARNING—A MATHEGENICAL APPROACH

Chapter 6 examined teaching methods that focused on the principal persons involved in the educative program, namely, the teacher and the learner. Both foci are legitimate and valuable in various circumstances, and both have produced effective results. However, in this chapter, I want to extend the thinking to a third focus, which moves away from agents to agency, from teacher/learner to the process of learning, which in turn puts the emphasis on producing a capable autonomous learner. Accordingly, this chapter builds on those previous chapters by exploring the potential and processes of mathegenical pedagogy. A mathegenical approach is not a substitute for nor indeed opposed to the previous methodological approaches. On the contrary, it uses those and other methods in a holistic approach to developing lifelong independent learners, with a capacity to analyse, think critically, explore new knowledge, address issues of vitality, and to function effectively beyond their teachers' input in addressing as yet unanticipated issues. This sort of holistic development is key to mathegenical teaching.

A. THE IMPORTANCE OF PROCESS

So, what does 'a mathegenical approach' mean?[1] I have coined the term for my own purpose here from its Greek origins of *manthano* ('to learn' as in 'mathematics', which is also the base of *mathetes*, 'learner' or 'disciple') and *ginomai* (to 'produce' or 'generate'). My Arndt and Gingrich *Greek-English Lexicon of the New Testament* includes the following definition of *manthano*: 'learn, appropriate to oneself less through instruction than through experience and practice'. The combined sense of the root terms is that of 'producing learners'. Hence, the concept of mathegenics centres on the learners' learning to learn, that is, how they can and will continue to learn long after content has become obsolete or performative skills have become redundant. This concept can be applied to any age group and is arguably the highest form of higher education. As such, it is the core thesis of this book, namely, that *the most effective concept of theological education is that of generating learners, who will not only learn theology and master techniques, but will also become accomplished in the art of learning, grounded in the ongoing engagement with theological inquiry and advancement.*

This philosophy requires learning methods that promote the art of independent and lifelong learning, not just the limited content of unit material and/or the transient skills of vocational practice. Much has been written in recent literature of the aspiration to integrate knowledge, skills, values, and character in education, yet little progress in the attainment of such an aspiration has been documented. If we are looking to graduates to be the embodiment of such integration upon their graduation, we are probably doomed to be largely frustrated because it is difficult to envisage any graduate of a three- or four-year course as a complete product—I cannot readily identify one in my long career as a theological educator. However, I can identify a significant number who have clearly demonstrated that they now know how to learn, and their subsequent careers have demonstrated that very clearly, as they have advanced in their learning beyond their teacher in so many ways. Indeed, it is that reflection that has led me to posit my thesis of the priority of generating learners as the ultimate goal of theological teaching. If we as theological teachers have a corpus of inherited sacred knowledge to convey, and if we recognise the adult status of our students, then we do well to merge those elements into generative learners

---

1   I stress at the outset that this is not to be confused with recent educational terminology of 'mathetics', which refers to programmed reinforcement learning, especially in primary school writing programs.

who will be independent of, or will even transcend, their teachers as they learn to inquire, research, evaluate, apply, and create in ways that surprise both teachers and learners.

A recent example of this sort of pedagogical approach can be observed in Stephen Smith's application of complexity theory to work-integrated learning.[2] Noting that students are now confronted by the 'emerging truth of postmodernity' rather than the previous 'certain truth of modernity', Smith advocates a corresponding pedagogical shift from instruction to inquiry, with the workplace viewed as the ideal living laboratory for the execution of the necessary sense-making agenda. When a culture of learning is blended into a context of a living system, the learner is exposed to and is shaped by the constant and dynamic interaction of all forms of knowledge: simple and complex, chaotic and complicated, as well as the ultimately unknowable. While Smith's focus is on workplace settings, his notion of the complexity and fluidity of knowledge has wider application. As he states, it is not about the workplace, it is about the quality of the learning. In all such applications, the underlying quest is to lead the learner into making sense of whatever is encountered. To achieve this, learning needs to move away from linear mechanistic thinking to living systems thinking, in which learners will be constantly evolving as they learn how better to learn.

The focus of this methodological approach is on developing the learners, with teacher and learner being integral partners in the enterprise. Key elements of mathegenical education are motivation, facilitation, consolidation, and creation: motivating the learners to seek new and lasting ways of learning; facilitating and guiding the processes of such learning; constructing learning activities that will consolidate such processes; and learners' creative production of artifacts as outcomes of such learning. The ultimate quest is the holistic integration of all aspects of learning in the person of the learner: the knowing, the doing, and the being components of a graduate who is equipped to confront the host of new and unpredictable learning demands that will follow formal education.

> *Critical Reflection.* What mathegenical approaches do/could you employ in teaching your programs?

The pedagogical methods that are conducive to such development are those that embrace independently motivated inquiry and production. As we have

---

[2] Smith, 'Moving from Instruction to Inquiry', 35–51.

noted earlier, different kinds of learners will find motivation in different kinds of activities, but the need for personal meaningfulness is common to all, so that needs to be the trigger for mathegenical teaching. Addressing the 'why' question is typically a feature of such learning, but it needs to be expanded to 'Why do I want to learn this? How can I ensure I learn it well and make something out of it that will have ongoing value?'. The learner needs to be a part of the process design not just the topic selection. This can be difficult when units and assessments need to be predetermined for logistical purposes, but even such pre-set learning tasks can be crafted in ways that allow flexibility and thereby individual ownership of the required tasks. That word 'ownership' is significant because it is in the appropriation—the making it one's own—that integration occurs. In other words, this approach to learning and teaching has as much to do with process as it has with content. The content is not debased, but the processing of that content is what adds the level of integration, and it is that processing that needs to be constructed and facilitated by the teacher. The most successful process of ownership will result in the learner's consolidation of their learning in the form of a usable artifact to be available for their ongoing life or vocation. By drawing on the tenets of methodology introduced previously to suit various teaching objectives, we can employ various approaches to learning that incorporate desired integrating processes.

Critical Reflection. (How) can you advance the need for students' personal meaningfulness in your teaching programs?

B. SOME MATHEGENICAL APPROACHES TO THEOLOGICAL INTEGRATION

We turn now to some samples of the kinds of pedagogical approach that may prove useful in the generation of an integrated theological learner. The stages of three common types of such learning are depicted in Table 7.1. Each approach has a basic underlying motivational assumption that prompts the methodological starting point that drives the process through to the production of an active outcome.

Table 7.1: Learning Approaches

Problem-Based Learning	Inquiry-Based Learning	Group Project-Based Learning
'Felt need' Identification of a problem	Appreciating Valuing the best of 'What is' or 'Where I have come from'	Defining a possibility Articulating aspirations and identifying 'like minds'
↓	↓	↓
Analysis of causes		Establishment of a working group
↓	↓	↓
Analysis of possible solutions	Envisioning 'What might be' or 'What I might become'	Analysis of situation and resources
↓	↓	↓
Action plan (treatment)	Dialoguing 'What should be' or 'What I should become'	Establishment of possibilities
	↓	↓
	Innovating 'What will be' or 'What I will become'	Establishing course of action
		↓
		Implementation of action
Basic assumption: Person has/organisation Is a problem to be solved	Basic assumption: Person is a continuing work in progress with past/existing successes that can be built on	Basic assumption: Group dynamic maximises energies with potential to incorporate PBL and IBL

(a) Problem-Based Learning Methods

Problem-based learning (PBL) is common in higher educational courses focused on curative or remedial processes. The process of investigating and solving real contextual problems involves discovering problems, understanding their nature, and reaching an appropriate solution. Thus, PBL is not really teacher-centred or learner-centred. Rather, its focus is on learning that generates knowledge through the process of solving real-life problems. That is, its focus is on the process of learning rather than on the product of learning.[3]

The basic motivational assumption of PBL is that there is a problem to be solved that requires a treatment plan to be produced, which has obvious application to areas such as medicine, and obvious but hopefully not so prevalent application to church life. However, it should not be viewed as the sole method for all learning, as (hopefully) not all of life is problematic.

A major strength of PBL lies in its being grounded in real-world contexts in which specific problems can be identified and addressed in ways that foster higher-order learning. The inclusion of topics in the curriculum that connect to the known or potential problem areas actually or likely to be faced by the learners provides a strong connection to the experiential reality of their lives and thereby provides strong motivation to learn. The methods of PBL then facilitate growth in desired learning approaches. Such contextualised learning combines several phases of learning, including the activation of the learner's prior experience in defining the problem, the demonstration and application of skills in data gathering and analysis, and the integration of those skills in real-world action.[4] It is this creative integration that is the mark of genuine mathegenical learning.

Two common forms of PBL are observation and analysis of identified problems, and case studies. Observation and analysis may be carried out by means of literary research, through which the published observations of others may be analysed, or by field observations, conducted and analysed by the individual learner or other groups. Case studies have several forms. They may be remote studies, which are done via documentary analysis; they may be detached studies, which are done by field observation as an 'outsider'; or they

---

3   Jusu, 'Problem-Based Learning in Advanced Theological Studies', 211. This chapter serves as a primer in approaching this form of learning in ways that are specifically geared to higher level theological education. It ranges across characteristics, processes, players, assessment, and implementation of problem-based learning.
4   Joseph, 'Contextualized Curriculum Design', 95–96.

may be participatory studies, conducted via the field engagement of an 'insider' operating within the system under analysis. All such case study formats are valuable, although they come with increasing intensity of ethical and emotive issues as they progress from the classroom to the field.

PBL also lends itself to dramatic role plays and scenario learning. Classroom role plays may be very short scenes in which students portray an incident and work to resolution of a problem as a starter to class analysis and development, or they may be more developed performances illuminating a common problem. Such performances lead naturally to scenario learning, in either a static or a developing form. Static scenarios posit a specific problem requiring a workable active solution. Conversely, developing scenarios seek not a 'correct' answer, but agile responsiveness to a fluid and changeable scenario dependent on prior responses is employed. James Dalziel, a leading exponent of scenario learning, presents a sophisticated approach to developing scenario learning. In this approach, learners engage in a scenario, make their suggestions for resultant action, but then have to reconnect with the outcomes of those initial recommendations, and so continue to process issues that arise in previously unanticipated ways or that have further variables injected. Thus, the developing scenario portrays a more realistic and fluid situation than a static scenario.[5]

Example of a Developing Scenario Exercise

> In a local church, a group of young people has been vocal in expressing that they do not believe preaching is a good mode of communication in a postmodern world and that the church should scrap its approach to church services and find interactive ways of communicating. Further, a leading member of the group declares that he is going to quit attending church because he cannot see the value of sitting and listening to one person speak to a large group of people who have different needs, questions, and issues and who are not allowed to challenge the speaker's view or theology.
>
> Trace the possible evolution of this scenario with a view to a practically workable and theologically appropriate resolution.

---

5 Dalziel, 'Developing Scenario Learning to Theological Education', 17–29.

(b) Inquiry-Based Learning Methods

Inquiry-based learning (IBL) can also take many forms. A common form is that of literary research to seek understanding of key concepts or issues. Such inquiry is based on a defined topic where the learner has limited if any knowledge and is prompted to 'find out' what is going on, why, how, and with what outcomes. This is standard fare for historical and philosophical study. Yet it is more than simply setting a topic. It requires a preliminary motivation of its intrinsic value to the learner for it to be undertaken effectively. Other forms include surveys, focus groups, and interviews, in which 'real-world' data may be collected and reviewed for understanding. In all these interpersonal formats, careful structure of components is needed because simply asking any questions may be too random and chaotic to be valuable. However, carefully constructed instruments to guide these investigations can be most productive.

A specific form of IBL that is particularly appropriate for mathegenical learning is *appreciative inquiry*. The basic assumption of appreciative inquiry is that the learner is a work in progress, with an established base that has worth that can be used as a starting point to add value. The learner is encouraged to identify and analyse past personal successes, then to articulate ways those past successes may be developed to generate ongoing successes. This strategy takes genuine cognisance of where a learner has come from and where the learner is potentially going. Whereas PBL begins from the identification of a problem to be healed, appreciative inquiry starts from a success that can be positively enhanced in a new application. It strategically encourages creative innovation in thought and practice. This approach commonly includes literary research (to further an inchoate interest); surveys, interviews, or forums (to garner a wider data base for more informed personal development); focus groups (not as a means of imposing views but as a means of participatory research that values community input). The key thing is that the learner's own successful experience and real future aspirations are the springboard for effective engagement in and application to a new and creatively extended setting. James Arkwright and Clement Chihota have compiled an insightful report on an appreciative inquiry project conducted at Bethlehem Tertiary Institute, New Zealand. Their report traces the main elements in appreciative inquiry under the headings define, discovery, dream, design, and destiny, within the context of a Christian tertiary institution. While it focuses on a specific research project, its findings can be applied in a wider educational context.[6]

A less typical but very powerful method is that of *narrative inquiry*, which allows learners to articulate their experiences through their stories and to 'offer a perspective about their perspective'. By encouraging people to reflect on, explore, and share their stories, narrative inquiry provides a means of developing their understanding of themselves and uncovering meanings through dialogue. Narrative inquiry has the potential to foster students' critical reflection during their course of study, potentially leading to evidence of transformation of other habits of mind, especially if learning is embedded in a context that supports the establishment of relationships which facilitate discourse.

A simple example which embraces group work, appreciative inquiry, narrative inquiry, and peer critical reflection is provided below.

Example of Appreciative and Narrative Inquiry

>(One-hour session, based on a group of eight, but other sized groups will suit)
>
>Objective: Each member will identify, articulate, and reinforce personal capabilities for ongoing success in future action.
>
>*Step 1: Individual (5-10 minutes)*
>
>Identify an idea, an event, a lesson, or a staff activity for which you had primary responsibility to manage or implement and which worked successfully.
>
>Write a brief note describing the event, your role, and what personal strength or action of yours made it work well.
>
>*Step 2: Pairs (10 minutes)*
>
>In pairs, both members relate their story to their partner.
>
>Discuss in particular what you view as the 'success point' of your partner's story.
>
>Each member suggests ways in which their successful approach/identified strength could be re-applied in a new venture or context.

---

6 Arkwright & Chihota, 'Using Appreciative Inquiry and Multimodal Texts', 259–269.

Try to co-create a mood of curiosity, inquiry, and respect in your dialogue, rather than a detached analytical interview. Try to get to know each other, be interested to discover and to understand what has influenced and shaped their performance. Take short notes, ask questions, and respect silence. Be ready to give a quick synopsis of your partner's story to a wider group.

Step 3: Small Group of Four (Two pairs join) (15 minutes)

Each member relates the story and success point of their original partner to the other pair.

Distil from the accounts the main causes of success that emerged across the group.

Appoint one member from the group to act as spokesperson for the group in Step 4.

Step 4: Plenary Group (15–20 minutes)

The small group spokespersons report on their group's findings about what led to success and what potential developments have been identified.

Plenary group compiles summary of key principles and practices that can be used to further success.

Individuals make notes of their own projected potential action/s.

(c) Group Project-Based Learning Methods

Group project-based learning methods combine elements of PBL and IBL. They work on the basic assumption that working in a group maximises the overall learning dynamic, as group members are accountable to and engage more relationally with peers. Thus, a mutually beneficial climate is established. Such peer learning provides learners with the opportunity to gain knowledge and skills by working for an extended period to investigate and respond to an engaging and complex question, problem, or challenge. In this way, peer learning addresses the oft-neglected issue of learning to work in a group, one of the chief failings noted in most student evaluations of tertiary courses. The project is focused on student learning goals, including content and skills such as critical thinking/problem solving, collaboration, and self-management. It is framed by a meaningful problem to solve or a question to answer, at the appropriate level of challenge, featuring real-world contexts, students' personal concerns, interests, and issues in their lives. Students and teachers are engaged together in an extended process of asking questions, finding resources, and applying information. Together, they reflect on learning, the effectiveness of their inquiry and project activities, obstacles and how to overcome them. Throughout, students make significant decisions about the project, including how they work and what they create, and they give, receive, and use feedback to improve their process and products. Finally, students make their project work public by explaining, displaying and/or presenting it to people beyond the classroom.

Michael Marquardt details such group learning in a business context. He outlines six underlying concepts and components of what he calls 'action learning', defined as 'a process that involves a small group working on real problems, taking action, and learning as individuals, as a team, and as an organisation while doing so'. The components of such learning are (1) a problem (project, challenge, opportunity, issue, or task), which is significant and urgent for the team to solve; (2) an action learning group or team, a diverse group of four to eight individuals who examine an organisational problem that has no easily identifiable solution; (3) a process of insightful questioning and reflective listening, which emphasises questions and reflection above statements and opinions to clarify the exact nature of the problem; (4) an action taken on the problem, which enhances learning as it provides a basis and anchor for the critical dimension of reflection; (5) a commitment to learning, which places the same emphasis on the learning and development of individuals and the team as it does on the solving of problems; and (6) an action learning coach, who enables group members to reflect critically on how they listen, how they may have reframed the problem, how they give each other feedback, how they are planning and working, and what assumptions may be shaping their beliefs and actions. Action learning in a group will be at its peak when all six components are operational.[7]

---

[7] Marquardt, *Optimizing the Power of Action Learning*, 1–23.

Example of a Group Project Exercise

A college mission team is to undertake a two-week program in a local church. The congregation is around twenty-five to thirty people, mainly elderly (sixty to eighty years old), in a suburb which has experienced considerable demographic change from a predominantly young family area to mainly units occupied by singles or couples. The remaining residents are mainly long-term elderly people. The church provides a number of mid-week social functions often attended by these long-term residents, although most are not members or involved in worship at the church.

The church is in serious decline and has asked the college team to 'give it a lift' as a last attempt to avoid closure. The team of six mainly young (twenty to thirty years old) and extroverted enthusiasts has six months' preparation time, alongside their regular studies.

Formulate an approach for executing this project.

(One approach could be to follow the four steps of Osmer's practical theology framework as noted previously.)

(d) Curiosity-Based Learning

A field of learning that fits very well within a mathegenical learning framework is that of curiosity-based learning (CBL). This is not so much a discrete method, but more a motivational base that can adopt a variety of methods of proceeding. The fundamental distinctive of this approach is its focus on the role of innate curiosity as a powerful motivator of stretching learning, that is, the type of learning that stretches the boundaries of a learner's capacity to grow in understanding and wisdom, to learn, to adapt, and to change. Curiosity is a questioning aimed at knowing more, that is, it prompts a desire to learn. Curiosity motivates exploration into previously unknown areas of knowledge and discovery and leads to immersion in the field of exploration that far exceeds superficial knowledge acquisition. A basic element in mathegenical teaching is the sparking of such curiosity within the learners. Once that spark has been touched off, it needs to have resources and structures for fulfilling exploration, discovery, and growth. Stephen Smith and others present two models of how CBL can be employed: a stretch learning matrix and an action coaching approach.[8]

Figure 7.1: Stretch Learning Matrix

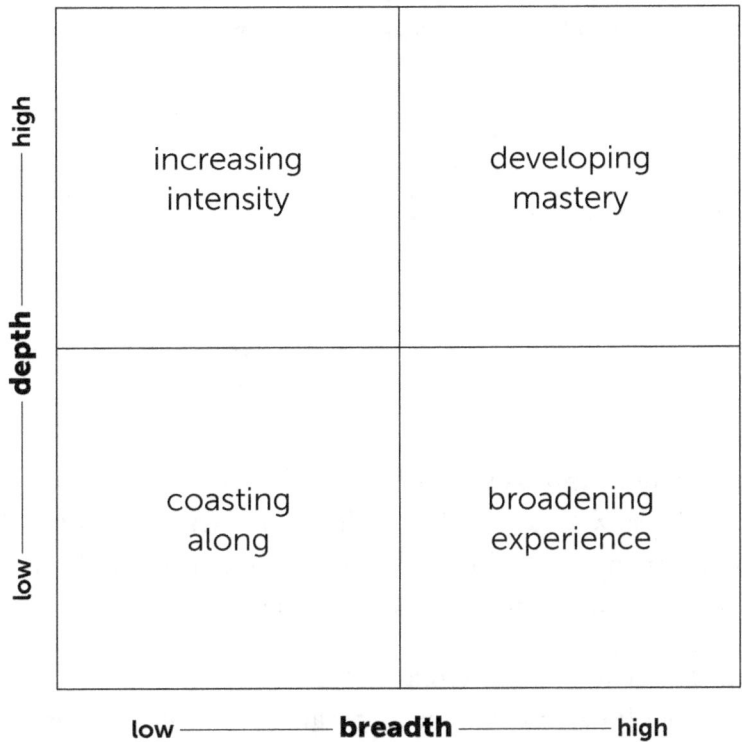

The stretch learning matrix involves being stretched in two directions: depth and breadth. Depth refers to increasing the intensity of work in an area already known and breadth refers to broadening work beyond the usual areas of work. That is, depth increases intensity and breadth broadens experience. The stretching occurs in both directions, not necessarily simultaneously, but in different ways by providing different kinds and levels of challenge and aspects of responsibility for their own learning.

---

8   Smith, Bingham & Kleemann, 'Curiosity-Based Learning', 435–449.

Figure 7.2: Action Coaching Approach

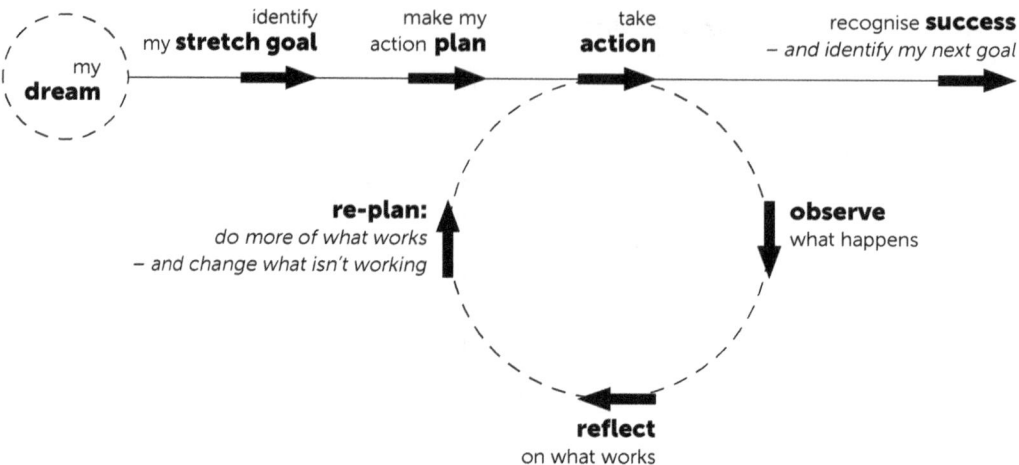

The action coaching approach works on the basis of iterative cycles of curious questions, such as: What did I plan to do? What action did I take? What did I observe? What are my reflections? The cycle of action and reflection is repeated, leading to further inquiry and action for change.

> *Critical Reflection.* Choose one of the learning types discussed above and consider how you could incorporate it into one of your units.

C. CRITICAL THINKING

A key component in all the methods listed above is the development of learners' capacity for independent critical thinking, which is essentially a process of appraisal of underlying assumptions in the things we believe and do. Thus, it is not simply a case of demolishing arguments, but it is a process of confirmation or correction, of modification or renewal, and sometimes even the abandonment of views or practices. This involves the identification, analysis, and evaluation of held assumptions (those of themselves, of others, of their institutions, of their study disciplines); the astute marshalling and interpretation of evidence; empathetic engagement with and respect for a range of ideas and perspectives; and social sensitivity to contexts (both individual and institutional). These critical faculties need to be developed in the learner, which also means they need to be modelled and facilitated by the teacher. The teacher needs to be open to receiving and giving critical feedback as a demonstration of authentic critical thought.

Brookfield lists a number of principal ways in which critical thinking may be strategically developed in learners. First, and most important, is the need for teachers to model and draw explicit attention to the operation of critical thinking in their own life and work, which admittedly leaves them vulnerable to criticism, but that is itself a core component of the development of the art of criticism. Students typically respond positively to critical thinking as a social experience, in which peers serve as critical mirrors on assumptions, and when activities are grounded in concrete experience through such things as case studies, critical incidents, simulations, or scenarios.[9]

A more challenging form of critical development comes through the judicious insertion of a disorienting dilemma, whereby students are deliberately shaken (but not too violently) out of their comfort zone as a means of challenging common (and deeply rooted) assumptions as a start of the critical thinking process. In my introduction to hermeneutics, which was located in the second semester of an undergraduate theology degree, I would casually ask the class of fervent evangelical students, 'What is your basis of authority of Christian truth?' to which the typical response was, 'The Bible'. My riposte: 'No, it isn't—it's your interpretation of the Bible'. This was a distinctly disorienting moment for these biblical idealists, who started to formulate opinions of me ranging from merely an *agent provocateur* through to an outright heretic atheist. However, over the following weeks, the class grew in appraising their hermeneutical assumptions and the way in which they shaped their core convictions, which led in the main to a strong affirmation of their faith, reinforced by a new and more critically informed way of thinking – they even concluded that perhaps I was, after all, an acceptable Christian.

In all the above approaches, it is important to ensure that critical thinking is facilitated in a developmentally sequenced way, beginning from non-threatening real or hypothetical settings and progressing through to students' own life and experiences. This provides the necessary safety net for constructive development because too heavy a challenge in the early stage can mortify rather than motivate and can thereby be more disastrous than developmental. In my hermeneutics class, the safety net had been established in the good rapport I had developed with the class in the previous semester, my respectful treatment of conflicting

---

9   Brookfield, *The Skillful Teacher*, 155–167.

views that arose within the class, my personal story of growth from a naïve understanding to a deeper critical position, and my knowledge that I had an ongoing term to develop the critical faculties that I was introducing. By the time that class reached their advanced biblical studies, they had a well-established framework of critical biblical thinking.

An effective way of demonstrating authentic critical thinking is team teaching. It is not uncommon for theological faculty in different departments (or even within a single department) to hold variant views on important topics. When students encounter this among their individual teachers, confusion as to who is 'right' (with its inevitable corollary) can be disturbing, to say the least. An effective way of overcoming this potential divisiveness and of expanding the critical horizons of students is to embrace the difference by teaching as a team, whereby such divergent views are openly presented and critically evaluated, in an atmosphere of respectful discussion and debate, with the inclusion of the students in the process. In a way, team teaching injects the elements of risk-taking and uncertainty, as teachers expose themselves to the critical judgement and potential disagreements of their teaching colleagues as well as the students. However, such uncertainty within diversity lies beneath all critical development, and so this faculty modelling is itself a contributing factor, as the richness of teacher input is thereby enhanced and the learning experience is expanded. It is important that in such a team environment, the team acts together by being all present in the room at all times so a genuine teamwork is demonstrated. Such an approach can have an immense impact on the development of respectful critical thinking because it is powerfully demonstrated by the group and thereby serves as an expression of the institution.

Two brief examples from my own experience of the power of team teaching may serve as illustrations, one in which I was involved, the other which I observed at close quarters. An issue had arisen concerning the ordination of women, which was troubling the student body. To address this, a forum was arranged in which four faculty members from different disciplines—biblical studies, theology, pastoral studies, and education—would present various perspectives on the issue, with a critical summary to conclude. The perspectives varied widely, with some irreconcilable polarisation of ultimate positions emerging within the faculty. The high degree of authentic respect that existed among the differing faculty positions and persons was well received and the overall result was not so much a resolution of the contention, but a deeply entrenched commitment to legitimate searching through reasoned discourse.

The other example was in a consortium of three denominational theological colleges, where an Introducing Theology class was team taught for a semester by three ordained clergy representing the denominations, with all presenting theology from their tradition's perspective, with all three lecturers in the room at all times, with students from all three denominations simultaneously in the class. Again, the perspectives differed greatly and were presented with equal vigour, accompanied by respectful yet robust discussion. In reviews of the consortium programs conducted among graduate students, this class was universally rated as the most helpful offering in the promotion of critical and respectful relations among the denominations, both during and after their formal course.

> *Critical Reflection.* Are you more likely to feel comfortable or feel challenged in a team teaching setting?

A final word is warranted regarding online teaching. This is more about the mode of course presentation than it is pedagogical method, but the two are not entirely separable. Some institutions deliver courses solely online, but even those who conduct all classes in face-to-face mode use a degree of blended learning, if not formally in teaching by teachers, then certainly in learning by students. As noted earlier, the divisive question, 'Can theological education be authentically delivered online?' has pretty much evolved into the developmental question, '*How* can theological education be authentically delivered online?'. We have also observed that online teaching is not essentially qualitatively different from face-to-face teaching, since it follows similar fundamental principles of good teaching. Online delivery does have its own set of logistical and learning management conditions, which are beyond the scope of this chapter, but most of our suggestions concerning pedagogy in general apply equally to online mode. However, certain fundamental issues of method pertinent to online delivery can be indicated.

The first thing to emphasise is the need for absolute clarity in communication. Too much information is far better than not enough. Because online teaching is usually asynchronous, students do not have the luxury of the immediacy of communication that accompanies direct or incidental contact with teachers in the classroom and corridors, so they need to know precisely what the expectations of their study are, in terms of institutional administration and, for our purposes, in terms of learning activities, demands, and methods involved.

All this needs to be communicated clearly at the outset and there should be ongoing access to this information throughout the course. Establishing early and clearly the expectations of the program and the students, as well as setting ground rules for communication, both with the teacher and with the other students, will help to keep the course and the learning on a clear trajectory. Of course, as with all forms of teacher-student interaction, there will be room for evolving ground rules, but setting a base early in the program is always helpful.

The second thing is to establish a teacher presence online, which is the single most important predictor of online students' satisfaction.[10] Much of the criticism of online learning relates to the distance separating teacher and learner, so regular group and/or individual connection opportunities are needed. Every learner needs to be confident of being important to the teacher and that the teacher is an accessible ally in learning. The online teacher needs to establish a personal presence that connects meaningfully with the learners and that is both dialogical and inclusive. An effective way of doing this is the establishment of a community of inquiry, which can be well suited to the online medium.[11] There are three main types of teacher presence: social, teaching, and cognitive. Social presence is defined by Maddix as the 'ability of learners to project their personal characteristics into the community of inquiry by presenting themselves as real people'.[12] That is, students are not words on a screen but people who have their own likes, dislikes, experiences, and hopes. Learning to engage with the person *behind* the words brings the teacher (and other students) into the world of the student in a risk-free and supportive setting. The purpose of doing this is to enhance the teacher's cognitive presence. This is where interaction with the student builds meaning, as it involves the exchange of information, analysing new ideas, and connecting ideas. The primary focus here is to ensure that online discussion includes learning that fosters critical thinking. Finally, teaching presence brings the social and cognitive aspects together in the focused attainment of learning outcomes and course requirements. The teacher has the role of setting the parameters within the curriculum and focusing the discussion to lead to critical sharing of personal meaning. Together these elements make up a community of inquiry.[13]

---

10   Brookfield, *The Skillful Teacher*, 179.
11   In this treatment of a community of inquiry, I am greatly indebted to my colleague Associate Professor Peter Laughlin for his insights in this field, which I include here with his permission.
12   Maddix, Estep & Lowe, *Best Practices of Online Education*, 109.
13   Garrison & Anderson, *E-Learning in the 21st Century*, 29.

There are various ways a teacher can construct such a community, such as synchronous group discussion meetings to establish group identity; asynchronous forums where the teacher engages actively in the dialogue to guide, focus, affirm, challenge, extend the discussion; use of plenary emails rather than one-to-one emails concerning learning elements; cross-referring students with one another for peer engagement; and quick response systems for student queries. However, whatever the techniques employed, the key is intentionality and consistency. The teacher must be proactive and reliable in engaging the students meaningfully throughout the course of the teaching term.

> *Critical Reflection.* How effectively can you establish a meaningful 'teacher presence' in online teaching?

But all that is the stuff of the mode. Methodologically, there are two major areas of focus: discussion and assessment. Most online units incorporate some form of online discussion. Such activity needs to have clear ground rules and, most important of all, they need to be clearly and integrally linked to stated learning objectives. If the teacher cannot show (or has not shown) in advance how such a connection exists, it is probably not connected, and is even less likely to have such a connection made by the student. Associated with this is the need to ensure the discussion remains focused. When a discussion topic is too broad or ill-defined, the scope for divergence is huge: a small degree of individual divergence early in the discussion can lead to a global meandering by the whole group. It is advisable to keep discussion topics narrow in scope so depth of discussion can occur. Further, the topic and demand of the discussion need to be suited to the level and distinctive ethos of the unit and not simply be a convenient 'one size fits all' for a combined class grouping.

Perhaps the major source of online student angst occurs in assessment tasks and processing. Assessment tasks need to follow the same principles as discussions: to be well defined not vague, to have clear directions for the processes involved, with clearly articulated linkage to learning outcomes, and indications of suitable and sufficient resources for the attainment of the task objectives. While the task itself needs to be clear and focused, the evaluation provided also is of paramount importance. In light of the less direct personal connection between teacher and student, the most significant part of the evaluation is not the summative mark awarded, but the verbal feedback provided. Positive feedback needs to be focused on what has been done well, with specific evidence from the assignment by way of explaining precisely where this good quality has been demonstrated. Without such specifics, the student will be left feeling affirmed, but unclear as to why. Similarly, negative feedback will note the worthy elements but place more emphasis on exactly where the shortcomings occurred, with clear explanation of why this was so, and how the shortcoming can be addressed in future efforts. Without such specifics, the student will be left feeling ashamed and inadequate but with no idea of how to improve. General platitudes of 'Good work' or 'Unsatisfactory performance' without elaboration have no value to the student. It is also helpful if evaluation of a subsequent assessment item can refer to previous feedback, by way of relevant affirmation or continuing remediation. The more pertinent detail the marker can provide, the more the student is likely to be assisted in learning, and the more the teacher will be seen to be genuinely vested in the learner's progress. A helpful element in all of this is the creation of detailed and clear assessment rubrics to be provided to the learner at the outset and to be the basis of formative and summative feedback in due course. More specific details of this aspect will be provided in the next chapter.[14]

> *Critical Reflection.* Review the pedagogical methods employed in your own theological (or other) education. As a learner, how did/would you respond to such approaches?

---

[14] A helpful book on constructing and delivering online programs is Thormann & Zimmerman's *The Complete Step-by-Step Guide to Designing and Teaching Online Courses*, especially 'Course Design and Development', 9–34. As the title suggests, this is a chapter from a practitioner's handbook for constructing online educational programs. Its focus is on schools, with several local American school references, but its coverage of the underlying philosophy of online education is worth examining, as too is its array of pedagogical practices that can be effectively utilised.

8 | INTEGRATING PEDAGOGY— BRINGING IT ALL TOGETHER

This final segment on pedagogical issues attempts to bring together the various elements of the preceding chapters with a focus on the key aspects of assessment and integration. It is a fundamental premise of pedagogy that effective assessment activities are those that exhibit clearly an expression of pedagogic intent and style, not a separate traumatic event. Hence, assessment is itself a key learning activity, since it is the sharp end of what all students look to as a marker of their successful learning. As such, it often tends to drive the learner's whole approach to a unit and so it needs to embody the same deep learning principles that good teaching incorporates. Assessment should never come as a surprise—or worse, a shock—to learners. The importance of an appreciation of the nuances of award levels in higher education is also featured because this is an area of increasing significance with the now-common educational move away from norm-based to standards-based assessment. Finally, as a conclusion to this section, an exhortation to integrative learning is offered as a means of providing a coherent reinforcement of the learner's development. Since integration is a global aim of all mathegenical teaching, this serves as a salient *conclusio* to our discussion of pedagogy.

A. ASSESSMENT

There are arguably, albeit somewhat simplistically, two basic camps when it comes to the aim of setting assessment tasks: (1) to demonstrate what students know; or (2) to demonstrate what students do not know. I stand unapologetically in the first camp and strongly opposed to the philosophy of the second camp.

Assessment should be viewed as nothing other than an authentic learning activity, which provides learners a vehicle for demonstration of the learning that they have mastered. As various pedagogical purposes and learning styles have dominated our consideration of teaching and learning, so too they should dominate our discussions of assessment.

Assessment grounds the principles of deep learning, which results from good pedagogy and should reflect such pedagogy. How the learner has been guided to learn should also be the way the learning is assessed. It is often said that deep learning is driven by integration, while surface learning is driven by assessment. However, I suggest that this is a false dichotomy, born of common practice rather than good practice. Activities that *facilitate* deep learning, such as connecting with existing frameworks of reference, relating to learners' aspirations, and engaging learners in designing and assuming responsibility, can readily translate to activities that *demonstrate* deep learning, by allowing expression of attainment of outcomes in a variety of ways and allowing a variety of learners to express attainment of outcomes via different learning styles. Therefore, assessment of learning that retains a clear relationship between assessment and learning approaches will enhance deep learning by focusing on a learner's collection and interpretation of evidence as a means of making judgements on their progress towards achieving outcomes. Charles De Jongh has listed seven principles of assessment that incorporates deep learning that should be kept consistently in mind:

1. Assessment is integral to course design and should be centred on the students' envisaged achievement.
2. Assessment requirements focus on the significant principles and structures of the course.
3. Assessment is based on clear and stated objectives and outcomes, which are directly associated with the aims and purpose of the course.
4. Assessment for deep learning makes use of a wide variety of methods and types.
5. Assessment requirements and criteria are clearly and explicitly stated.
6. Assessment for deep learning is supported by good preparatory guidance, material and personal support, and appropriate resourcing.
7. Assessment gives early and comprehensive feedback, with the intention of addressing weaknesses and improving learning.[1]

---

1 De Jongh, 'The Contribution of Theories of Multiple Intelligences', 95.

Critical Reflection. How can you ensure that assessment activities are authentic deep learning activities? Give some examples drawn from your own teaching.

Historically, assessment has been used typically as a measure of relative performance of learners, with notions of normal distribution of results shaping assessment practices to establish an order of merit among students. Significantly, such an inherently competitive approach seems not to engage any of the above principles. Today, a fundamental change operates, which places the emphasis on standards of individual performance without reference to others' performance, but simply as a measure of the student's own attainment of stated standards of learning. Consequently, we no longer 'grade on a curve' but we base assessment on clearly identified and published standards. This is a relatively new, at times daunting, philosophy for many experienced tertiary teachers but it is a fundamentally just and educationally sound approach. The core element in this approach is the establishment of standards, which demands a high level of pedagogical finesse on the part of the assessor, at both construction and grading stages.

The task of establishing standards is effectively done by articulating a clear expression of the requirements and the markers of such learning standards, so both teacher and learner are literally working from the same page. This is efficiently done by creating a sound assessment rubric in advance of delivery of the unit as a guide and reference point for both the activity and its assessment. In this way, a teacher will hone the learning objectives and provide a clear focus for the learners to guide their study as well as their assessment. In my experience, an irritatingly common statement from too many teachers has been along the lines of, 'Well, I can't spell out in precise detail what I am looking for in an assignment, but I will recognise it when I see it'. I must admit that I have never been convinced of the legitimacy of such a claim. Rather, a standards-based approach to assessment requires the teacher to analyse exactly and to articulate precisely what is being sought in the assessment as an expression of the desired learning outcomes.

In constructing a viable assessment rubric, there are three basic and essential components: criteria; standards; and descriptors. James Cook University has produced a workable approach to the creation of rubrics that contain all these elements presented in a clear format.[2] In this approach, criteria are the properties or characteristics by which to judge the quality of the assessment task, while not making any assumptions about actual quality; standards are defined levels of quality of achievement or performance; and descriptors indicate the qualities required to demonstrate achievement of each standard for each criterion.

In developing criteria, transparency of expectations is important. Whatever elements form part of the assessment (for example: biblical knowledge; understanding of theological significance of sacraments; coherent articulation of theories; historical causation and outcomes; practical applications; and creativity or accuracy in expression) should be included, with care being given to ensure all such assessment expectations are in fact part of the stated learning outcomes of the unit of work. In identifying standards, a limited number of three to five grade zones should be set. It is usual to identify what is the best possible standard that could be expected for this level of work; what is the least or threshold standard that is acceptable; what is an unacceptable standard; and a very small number of mid-points as relevant. It does not matter if a letter grade, a percentage band, or a combination of both is used, so long as the standard is clearly stated. Creating standards descriptors is perhaps the most challenging element, as here the rubric designer must be astute in discerning what level of difficulty is appropriate and what nuances of performance match the stated standards. Descriptors should ideally be brief, clear, and specific, but should not be reduced to laboriously detailed mechanistic formulae—in all assessment, there will be an inevitable degree of subjectivity of assessor judgement, but that should be compatible with what the learners expect. No matter what format of rubric is designed, these three components should be clearly present, and the overall assessment should be a coherent combination of the sectional marks awarded.

There are various ways of constructing assessment rubrics, ranging from a simple holistic table that can serve as a 'one size fits all' template, through a more focused matrix that serves a suite of units with comparable outcomes, to a more specifically focused rubric tailored to match a single unit. Thus, the

---

2   See 'Developing Assessment Rubrics. Guidelines for JCU Subject Coordinators'. This is an excellent introduction to the art of creating a rubric, which I am largely following in these paragraphs. https://www.jcu.edu.au/__data/assets/pdf_file/0009/496269/Developing-assessment-rubrics.pdf
    A more detailed discussion of the principles and possibilities of Standards Based Assessment can be found in The University of Queensland's guidance document 'Designing Rubrics For Better Assessment'. https://itali.uq.edu.au/files/1234/Discussion-paper-Designing-Rubrics-For-Better-Assessment.pdf

degree of focused precision can be varied to suit different contexts. The important thing is to establish and articulate the standards, criteria, and descriptors so that all learning will be appropriately guided. A few sample rubrics that have been recently developed follow, as they demonstrate three approaches to creating an analytical rubric.

The first sample (see Figure 8.1) is a generic 'one size fits all' rubric intended for use as a college-wide tool for all units. As such, it has more criteria than normally recommended, as it seeks to be broadly used. The second sample (see Figure 8.2) is designed as a unit-specific rubric for a set research essay in Theology, very much tailored to the precise assessment task. The remaining two samples are intended as discipline-specific rubrics, which can be used for all Church History units at differentiated award levels (see Figure 8.3: Undergraduate and Figure 8.4: Postgraduate). The History samples are constructed on the premise that comparable criteria and standards apply across the group of introductory History units, in line with their corresponding learning outcomes, but with a nuanced discrimination between the corresponding undergraduate and postgraduate levels. Together, these four examples demonstrate a variety of approaches without mandating any one. That is, they should be considered as samples rather than paradigms. The key thing is the provision of meaningfully focused and constructive feedback to help students improve their learning and to develop more autonomy in that learning.[3]

---

3   I acknowledge the collaborative contribution to these samples by my colleagues at Australian College of Ministries and Professor Gerard Kelly of the Catholic Institute of Sydney. The samples are used here with their permission.

Figure 8.1: Generic Assessment Rubric

Assessment Criteria	Fail (<50%)	Pass (50-64%)	Credit (65-74%)	Distinction (75-84%)	High Distinction (85-100%)
General Description	Work that fails to attain the required outcomes(s), lacking in basic knowledge, understanding, analysis, and presentation	Work that satisfactorily attains the required outcomes(s), with adequate knowledges, understanding, analysis, and presentation	Work that soundly attains the required outcomes(s) showing a good level of knowledge, understanding, analysis, presentation and some evidence of critical interpretation	Excellent work that substantially attains the required outcomes(s) showing a high level of knowledge, understanding, analysis, critical interpretation, presentation and some originality	Outstanding work that comprehensively attains the required outcome(s) showing superior knowledge, understanding, analysis, critical interpretation, presentation and originality
Resources Up to 10% of total mark	Inadequate evidence of having used appropriate resources	Evidence of having used some appropriate resources	Evidence of sound understanding of appropriate resources	Evidence of relevant use of resources beyond expectations	Evidence of wide, relevant, and independently gained resources
	☐ Fail	☐ Pass	☐ Credit	☐ Distinction	☐ High Distinction
Knowledge of Topic Up to 30% of total mark	Inadequate factual and conceptual knowledge	Demonstrated satisfactory factual and conceptual knowledge to serve as a basis for further study	Demonstrated extensive factual and conceptual knowledge	Demonstrated substantial factual and conceptual knowledge incorporating highly distinctive insight into deeper and more subtle aspects of the topic	Demonstrated outstanding factual and conceptual knowledge incorporating highly distinctive insight into deeper and more subtle aspects of the topic
	☐ Fail	☐ Pass	☐ Credit	☐ Distinction	☐ High Distinction
Articulation of Argument Up to 20% of total mark	Insufficient construction of a coherent argument	Ability to construct sound argument based on evidence	Ability to construct well-reasoned and coherent argument with discriminating use of evidence	Argument contains evidence of imagination, originality, and independent thought	Sustained evidence of imagination, originality, and independent thought throughout the argument
	☐ Fail	☐ Pass	☐ Credit	☐ Distinction	☐ High Distinction
Analytical and Reflective Skills Up to 15% of total mark	Insufficient evidence of analytical and reflective skills	Evidence of analytical and reflective skills	Evidence of developed analytical and reflective skills	Evidence of well-developed analytical and reflective skills	Evidence of highly developed analytical and reflective skills
	☐ Fail	☐ Pass	☐ Credit	☐ Distinction	☐ High Distinction
Application Up to 15% of total mark	Insufficient evidence of appropriate application	Evidence of some appropriate application	Ability to apply some of the concepts to specific situations.	Ability to apply concepts to challenging problems	Ability to apply to non-routine or very challenging problems
	☐ Fail	☐ Pass	☐ Credit	☐ Distinction	☐ High Distinction
Expression and Presentation appropriate to the Discipline Up to 10% of total mark	Inadequate skills in expression, presentation, and documentation	Adequate skills in expression, presentation, and documentation	Good skills in expression, presentation, and documentation	Well-developed skills in expression, presentation, and documentation appropriate to wider audiences	Highly developed skills in expression, presentation, and documentation appropriate to wider audiences
	☐ Fail	☐ Pass	☐ Credit	☐ Distinction	☐ High Distinction

Comments on essay (minimum 100 words):

All marks returned to students with assignments are conditional only.
They may be adjusted as part of the SCD result monitoring process.

Final Mark: #DIV/0! / 50   Grade: #DIV/0!

Figure 8.2: Undergraduate Theology Research Essay Rubric

Standard	Fail	Pass	Credit	Distinction	High Distinction	Comments
Criteria	Work that fails to meet the criteria, lacking in basic knowledge, understanding, analysis, and presentation	Work that satisfactorily meets the criteria, with adequate knowledge, understanding, analysis, and presentation	Work that soundly meets the criteria, showing a good level of knowledge, understanding, analysis, presentation, and some evidence of critical interpretation	Excellent work that substantially meets the criteria, showing a high level of knowledge, understanding, analysis, critical interpretation, presentation, and some originality	Outstanding work that comprehensively meets the criteria, showing superior knowledge, understanding, analysis, critical interpretation, presentation, and originality	
Understands the Eucharistic doctrines relevant to the chosen topic	Does not identify the Eucharistic doctrines relevant to the chosen topic	Accurately presents some of the relevant doctrines	Shows a good understanding of the doctrines	Is able to analyse the doctrines in the context of the chosen topic	Brings insight into Eucharistic doctrines to an analysis of the topic subject	
Works with the sources of Eucharistic theology	Fails to identify the relevant sources of Eucharistic theology	Identifies and makes adequate use of relevant sources	Uses primary sources in conjunction with relevant secondary literature	Shows discernment in the choice of both primary sources and secondary literature	Uses primary sources and secondary literature to develop own understanding	
Shows the connection between the theological and the pastoral	Fails to identify either the pastoral or theological aspects of the topic	Recognises that the topic has both pastoral and theological aspects	Can diagnose the theological questions raised by a pastoral situation	Shows how the pastoral and theological inform each other	Is able to develop a coherent understanding of the Eucharist that informs and is informed by the pastoral context	
Essay presentation	Essay lacks clear organisation, has poor English expression and lacks appropriate referencing	Essay has a recognisable structure and is clearly written, but has errors of grammar and syntax. Footnotes and bibliography are poorly presented	Essay uses clear language generally free of errors; referencing of footnotes and bibliography is accurate and consistent	Essay uses clear and appropriate language free of errors; referencing of footnotes and bibliography is accurate and consistent	Essay is fluently and elegantly expressed, with accurate and consistent footnoting and bibliographical referencing, and a good sense of when to use footnotes	

Figure 8.3: Research Essay in Undergraduate Church History Rubric

Standard ↘ / Criterion ↓	N (0–49%) Does not Meet Standard of Historical Knowledge or Understanding	P (50–64%) Attains Minimal Standard of Historical Knowledge	C (65–74%) Presents a Good Understanding of Historical Events	D (75–84%) Sustains a Good Level of Historical Accuracy and Analysis	HD (85–100%) Performs at Highest Standard with Expert Analysis & Evaluation of Events & Movements	Marks
Processes Historical Information (40%)	Lacks sufficient accurate and relevant detail	Describes a limited amount of accurate and relevant historical information	Shows a clear understanding of main historical events and issues	Presents a clear analysis of major historical issues and movements	Presents skilful interpretation and evaluation of historical developments and directions	
Uses Primary & Secondary Historical Literature (30%)	Lacks engagement with primary literature and makes limited use of secondary literature	Makes adequate use of selected secondary literature but limited use of primary literature	Uses secondary material well and includes some relevant primary literature	Makes consistent use of appropriate primary and secondary literature	Presents skilful integration of well balanced primary and scholarly secondary literature	
Presents Historical Argument (20%)	Lacks clear organisation of thought and presents disjointed collection of data	Presents a clear descriptive narrative of events but lacks thematic unity	Presents a clear line of development of some important issues	Presents a clear line of development with effective base of specific evidence	Presents a coherent and cogent argument based on comprehensive historical evidence	
English Usage and Essay Writing Conventions (10%)	Contains too many errors in English usage and essay writing conventions	Contains significant errors but not to the extent of obscuring meaning	Uses generally clear expression and formatting with some minor flaws only	Makes good use of English language and essay writing conventions	Uses concise and well chosen language and correct essay writing conventions	

← Descriptors →

TOTAL = %   Grade =

Figure 8.4: Research Essay in Postgraduate Church History Rubric

Standard / Criterion	N (0–49%) Does not Meet Standard of Historical Knowledge or Understanding	P (50–64%) Attains Minimal Standard of Historical Knowledge and Understanding	C (65–74%) Presents a Good Understanding of Historical Causation	D (75–84%) Sustains a Critical Level of Historical Accuracy and Analysis	HD (85–100%) Performs at Highest Standard with Scholarly Analysis & Evaluation of Events & Movements	Marks
Analyses Historical Information (30%)	Does not justify selection of pivotal elements and lacks adequate accurate and relevant historical detail	Justifies the selection of key elements and relates the narratives accurately	Accurately identifies and analyses significant causes of main historical events and issues	Presents a clear statement of the interrelatedness of historical issues and movements	Presents an expert critique of the relative importance of the pivotal elements	
Uses Historical Literature (30%)	Lacks sufficient engagement with primary literature and relies on a limited range of secondary literature	Makes use of selected primary and secondary literature but lacks critical engagement with the scholarship	Uses a well chosen selection of scholarly secondary material and pertinent primary documents	Engages critically with a range of disparate approaches and interpretations at most points	Expertly combines a wide range of scholarly primary and secondary literature to analyse and interpret events	
Presents Historical Argument (30%)	Presents little more than descriptive narrative without explanation or interpretation	Presents a clear narrative highlighting the importance of the key elements	Presents a logical account of the causative factors and historical consequences of the elements	Argues from solid evidence to a logical evaluative conclusion	Presents a cogent argument based on diverse readings and reaches an independent summing up	
Uses Scholarly Presentation (10%)	Contains too many significant errors in English usage and essay writing conventions	Writes clearly but lacks appropriate academic essay conventions	Uses generally error-free English and suitable academic conventions	Writes accurately and concisely in fluent English	Presents a polished piece of scholarly writing suggesting potential for publishing	

← Descriptors →

TOTAL = %   Grade =

> *Critical Reflection.* Following any of the Guidelines or Samples of Assessment Rubrics, construct a simple rubric for a unit you teach or assess.

Assessors' feedback to learners is an integral part of teaching and learning in all modes of delivery, but most pointedly in online learning environments. An assessment rubric provides essential feedback on performance in terms of connection to learning outcomes, but there is still more to qualitative mathegenical feedback that focuses on furthering the learning capacity of the student. That is, the assessment rubric provides a point-in-time comment on what learning has been currently attained. Conversely, genuinely mathegenical feedback is not an isolated point-in-time communication. Rather, it is part of ongoing connections between teacher and learner and forms part of a developmental dialogue between the two parties, designed to provide input on how to enhance future learning. Constructive positive feedback reinforces the strengths of that relationship as it connects with what is already known and so advances those strengths. Constructive negative feedback is also connected because it shows pointedly and specifically the things that need remediation and shows the way to do so, all clearly in the interest of the learner rather than a punitive commentary. Such feedback is both time-consuming and critically demanding. However, it should be viewed not as a burden but as an investment in learning. This cannot be a box-ticking task because it needs to be tailored to the individual learner's context and capability, both demonstrated and potential. It needs to connect with what has been presented with clear direction for reinforcement, remediation, challenge, extension, or inspiration. This is a critical point of personal connection between teacher and learner that provides a powerful opportunity to collaborate meaningfully in the students' development of their learning capacity.

By way of illustration, I provide below several samples of what I consider effective qualitative mathegenical feedback by an experienced teacher. The setting is that of online learning, with both discussion forums and formal essays involved, in which the formal feedback on assessment items was part of an ongoing dialogue. The teacher had conducted a series of group video meetings; had always responded to student queries within a twenty-four-hour window (typically same day response); and had answered all student queries about the course work by way of whole class posts that acknowledged the value of the query and included the whole class in the response. She had engaged with learners actively in the forum discussions and guided those conversations by focusing the discussions, soliciting and respecting all participants' input, extending and challenging the learners to think ever more widely and deeply. That overarching atmosphere authorised her to make pointed comments as needed because the learners were confident in the mutual respect that had been established. So, her feedback on formal assignments became an effective instrument in learner development, that is, authentic mathegenical feedback. In the following samples, Sample 1 concerns a new postgraduate student in a Theology for Ministry unit, whose forum post was a little after the due date. The dialogue between teacher and student reveals a personalised connection and a growing sense of the value of the study. Sample 2 is the teacher-student dialogue in an introductory Church History unit, in which a very articulate student was the sole enrolment, so the teacher took on a more active partner role in the forum. Sample 3 is provided because it illustrates the need of serious correction leading to enhanced progress in the case of a modestly capable student. All samples illustrate the time and thought demand on the teacher and the clear focus of improving and extending the student's learning capacity as distinct from simply grading the work submitted.[4]

Sample 1: Theology for Ministry Forum Discussion (postgraduate)

Forum Topic

Didache or 'Teachings of the 12' document. The *Didache* is dated to either the late first century or early second century and so represents an interesting insight into the life of the early church. Read through it and then respond in a forum post to the questions that are listed at the end. That is, what were your initial reactions to reading the *Didache*? What surprised you? What did you appreciate most? What did you find confusing?

Student Forum Post

With regards to the practice of ministry in the early church, the *Didache* provided an interesting challenge to my theology of the relationship between a 'function' and an 'office'.

---

[4] Given the need to de-identify the students and thus the teacher, I have not cited sources of these samples. However, they are used by permission of the teacher as illustrative samples.

By way of context, I belong to a charismatic church movement that strongly emphasises every-member ministry. We read passages like Ephesians 4:11–13 (the five, or fourfold ministry, depending on your interpretation of the Greek) as describing 'functions' that any member of the body can carry out. This is as opposed to the idea that they are specific 'offices' or roles that are given to specific members of the church community.

I was surprised by the way the *Didache* clearly regards prophets and teachers as 'offices' within the church structure. While the scriptures do this to an extent, the *Didache* goes into far more detail, in particular describing the practice of hospitality for such individuals:

But every true prophet desiring to settle among you is worthy of his food. In like manner a true teacher is also worthy, like the workman, of his food. (13:1–2).

However, the fact that the early church regarded teachers and prophets as specific offices does not necessarily imply that we need to adopt these roles. Shaw argues that the stories we are given about the early church are not meant to be prescriptive of a particular model, but rather descriptive of the way the early church responded to its unique circumstances.

For example, Shaw addresses the appointing of the seven in Acts 6: 'Luke's concern in Acts 6: 1–6 was not to prescribe a model for church governance and decision-making procedures.' (p. 132).

In the same way, I suspect the *Didache* is not trying to mandate a church structure, but instruct its readers in how to work with the church structure that existed in the late first/early second century.

As we search the scriptures for instruction on how we structure our modern churches, we should be less concerned about any specific model, and more concerned about Shaw's main thesis: 'with respect to governance and church administration ... the preferred approach is one which best promotes the spread of the gospel.'

Teacher Response

Hi XXXX

I did not have time to engage with this post before the 'due hour', but I will do so now anyway.

I think you are exactly right to distinguish between biblical models as descriptive of functions rather than prescriptive of forms. Failure to grasp that concept is at the heart of so many church political problems. However, as the *Didache* demonstrates from a relatively early church period, later church communities so regularised this principle that they became quite legalistic in nature and, more problematically, in implementation. Fast forward a couple of millennia and where are we now? When we look at our own church governance models, how far have they been so regularised that they have become 'set in concrete' to the point that the function is obscured by the form? It is inevitable that any organisation (which the church is) requires rules of conduct, so how do we maintain the ethos and function of the gospel within the desire for orderly conduct?

Do you have any observations based on your own contemporary church experience?

(I realise this is now after the due date, but feel free to respond anyway if you wish.)

Student Response

Hey YYYY

I'll definitely be making an effort to get my forum posts in a little earlier from here! I'm normally the student that's a week ahead but I have some catching up to do this time around. Plus I find this kind of conversation invaluable to helping crystallise these ideas in my brain.

I like the way you better framed what I was trying to say—we often interpret scripture with legalistic mindsets and therefore get into trouble when my legalistic interpretation doesn't agree with yours.

Interestingly we have almost the opposite problem in [our church] ... with regard to both our governance and interpretation of scripture as a whole.

We're officially an 'association of independent churches', which means each church is loosely affiliated and gets to choose its own governance and structure. It usually ends up being a fairly typical Senior pastor/worship pastor/campus pastor kind of model but exactly what these roles mean is defined by the church (or sometimes, ill-defined).

I actually love this structure and the way it allows for the kind of missional-reactive model these papers talked about. It's just enough hierarchy to fix problems when they arise but when things are good it's whatever suits the church.

The only downside is sometimes we forget that there are 2000 years of church history we can learn from! Sometimes in [Our Church] we can shy away from tradition simply because it's tradition. This also comes to reading and interpreting scripture.

As my second subject in my masters this has been one of the biggest realisations for me – learning the history of Christian thought and why people believed what they did.

Sample 2: Introduction to Christian History Forum Discussion (undergraduate)

Forum Topic

What were the challenges to the survival of the Eastern Church traditions in the past and what are they today? In terms of healing splits or disagreements, do you have experience of reconciliation work in church or between church communities? Please remember to value others' experience and be respectful of difference.

Student Forum Post

There were many historical challenges to the survival of the Eastern Church. Some of these include:

CULTURAL

The rise of Latin culture threatened the Eastern church with its practical, formulaic, juridical approach to understanding of theology versus the Greek experiential, speculative and worshipful culture.

ROMAN PAPACY

The papal supremacy of Rome was a large challenge to the Eastern Church. Not only was Rome influenced by Latin culture, but it acted as the supreme authority in matters of 'doctrine or practice as if it did not need counsel from anyone else'. (Noll, 128). A great example was the addition of filioque to the Nicene creed which shifted a key aspect of doctrinal understanding.

ISLAMIC ENCROACHMENT

Further, a completely foreign religion, Islam, travelled in from the East challenging the Eastern Church and the Byzantine empire (Noll, 127).

CRUSADES

Finally, it seems that the Eastern Church was caught in the crusading crossfire, as the Western Church sent armed soldiers eastward to reclaim ground from Islam. Unfortunately, as opportunistic and commercially minded crusaders were travelling through Constantinople, they were seduced by its riches and decimated the city.

TODAY, there is ongoing political threat. Though not as prevalent now, Communism certainly impacted the Eastern Church especially through Europe. In many of those countries, the political environment has not yet stabilised (Noll, 137.)

Geographically, the Eastern church is often in close proximity to Islamic nations or peoples which presents major challenges, especially if Islam is the presiding religion in the nation.

On a personal note, over the last few years, I have taken some interest in the theology of the Eastern church. A long term friend of mine recently converted to the Greek Orthodox tradition and I attended his son's Christening. I was impacted by the detailed liturgy, especially with respect to the apparent Exorcism style declarations made over the young boy.

Also, in some earlier units I have come across theologian N.T. Wright who suggests Christus Victor is the pre-eminent motif *of the atonement. However, my reformed roots (my father grew up in the Dutch reformed church) heavily adhere to the Penal Substitution* motif *as the primary view of Jesus' atonement. Again, my view here is more consistent with the Eastern church (Noll, 127 compares Latin thinking of* 'Christ the Victim', vs Greek thinking of 'Christ the Victor').

I have had first-hand experience in a church disagreement, which did result in many members moving to other churches (not quite a church split though). It was over a reasonably common case of charismatic practice/belief being brought into a conservative environment. It's such a challenging situation to observe two very valid, but different viewpoints. This was an incredible learning time for me, and caused me to research my Bible thoroughly, to consult external wise counsel, and most importantly, to look inward at my own heart. It didn't take too long to discover a very combative internal attitude of 'They're wrong, and I'm right'!! Good thing I'm currently doing the Personal Formation unit, which should iron out some kinks!

But probably the most challenging observation from this experience, and one that I also observe back in history, is an attitude that essentially says, 'Theology is more important than relationships'. Perhaps this is an oversimplification, and I'm sure the forum response will set me straight!

Teacher Response

Again, a LOT of good stuff here XXXX. Your comment on the Roman Papacy is an excellent example of good historical writing. You make an incisive comment (Rome as supreme authority), support it by reference to the literature (Noll quote), and provide a relevant piece of specific evidence as illustration of that point (filioque). A good historical cameo.

In today's post-Communist Russia, it is interesting that the Orthodox Church, in emerging from the shadow of dominant Communism, has taken a position not unlike medieval Rome: increasing political power within the State, with oppressive control over 'dissidents'.

I also attended a Greek Orthodox ceremony—a wedding of a school teaching colleague—and was impressed by the high liturgy. But my lasting memory is of the half dozen or so youths waiting outside the church who needed me to translate the biblical Greek text that was inscribed over the church door: 'We've been coming here all our lives but no one has ever told us what that means'. Some modern cultural characteristics seem to transcend other traditions, it seems.

'They're wrong and I'm right' seems to be a universal tendency. It is particularly pernicious (and sadly, prevalent) in areas of such deeply held convictions as religion. One of the most precious things church history has given me is a much greater capacity to see many 'rights' even if they are different from mine. I don't see that as a doctrinal weakness, but as a greater measure of genuine respect for (as distinct from mere toleration of) a wider array of God's creation. Sometimes, the convictions we hold so strongly are really not much more than ego at play.

The attitude that essentially says, 'Theology is more important than relationships' is interesting. I doubt that too many would admit to holding such a view, but you are right, it has been prevalent throughout history. However, when we understand theology as being 'how we understand and express our understanding of God' rather than 'being God', we start to see our expression of belief (theology) as somewhat more transitional and evolving rather than a static dogmatic, and so it can become a means to enhancing our relationships (with God, with others) rather than dominating others.

I'm not sure that I have met your challenge of 'setting you straight', but I have enjoyed the conversation.

Student Response

Hi YYYY, thanks for your thorough comments, they're invaluable. I appreciate the added insight you offered especially regarding some of the difficult personal/relational issues that arise when we consider our differences. It's tricky to walk the line between mere tolerance and genuine respect for the 'many rights', but I can see this balanced attitude has been slow developing in my life also.

Sample 3: Introduction to Christian History: Feedback on three consecutive Assessment Items (undergraduate student who struggled to pass, but improved to an overall grade of Credit)

Assessment 1: Document Study

XXXX

I am afraid this essay has not done enough analysis or provided sufficient historical commentary. It offers a few general acceptable comments (as noted throughout) mixed with a lot of irrelevant detail and generalisations. It has all the marks of a rushed and poorly researched piece, which demonstrates an inadequate reading base that would be necessary to get a good appreciation of the emergence and impact of this most significant creedal statement. While you have listed a superficially large number of works in the bibliography, the reality is that there has been a gross over-reliance on a few quick but unreliable online sources. To appreciate the full significance of the Chalcedon Definition, you must read much more from established historical sources (e.g. MacCulloch, Gonzalez, Hill).

Since this result is a Fail, you may re-submit a revised version within 7 days of receiving this feedback, for a maximum possible mark of 50%. In that revision, there will need to be evidence of much more significant reading and a more detailed analysis of the actual terms of the document itself.

Grade: Fail

Assessment 2: Historiographical Essay

XXXX, this is a huge improvement on your first assignment. Most pleasing is the change of approach to resourcing the essay. The research base is solid and well incorporated, with evidence of both reputable secondary literature and primary references—well done.

The essay itself presents a good balance of argument, with some appropriate historical evidence (could be more, especially if some wordy passages were more concise, but what is provided is effective). Content of the essay is solid and shows some good sense of individual critical thinking. Expression in the main is acceptable, although some English errors could be worked on still.

Overall, a pleasing piece of work. Keep up this more industrious approach in future assignments.

Grade: Distinction

Assessment 3: Thematic Essay

XXXX, this is a bit of a mixture. There are numerous examples of accurate and documented historical details but there are also many omissions of significant elements. The indulgence issue and the general tenor of the church which prompted Luther to action is quite well handled. However, the printing press is rather fleetingly mentioned (although it was very significant). Similarly, the general Renaissance culture of humanistic inquiry and expansion of critical horizons was virtually absent, yet it was a foundational cultural mindset which spawned revolutionary reformist movements in art, politics, religion, and education, without which it is doubtful that such radical reforms could have been envisaged let alone achieved: virtually all the leading Reformers were first of all humanist scholars.

Your writing style is also a mixture. There is a certain attractiveness in the liveliness of expression, but in places it gets more flowery than factual—too many fine sounding phrases without any particular point. By all means cultivate your individual style of expression, but try to make it more consistently meaningful and, in academic work, supported by evidence not just nice sounds.

It is good to see you engaging with a wider range of literature.

Grade: Credit

B. WHAT ABOUT LEVELS?

A recent trend towards multi-streaming of courses has led to an urgent need to differentiate between levels across which similar content is being taught, although the need exists even when courses are not multi-streamed. Multi-streaming is the system of combining classes from undergraduate and postgraduate student cohorts in one class for the delivery of courses, commonly on the ground of economic delivery especially to small classes. A problem occurs when the learning emphasis is content driven, since the lecturer generally conveys identical content to both cohorts and so their performance is indistinguishable, apart from occasional variations in length of assignments or other quantitative demands. Familiarity with guidelines for different levels of awards makes it clear that this is not appropriate since awards have significant qualitative discriminators. The AQF is typical of award statements issued by accrediting bodies. Its organising framework is 'a taxonomic structure of levels and qualification types each of which is defined by a taxonomy of learning outcomes ... designed to enable consistency in the way in which qualifications are described as well as clarity about the differences and relationships between qualification types'.[5] The framework not only spells out mandatory accreditation regulations, it also details the nuanced nature of the various levels of awards and the expected standards and characteristics of awards. While the framework's arrangement of criteria around the three categories of knowledge (what a graduate knows and understands), skills (what a graduate can do), and application of knowledge and skills (the context in which a graduate applies knowledge and skills) is arguably in need of refinement, the principle of qualitative differentiation across award levels is exemplary. In practical terms, since assessment and learning are integrally linked, when assessment for two groups is qualitatively identical, then it follows that there is a failure to deliver qualitatively distinguished levels of learning.

Whether we are teaching separate parallel classes for the various award levels or teaching combined classes that feature common content, there is the same requirement for a clear grasp of pedagogical differentiation across the levels. To take a common tripartite approach, we can consider diploma, bachelor, and master courses, which are the common levels of teaching at many theological institutions. It is the *pedagogical aspirations and descriptors of these*

---

5   *Australian Qualifications Framework* 2013, 11–18.

awards that provide authentic discrimination, rather than the notional content. For example, it is often said that an introduction to the Bible has a defined textual corpus, which has to be introduced to students who are beginning their theological studies regardless of award level, and so differentiation is inevitably minimal and assessment is often distinguished by 'marking harder' at the higher level. However, such an approach neglects the pedagogical nuances of higher education. It is not the content of the New Testament that differs between Bachelor of Theology and Master of Theology; it is the processing of that content expected of the two cohorts that differs markedly. Throughout our discussion of pedagogy, much has been made of pedagogical process, and perhaps nowhere is that more telling than at this point. A Master of Theology is not a Bachelor of Theology + 10%; it is a different kind of award, with different aims and requiring different pedagogies.

So, what pedagogies suit different awards, noting that this question addresses simultaneously the demands of learning and assessment activities? It is important to appreciate that unit content is not the main driver of learning tasks: rather, the higher the award level, the higher the pedagogic demand. Following the simple tripartite categorisation mentioned above, some specific illustrative examples follow.

At undergraduate diploma level, the learning emphasis is on teacher-assisted location and identification of relevant knowledge pertaining to a stipulated topic within a known context. Assessment requires the demonstration of the student's capacity to report such knowledge accurately. The following examples illustrate a degree of teacher guidance in terms of specifying the scope and directing the process:

A. New Testament

Assessment Item 1: Textual Analysis

Read the Parable of the Sower in Matthew 13;1–13; Mark 4:1–12, and Luke 8:1–10.

Make a list of the details that are common to all three accounts.

Make a list of the details that are different across the three accounts.

How do you account for (a) the similarities and (b) the differences?

Assessment Item 2: Essay.

Select one major theme relating to the practice of the Christian life from the book of Acts or one of the Epistles that you have found most significant.

Summarise the teaching of this theme, explaining how it related to the culture of its day and showing how you could use it in a ministry situation (for example, teaching, preaching, giving advice to an inquirer, and do on).

You may limit your essay to one particular biblical book or a group of associated books.

B. Church History

Assessment Item 1: Essay

Select one of the 'turning points' identified by Mark Noll in his book *Turning Points: Decisive Moments in Christian History* [the set textbook]. Write an essay that traces the historical development of the key theme surrounding this turning point, noting the major issues, events and people involved in its development, and showing how its development contributed to this particular turning point in the history of the Church.

You should begin your reading for this essay with the relevant chapter(s) in Noll's book and the thematic study guides provided in the relevant Sessions of this unit. However, your reading should not stop there, as your essay is intended to be more than just a summary of one chapter of a book. It is important that you read as widely as you can on the issue, rather than simply accept the perspective of one scholar (never a wise move). Refer to at least five or six other secondary reference works to see if there are additional viewpoints to be considered and include where possible references to primary historical material to support your informed ideas. For assistance in referencing your reading in the appropriate way, refer to the various guides to writing assignments in the Higher Education Handbook and in Student Support resources at *Writing Skills*.

Undergraduate bachelor degrees emphasise analysis and application of such knowledge in a wider range of known contexts, commonly requiring a broader range of both primary and secondary reading, less dependency on teacher guidance, and evidence-based argument. Assessment will require the student to demonstrate an increasing capacity for such evidence-based analysis and critical argument. The following examples incorporate these analytical and evaluative dimensions which call for the learner's independent judgement:

A. New Testament

Assessment Item 1: Essay

Write an essay on ONE of the following topics:

a) Discuss with reference to Romans the place of 'law' in the life of the Christian.

b) In the light of Paul's thematic statement in Romans 1:16–17, discuss the unity and progression of his argument in Romans 6–8.

Assessment Item 2: Exam

What is the meaning of 'righteousness' in Romans?

B. Church History

Assessment Item 1: Essay

Assess the place of Menno Simons and his followers within the Anabaptist or 'Radical' Reformation movement in the sixteenth century.

Assessment Item 2: Exam

How far did the achievements of Queen Mary's reign match her ambitions for the English Church?

The postgraduate master level focuses learning on more critical judgement in terms of independent evaluation and synthesising of students' own arrangement of a wide range of information and perspectives, with creative application to a wider range of contexts. The following examples illustrate the requirements of wide research of disparate views and critical processing of such information, with personalised synthesis and increasing autonomy of learning as a result:

A. New Testament

Assessment Item 1: Research Assignment

A Masters Seminar will be convened in Lecture Weeks 6–8. At this seminar, students will present a paper to the class. The paper will not be a formal paper for submission at this stage but will be a report to peers detailing the state of their research in preparation for the major assignment and should be geared to provoke scholarly discussion. Details of the assignment are given below. By the end of Lecture Week 3, all students are to consult with the lecturer regarding their choice of scholar for the assignment.

Task: Review and critique the contribution of ONE or MORE of the following scholars to the New Perspective debate, with particular reference to the interpretation of Romans:

James DG Dunn; NT Wright; Don Carson; Another scholar (with prior approval).

Students will submit a formal essay on this topic by the end of semester.

Assessment Item 2: Exam

How does Paul reconcile his teaching on the Law with his concept of Christian liberty in Romans?

B. Church History

Assessment Item 1: Research Essay

Recent histories have suggested that Anabaptism did not originate in one place, but in fact had a 'polygenesis.' Present a case for either a single origin or a polygenesis of Anabaptism.

Assessment Item 2: Exam

According to Christopher Haigh, the English Reformation can be viewed as having been 'rapid' or 'slow,' and as having been introduced 'from above' or 'from below.'

Which of these categories best suits your understanding of the English Reformation?

In all the above examples, there is a clear gradation from teacher-directed learning at diploma level through to autonomous learning at master level and a progression from knowledge location and marshalling through to wide research and critical judgement in analysis and creativity. Such a scaffolded approach to assessment is as important as the corresponding scaffolding of curriculum and all other learning activities.

While most teacher-learner engagement is involved up to master level, the issue of doctoral or higher degrees by research should not be neglected. While such programs are typically pursued on the basis of personal interest or need defined by an individual candidate, the role of the supervising teacher as facilitator and guide is important. Pedagogically, most research projects are designed within established discipline methodologies, so the die is well cast in advance, namely, as a somewhat rigid, linear, step-by-step empirical approach to reasoning. However, Perry Shaw stands as an advocate for innovative methodology and diversification within the current understandings of globally recognised criteria of higher research degrees.[6] In his review based on Bloom's taxonomy, the European Union's Dublin Descriptors, and the International Council for Evangelical Theological Education (ICETE) Beirut Benchmarks, he puts the focus not on the form of thesis production, but on the demonstration of depth of learning and understanding. Evaluation and creativity involving original contribution and critical thinking are married to a high level of self-reflective and self-critical skill in the capacity of assessing critically the strengths and weakness of the ideas of others and of self. There is also the Dublin addition of a passion for knowledge and learning that the doctoral graduate will pass on to those with whom he or she interacts and the Beirut emphasis on the need for missional impact.[7] Throughout a doctoral program, the supervising teacher needs to be attuned to opportunities to enhance the candidate's capacity for such highly developed capacities for personal awareness and growth as well as the contribution to knowledge. The learner's capacity to inform and impassion others needs to be nurtured within the doctoral learner.

In all the above discussion, we can discern an obvious alignment with the hierarchical scale of Bloom's taxonomy, with diplomas located lower in the pyramid than the more synthesising and creative postgraduate awards. These sorts of qualitative discrimination apply regardless of prior familiarity with content since they are the pedagogical markers of the award rather than merely a statement of content complexity.

> *Critical Reflection.* What pedagogical distinctives do you implement when teaching common content to different award levels? Is there room for more nuanced discrimination in pedagogy and assessment in your approach?

---

6   Shaw, 'Innovation and Criteria', 43–58.
7   Shaw, 'Innovation and Criteria', 45–52.

C. FORMATION, TRANSFORMATION, INTEGRATION

To bring this section on pedagogy to a close, I want to return briefly to the topic of pedagogic purpose. This final component is shaped largely by my personal experience and research, so it may well be little more than the musings of a reflective teacher. I have noted, especially over the past decade, that there has been much discussion (in Australia at least) as to the 'correct' purpose of theological education, specifically, is it formation or transformation? This has arisen pointedly from the impetus sparked by the Transforming Theology project (2010–2012), which sought to test the common claim of theological institutions that they provided a transformative experience (which ultimately seemed to be more aspirational than demonstrable). But what is the difference between formation and transformation? The question is not moot, as the answer will influence greatly our approach to pedagogy, as purpose and pedagogy are virtually inseparable, and our preference for a pedagogical style will match our pedagogical purpose. I will proceed on the basis of my own understanding at this point (although I acknowledge that such an understanding is as contestable as it is fluid).

Formation carries within it the implied notion of forming a learner into a pre-determined model of operator, with a common reference to the goal of vocational performance. In itself, that does not mean manipulative cloning or anything comparably sinister. Rather, it starts from an understanding of what is required to perform a certain role and seeks to equip the learner to fulfil that role. The role may be vocational, such as that of a minister, a youth leader, or a chaplain, and so the teacher sets out to teach the essential knowledge that such a role requires and to develop the performative skills and personal disciplines required for an authentic fulfilment of that role. It may equally be personal, such as spiritual growth, and so the teaching is geared to communicating the sort of knowledge and disciplines that are known to equip a person for a fulfilling personal experience in their life. Such formative purposes are legitimate and carry with them a preference (by both teacher and learner) for a didactic pedagogy with the teacher as driver and the learner as absorber of content and wisdom, a process that contributes ultimately to the appropriate forming of the graduate learner, who is thus deemed suitable for vocational service. Such a commitment to formation is typified by the conveying of necessary content, the analysis of acknowledged processes, and the development of suitable skills.

Transformation carries within it the implied notion of essential change within a learner, without any pre-determined outcome of that change. It involves what Mezirow called a disorienting dilemma, which prompts a change of world view in the learner and so leads into unforeseeable destinations. Its aim is to facilitate the learner's growth into all that he or she is capable of being, rather than teaching how to fulfil a traditional role in a traditional way. This too is a legitimate purpose because it leads to innovation and creativity and has more world-changing potential. However, it comes with high levels of risk, not least in terms of the vulnerability of the learner during the process of disorientation and the lack of apparent control by the institution of a course of learning. Transformative learning pedagogy is driven largely by the learner with a teacher as facilitator rather than determiner of the program. The teacher contributes by shaping experiences which will allow the learner to grow in individually helpful ways, but not allowing the abandonment of the learner. The teacher needs to be cognitively and personally agile in responding to the unexpected, which places high demands of competence and confidence on the shoulders of the teacher. Put simply, transformative teaching is as risky as transformative learning. Methods are typically flexible, heuristic, experiential, and expressive rather than absorptive and ordered.

In applying such a discrimination to the sphere of Christian education, Irene Alexander draws a distinction between formation (the forming of a person for a vocation) and transformation (which, in Alexander's terms, includes the element of healing, the intervention of the Spirit, and the call to kingdom thinking). Her approach takes Jesus as exemplar of combining both dimensions of formation and transformation in his purpose and practices. In this way, she also draws a distinction between a task leader and a teacher, with a task leader's responsibility being to assess the task and the participant's ability to do it, while the teacher's responsibility is to teach in a way that can be received and understood. Alexander sees no dichotomy between formation and transformation; rather, she presents them as complementary aspects of Christian teaching. The final heading in her chapter encapsulates her perspective on transformative learning in a college situation: 'Transformed—Patterned Yet Unique'.[8]

My own position is a little different from Alexander's. Having worked my way philosophically and practically through stages of formative and

---

8   Alexander, 'A Glimpse of the Kingdom, 85–99.
    See also, Norsworthy, 'Transformative Learning', 91–99. This is a report on the perspectives of a limited sample of first year students on their learning experience. It is a qualitative analysis of how learners' perceptions of themselves as learners developed through their first year in a Counselling degree. It provides observations on methodology, which has potential for teachers to employ in transformative learning.

transformative teaching and learning, I find myself somewhat paradoxically at once affirming and rejecting both. I affirm the legitimacy of both approaches, but I reject the exclusivity of both. Rather, I have come to a preference for the concept not of dual or parallel streams of objectives but of integration as the optimal form of learning that we can help our learners to attain. Formation is legitimate, but it may not be for everyone; transformation is legitimate, but it may not be for everyone; integration, on the other hand, incorporates the potential for both polarities, with the overarching purpose of producing a 'together' graduate, one who has learned the art of coalescing knowledge, skills, and values in a consistent expression of person and role, whatever that role (or those roles) may be. Integrative learning is driven by both teacher and learner as collaborative learning allies. It reaches holistically across the curriculum as adults-to-adults and sustains a creative ethos, culminating in a relevant educative experience that clearly expresses the learner's mastery of the art of learning.

I suggest that there are three domains of such integrative learning, which operate at different cognitive levels, which can be related to different kinds of institution, and which will lead naturally into a variety of pedagogical approaches. The primary domain of knowledge transmission is associated with institutions which see themselves primarily as conservators of a received heritage. The secondary domain of data processing and application is associated with institutions which see themselves essentially as entrepreneurial and contemporary. The tertiary domain of concept appropriation is associated with institutions which see themselves as intentionally transformative, of both individuals and society. Each has its own sense of legitimacy, and each has associated learning characteristics. The optimal integration occurs when all three domains merge—and this is my pedagogical aim.

Table 8.1: Domains of Integrative Learning

Domain	Level	Institutional Ethos	Learning Characteristics
Knowledge transmission	Primary	Conservator	• Collection of information • Recall of information • Presentation of information
Data processing & application	Secondary	Entrepreneur	• Critical analysis • Evidence-based argument • Cogent evaluation • Competent performance
Concept appropriation	Tertiary	Transformer	• Synthesis of perspectives • Holistic integration • Active implementation

Critical Reflection. Formation. Transformation. Integration. Which one is targeted by your current teaching methods? Is any modification warranted?

Critical Reflection. Where would you locate your teaching institution in the Domains of Integrative Learning? How does this manifest itself in the dominant pedagogical practice of the institution? Do you fit comfortably within that location?

As a final statement, I refer once again to Brookfield's work that I have found so helpful. The final chapter of that work concludes with a set of maxims for retaining teacher sanity. These maxims are worth re-visiting periodically, especially his Maxim #16: 'Don't trust what you've just read'.[9] I fully concur with his exhortation to treat all that is written—here and elsewhere—with critical scepticism, as all teachers are always learners, critically processing material and adapting to it, assimilating it into their own conceptual world, or rejecting it as irrelevant or unsuited to their context. As I have frequently said to students over the years, 'That's what I think. Consider it, take what you find valuable, and leave the rest'.

---

9   Brookfield, *The Skillful Teacher*, 265–277.

CONCLUSION: HOW THEN SHOULD WE TEACH?

The opening statement in the introduction to this book was 'How should we teach?' Following the intervening discussion, I reiterate that sentiment, 'How then should we teach?' Throughout this book, I have been seeking to extend the educational conversation beyond the pedagogy v. andragogy contest to establish a more integrative perspective. One of the unintended shortcomings of the pedagogy v. andragogy conversation has been the predominant focus on comparing methods of teaching and delivery, which tends to treat methods in isolation from other essential components of education such as purpose, contexts, agencies, and outcomes. An integrative approach to learning is grounded in a strategic coalescence of all such components in a cohesive educational program.

This book advocates the philosophy and practice of a mathegenical approach to theological teaching and learning in the quest for realistically achievable and permanently valuable graduate outcomes of any theological program. Many statements of desired graduate outcomes that describe a polished theologate are generally more wistful and wishful than realistic or attainable within the limits of a formal educational course of theology. A mathegenical perspective puts the focus not on a polished theological product but on a progressing learning person, that is, one who is learning efficiently under guidance and who will continue to learn autonomously and proficiently after graduation. Whether we wish to form a ministerial persona or to transform a world-changing pioneer, we will do it best by teaching our students how to learn what they need to know, whatever that is or may be, wherever it may occur, whenever it will emerge. My most outstanding graduates are those who, long after graduation, have continued to be passionate and proficient learners in ways that I could never have anticipated, but in ways that I can recognise as having been initiated during their theological studies. On considered reflection on a lifetime of teaching, that desire to produce such learners is a crystallisation of any and all success I can claim to have had. If my students have not learned to learn, it is because I have not taught them well enough.

In developing an integrative mathegenical approach, three elements have to coalesce: world view, curriculum, and pedagogy. Meaningfully grasping the significance of world view is admittedly problematic, yet it is a major factor in influencing and shaping the nature of the entire educative process. The institution and its teaching membership have a well-formed philosophical and educational framework in place, which is often unacknowledged but always present. Teachers and students alike need to be aware of such a governing climate of operation and to understand their place in it and their relationship to it. Similarly, the world inhabited by the students—past, present, and future—is a vital consideration. A student's entry into a theological study program is not the beginning of that student's theological development, nor will that program be its end. The commencing students bring with them an already formed world view that has led them to their enrolment. That world view needs not only to be recognised but also to be respected, and we should seek to use it as a seedbed for their growth, not a field to be ripped apart.

That last comment is worth developing. We should set out not to demolish but to develop their understanding of their world. Too radical a challenge to the comfort of an established position may be damaging. Most theological students will come from some sort of churchly tradition and their teachers need to take cognisance of such bases. Catholics value tradition and sacraments; Evangelicals value scriptural authority; Pentecostals value spiritual gifting. Content and processes of teaching need to be selected and treated to allow students to grow from their respective locations, towards a more solidified or modified understanding, without being force-fed content and processes that they cannot yet digest.

Then there is the aspect of the prevailing world view of context, both ecclesiastical and secular, which in some form will be the milieu in which the student will live and work following graduation. The ambient world view of church and society needs to be understood, as does the embodied world view of the individual learner, sometimes by way of defending the faith against conflictual positions, sometimes by way of constructing bridges to span the gulf between seemingly incompatible perspectives. But in all cases, both ambient and embodied world views will be a pervasive element in any educational program and so they need to be constantly and strategically incorporated in a cohesive integrative educational offering. When such prevailing world view factors are not a consideration in our educational program, that program runs a real risk of dis-integration.

Curriculum innovation is a commonly neglected element of theological education, perhaps because of the inherently conservative approach by ecclesiastical traditions or because of increasing uniformity imposed by accreditation agencies in the interest of benchmarking. Whatever the cause, there is a clear need to revise the way theological education is structured if we wish to achieve the goal of producing proficient learners. What has been largely missing from curriculum studies is the role of curriculum in developing these desired graduate outcomes. It is not merely the teaching and learning styles that are involved, but the very architecture of the overall curriculum design. We have reviewed the features of various approaches to curriculum design which emphasise comprehensive content and skills mastery, with a nod to values development. I have put forward the concept of a carefully structured scaffold for curriculum design, based on a taxonomic framework.

Such a taxonomic approach incorporates curriculum design, teaching methods, and learning activities, all of which need to be treated symbiotically not disparately. Such a curriculum approach features progressive complexity of both content and processes, of kinds of knowing (from factual through to metacognitive) and kinds of processing (from remembering through to creating). The curriculum needs to be structured so that these graduated levels of content, processes, and elements of world views are coherently leading learners from where they are to where they need to be and, ultimately, to where they are capable of arriving. An integrative curriculum is one that provides an early introduction to key understandings of world view, core content, and basic skills of thinking and processing, all within a spiritual, intellectual, and performative 'safety net'. That introduction is followed by an increasingly complex processing of increasingly challenging content, arriving finally at a point where a learner is enabled to make cohesive sense of the totality of learning to date. Thus, the learner is equipped with the tools of autonomous learning demonstrated in personal shaping of inquiry, research, and finding their own creative solutions or producing their own creative artifacts or tools for ongoing application. Throughout this progression, there needs to be a constant correlation of complexity of knowledge and complexity of processing. That sort of generalised structure needs to be attuned to the level of course involved, but all these components can be so tailored to suit the individual settings involved. The role of curriculum is to construct the framework that allows, even requires, the implementation of suitable learning activities to attain such mathegenical outcomes.

A mathegenical perspective on pedagogy sees value in all forms of teaching delivery but seeks to be judicious in matching methods to stages and kinds of learning. The traditional pedagogy of direct instruction is a teacher-focused approach wherein a pre-determined set of content needs to be delivered in some form for learners to receive, understand, absorb, and process. Especially in a new discipline such as theological study, there is a need for such efficient introductory methods of delivery. The technicalities of language study, the tools of discipline-specific analysis, the paradigms for practical analysis need to be communicated clearly as they form the base of ongoing learning. The key factor in this method is the focus on the teacher, who will select and shape the content which is deemed essential to learning. Then there is the classical andragogical approach of active learning which focuses on the learner as an active participant in the learning process, as guided by the teacher. This typically involves various forms of student-centred inquiry by way of research, problem-solving, presentations, or group collaboration, with specific application by the student to an area of personal interest or meaning. In this approach, the teacher sets the parameters of inquiry for the students' activity.

In incorporating such a variety of teaching and learning approaches, a mathegenical perspective focuses on collaborative learning development, whereby the learner is developed as a learner, with increasing independence in shaping and conducting the learning and its outcomes and applications. This will involve all forms of learning methods but will have an overarching ethos of individual discovery and a growing confidence and competence in the self-awareness of the learner. A mathegenical pedagogical approach will seek to have learners engaged in determining the scope of their study, in establishing the parameters and methods of study, and in taking responsibility for the outcomes and their personal development. The key lies in the learners' continuing to be shaped as learners, with not always predictable learning outcomes, facilitated and enhanced by the teacher in collaboration with the student.

A mathegenical approach to teaching is not an attempt to remediate flawed approaches to learning. It is an attempt to enhance our understanding and practice of teaching and learning by embracing as many of the constructive components of various approaches as it can encompass. Mathegenical outcomes derive from a congruence of educational purposes, world view articulation, curriculum design, and pedagogical delivery, with the consistent fusion and graduated progress of these elements through an increasing complexity of concepts, processes, and critical thinking that typify a program of study at any level of tertiary operation. Mathegenical teaching is not really a teaching method; it is rather a teaching disposition. The purpose of mathegenical teaching is not to produce learning for learning's sake, but to produce a learner who has a passion to learn, the skills to expand that learning, and the *habitus* of learning as a productive ongoing way of life.

BIBLIOGRAPHY

A. Recommended for Professional Reading

Bolt, P.G. & P. Laughlin (eds.)   *God's Exemplary Graduates. Character-Oriented Graduate Attributes in Theological Education* (Macquarie Park, NSW: SCD Press, 2021).

Brookfield, S.D.   *The Skillful Teacher* (3rd edn; San Francisco: Jossey-Bass, 2015).

Deininger, F. & O. Eguizabal (eds.)   *Leadership in Theological Education Volume 2: Foundations for Theological Curriculum* (ICETE Series; Carlisle, UK: Langham Global Library, 2017).

Dockery, D. (ed.)   *Theology, Church, and Ministry: A Handbook for Theological Education* (Nashville, TN: B & H Academic, 2017).

B. References

Alexander, I.   *A Glimpse of the Kingdom in Academia* (Eugene, OR: Cascade, 2013).

Allder, B.   'Theological Education Models Reconsidered' (Unpublished paper; Nazarene Theological College, Qld, 2018).

Anderson L.W. & D.R. Krathwohl (eds.)   *A Taxonomy for Learning, Teaching and Assessing: A Revision of Bloom's Taxonomy of Educational Objectives* (New York: Longman, 2001).

Arkwright, J. & C. Chihota   'Using Appreciative Inquiry and Multimodal Texts as Transformative Tools Within a Christ-Following, Missional, Learning Community', in J.M. Luetz, T. Dowden, & B. Norsworthy (eds.), *Reimagining Christian Education. Cultivating Transformative Approaches* (Singapore: Springer, 2018), 259–269.

Astley, J.   *Ordinary Theology* (Aldershot, Hants: Ashgate, 2002).

Australian Qualifications Framework, 2nd edn., 2013. https://www.aqf.edu.au/sites/aqf/files/aqf-2nd-edition-january-2013.pdf [accessed 1 April 2021].

Bailey, M.L.   'The Foundation and Shape of Theological Education', in D. Dockery (ed.), *Theology, Church, and Ministry: A Handbook for Theological Education* (Nashville, TN: B & H Academic, 2017), 23–42.

Bain, A.M.   'Theological Education in Early Christianity: The Contribution of Late Antiquity' in A. Bain & I. Hussey (eds.), *Theological Education. Foundations, Practices, and Future Directions* (Eugene, OR: Wipf & Stock, 2018), 47–59.

Bain, A.M. & I. Hussey   'Five Years On: The Long-Term Value of Theological Education', in A. Bain & I. Hussey (eds.), *Theological Education. Foundations, Practices, and Future Directions* (Eugene, OR: Wipf & Stock, 2018), 136.

Ball, L.	'The Role of Curriculum in Developing Character-Oriented Graduate Attributes with an Illustration from Church History' in P.G. Bolt & P. Laughlin (eds.), *God's Exemplary Graduates. Character-Oriented Graduate Attributes in Theological Education* (Macquarie Park, NSW: SCD Press, 2021), 251–264.
Ball, L.	'A Thematic History of Theological Education in Australia', in A. Bain & I. Hussey (eds.), *Theological Education. Foundations, Practices, and Future Directions* (Eugene, OR: Wipf & Stock, 2018), 88–100.
Ball, L.	*Transforming Theology. Student Experience and Transformative Learning in Undergraduate Theological Education* (Preston, Vic: Mosaic, 2012).
Ball, L.	'Where Are We Going?', in L. Ball & J.R. Harrison (eds.), *Learning and Teaching Theology. Some Ways Ahead* (Northcote, Vic: Morning Star, 2014), 11–20.
Bandura, A.	*Social Learning Theory* (Englewood Cliffs, NJ: Prentice Hall, 1977).
Belcher, C. & G. Parr.	'"Commonness", Diversity and Disequilibrium in Christian Higher Education: Narratives of and in Institutional Worldviews', *Journal of Christian Education*, Vol. 53, No. 3 (December 2010), 7–17.
Blair, E.	'Analysing Alignment in a Biblical Studies Unit' in P.G. Bolt (ed.), *Testing Us Testing God: Assessment and Theological Competency* (Macquarie Park, NSW: SCD Press, forthcoming).
Bloom, B. (ed.)	*Taxonomy of Educational Objectives: Handbook 1. The Cognitive Domain* (London: Longman, 1956).
Bolt, P.	'Deep Learning from a Shallow Surface? Encouraging Good Research in the Internet Age', in L. Ball & P.G. Bolt (eds.), *Wondering About God Together, Research-Led Learning and Teaching in Theological Education* (Macquarie Park, NSW: SCD Press, 2018), 352–372.
Boud, D. (ed.)	*Developing Student Autonomy in Learning* (London, UK: Kogan Page, 1981).
Brock, V.	'Integrated Curriculum Design for Holistic Student Development', in F. Deininger & O. Eguizabal (eds.), *Leadership in Theological Education Volume 2: Foundations for Theological Curriculum* (ICETE Series; Carlisle, UK: Langham Global Library, 2017), 281–315.
Budhai, S.S. & M. Williams	'Teaching Presence in Online Courses: Practical Applications, Co-Facilitation, and Technology Integration', *The Journal of Effective Teaching* 16, no.3 (2016), 76–84.
Budiselić, E.	'An Apology of Theological Education: The Nature, the Role, the Purpose, the Past and the Future of Theological Education', *KAIROS—Evangelical Journal of Theology* VII, no. 2 (2013), 131–154.

Chatfield, G.	'Models of Western Christian Education and Ministerial Training', in A. Bain & I. Hussey (eds.), *Theological Education. Foundations, Practices, and Future Directions* (Eugene, OR: Wipf & Stock, 2018,) 60–73.
Coley, K.S.	'How Would It Play in Peoria? Presenting Current Curriculum and Instruction Andragogy to Theological Educators in Santiago, Cuba', *Christian Education Journal* Series 12, no. 2 (Fall 2015), 415–417.
Cooper, T.	'Examples of Online Exercises' in L. Ball & J.R. Harrison (eds.), *Learning and Teaching Theology. Some Ways Ahead* (Northcote, Vic: Morning Star, 2014), 209–210.
Cronshaw, D.	'The Relational Teacher: Sharing Life as Vocational Essence', in L. Ball & P.G. Bolt (eds), *Wondering about God Together: Research-Led Learning and Teaching in Theological Education* (Macquarie Park, NSW: SCD Press, 2018), 338–351.
Cunningham, S.	'Creative Teaching Methods', in M.J. Anthony (ed.), *Introducing Christian Education. Foundations for the Twenty-first Century* (Grand Rapids, MI: Baker Academic, 2001), 140–146.
Dalziel, J.	'Developing Scenario Learning to Theological Education', in Y. Debergue & J.R. Harrison (eds.), *Teaching Theology in a Technological Age* (Newcastle, UK: Cambridge Scholars, 2015), 17–29.
Dalziel, J.	'Graduate Attributes and Theological Education', in P.G. Bolt & P. Laughlin (eds.), *God's Exemplary Graduates. Character-Oriented Graduate Attributes in Theological Education* (Macquarie Park, NSW: SCD Press, 2021), 90–104.
Das, R.	*Connecting Curriculum with Context* (ICETE Series; Carlisle, UK: Langham Global Library, 2015).
Deininger, F	'Developing a Learning Community in Theological Education', in Deininger & Eguizabal, *Leadership in Theological Education Volume 2*, 227–252.
DeJong, N.	*Education in the Truth* (Nutley, NJ: P&R Publishing, 1974).
De Jongh, C.	'Assessment of Learning in Curriculum Development', in F. Deininger & O. Eguizabal (eds.), *Leadership in Theological Education Volume 2: Foundations for Theological Curriculum* (ICETE Series; Carlisle, UK: Langham Global Library, 2017), 177–199.
De Jongh, C.	'Challenges to Learning in the Age of the Internet', in Y. Debergue & J.R. Harrison (eds). *Teaching Theology in a Technological Age* (Newcastle Upon Tyne, UK: Cambridge Scholars, 2015), 113–126.
De Jongh, C.	'The Contribution of Theories of Multiple Intelligences to the Promotion of Deep Learning through the Assessment of Learning', in L. Ball & J.R. Harrison (eds.), *Learning and Teaching Theology. Some Ways Ahead* (Northcote, Vic: Morning Star, 2014), 91–104.
Eckel, M.	'Interdisciplinary Education within Biblical Theology: A Scriptural-Philosophical-Educational-Practical Overview', *Christian Education Journal* 12, no. 2 (Fall 2015), 384–395.

Edgar, B.	'The Theology of Theological Education', *Evangelical Review of Theology* 29, no. 3 (2005), 208–217.
Forehand, M.	'Bloom's Taxonomy: Original and Revised', in M. Orey (ed.), *Emerging Perspectives on Learning, Teaching, and Technology* (2005), 1–9. http://www.coe.uga.edu/epltt/bloom.htm [accessed 20 March 2021].
Foster, C. R., L.E. Dahill, L. A. Goldman, B.W. Tolentino	*Educating Clergy* (San Francisco: Jossey-Bass, 2006).
Garrison, D.R. & T. Anderson	*E-Learning in the 21st Century: A Framework for Research and Practice* (New York: Routledge, 2003).
Hardy, S.	'Steps for Curriculum Design', in F. Deininger & O. Eguizabal (eds.), *Leadership in Theological Education Volume 2: Foundations for Theological Curriculum* (ICETE Series; Carlisle, UK: Langham Global Library, 2017), 57–78.
Harkness, A.	'The Role of Academic Leadership in Designing Transformative Teaching and Learning', in F. Deininger & O. Eguizabal (eds.), *Leadership in Theological Education Volume 2: Foundations for Theological Curriculum* (ICETE Series; Carlisle, UK: Langham Global Library, 2017), 135–175.
Harris, D.M.	'Theological Education and Spiritual Formation', in D. Dockery (ed.), *Theology, Church, and Ministry: A Handbook for Theological Education* (Nashville, TN: B & H Academic, 2017), 78–89.
Holy See, The	*Francis Apostolic Constitution Veritatis Gaudium On Ecclesiastical Universities and Faculties* (2017) http://w2.vatican.va/content/francesco/en/apost_constitutions/documents/papa-francesco_costituzione-ap_20171208_veritatis-gaudium.pdf [accessed 20 March 2020].
Joseph, E.	'Contextualized Curriculum Design', in F. Deininger & O. Eguizabal (eds.), *Leadership in Theological Education Volume 2: Foundations for Theological Curriculum* (ICETE Series; Carlisle, UK: Langham Global Library, 2017), 79–100.
Jusu, J.	'Problem-Based Learning in Advanced Theological Studies', in P. Shaw & H. Dharamraj (eds.), *Challenging Tradition. Innovation in Advanced Theological Education* (Carlisle, UK: Langham Global Library, 2018), 209–228.
Jusu, J.K.	'The Impact of Hidden Curriculum in Teaching, Learning, and Spiritual development', in F. Deininger & O. Eguizabal (eds.), *Leadership in Theological Education Volume 2: Foundations for Theological Curriculum* (ICETE Series; Carlisle, UK: Langham Global Library, 2017), 253–279.
Knowles, M.S., E.F. Holton III, R.A. Swanson	*The Adult Learner: The Definitive Classic in Human Resources Development* (6th edn; Amsterdam, Boston: Elsevior Butterworth Heinemann, 2005 [1970]).

Lawson, K.E.   'Historical Foundations of Christian Education', in M.J. Anthony (ed.), *Introducing Christian Education: Foundations for the Twenty-first Century* (Grand Rapids, MI: Baker Academic, 2001), 17–25.

LeFever, M.   'Learning Styles', in M.J. Anthony (ed.), *Introducing Christian Education. Foundations for the Twenty-first Century* (Grand Rapids, MI: Baker Academic, 2001), 130–139.

Maddix, M.A., J.R. Estep, M.E. Lowe (eds.)   *Best Practices of Online Education: A Guide for Christian Higher Education* (Charlotte, NC: Information Age Publishing, 2012).

Marquardt, M.J.   *Optimizing the Power of Action Learning* (Mountain View, CA: Davies-Black, 2004).

Martin, K.   'Theology of the iGeneration', in L. Ball & J.R. Harrison (eds.), *Learning and Teaching Theology. Some Ways Ahead* (Northcote, Vic: Morning Star, 2014), 147–157.

Marzano, R.J. & J.S. Kendall   *The New Taxonomy of Educational Objectives* (Thousand Oaks, CA: Corwin Press, 2000, 2007).

McEwen, R.   'Blended Learning: Curriculum Design for Effective Learning', in F. Deininger & O. Eguizabal (eds.), *Leadership in Theological Education Volume 2: Foundations for Theological Curriculum* (ICETE Series; Carlisle, UK: Langham Global Library, 2017), 201–223.

Miller-McLemore, B. J.   'Practical Theology and Pedagogy: Embodying Theological Know-How', in D.C. Bass & C. Dykstra (eds.), *For Life Abundant: Practical Theology, Theological Education, and Christian Ministry* (Grand Rapids, MI: Eerdmans, 2008), 170–190.

Mudge, P.   'Four Ways of Knowing (Jürgen Habermas): Instrumental, Hermeneutical, Emancipatory & Praxis/Wisdom, A Proposed Model for Pedagogy, Teaching/Learning, Knowing, Assessment, Reporting & Evaluation' (Unpublished paper, The Broken Bay Institute, Sydney, 2012).

Mudge, P. & D. Fleming   'The "What" of the Institution That Teaches', in L. Ball & P.G. Bolt (eds.), *Wondering about God Together: Research-Led Learning and Teaching in Theological Education* (Macquarie Park, NSW: SCD Press, 2018), 123–139.

Mudge, P. & D. Fleming   'The "Who" of the Teacher Who Teaches', in L. Ball & P.G. Bolt (eds.), *Wondering about God Together: Research-Led Learning and Teaching in Theological Education* (Macquarie Park, NSW: SCD Press, 2018), 106–122.

Newton, G.   'The Holy Spirit in the Educational Process', in M.J. Anthony (ed.), *Introducing Christian Education: Foundations for the Twenty-first Century* (Grand Rapids, MI: Baker Academic, 2001), 125–129.

Norsworthy, B.	'Transformative Learning: Insights from First Year Students' Experience', in J.M. Luetz, T. Dowden, B. Norsworthy (eds.), *Reimagining Christian Education. Cultivating Transformative Approaches* (Singapore: Springer, 2018), 91–99.
Osmer, R.R.	*Practical Theology: An Introduction* (Grand Rapids/Cambridge, MI: Eerdmans, 2008).
Ott, B.	*Understanding and Developing Theological Education* (ICETE Series; Carlisle, UK: Langham Global Library, 2016).
Payne, I.W.	'A Theology for Advanced Theological Studies', in P. Shaw & H. Dharamraj (eds.), *Challenging Tradition. Innovation in Advanced Theological Education* (Carlisle, UK: Langham Global Library, 2018), 167–183.
Pazmino, R.W.	'Philosophical Foundations', in *Foundational Issues in Christian Education* (2nd edn; Grand Rapids: Baker, 1997).
Pietsch, J.	'Educating for the Kingdom', in P.G. Bolt & P. Laughlin (eds.), *God's Exemplary Graduates. Character-Oriented Graduate Attributes in Theological Education* (Macquarie Park, NSW: SCD Press, 2021), 337–338.
Pullman, E.	'Life Span Development', in M.J. Anthony (ed.). *Introducing Christian Education: Foundations for the Twenty-First Century* (Grand Rapids, MI: Baker Academic, 2001), 63–72.
Shaw, P.	'Innovation and Criteria: Ensuring Standards While Promoting Innovative Approaches', in P. Shaw & H. Dharamraj (eds.), *Challenging Tradition: Innovation in Advanced Theological Education* (Carlisle, UK: Langham Global Library, 2018), 43–58.
Shaw, P.	*Transforming Theological Education: A Handbook for Integrative Learning* (Carlisle, UK: Langham Global Library, 2014).
'Simply Psychology'	https://www.simplypsychology.org/maslow.html#gsc.tab=0 [accessed 24 March 2021].
Smith, S.	'Moving from Instruction to Inquiry', in L. Ball & P.G. Bolt (eds), *Wondering about God Together: Research-Led Learning and Teaching in Theological Education* (Macquarie Park, NSW; SCD Press, 2018), 35–51.
Smith, S., M. Bingham, C. Kleemann	'Curiosity-Based Learning', in P.G. Bolt & P. Laughlin (eds.), *God's Exemplary Graduates. Character-Oriented Graduate Attributes in Theological Education* (Macquarie Park, NSW: SCD Press, 2021), 435–449.
Smith, S. & S. Healey	'On the Frontiers of Change: Designing Bespoke Learning Architecture', in Y. Debergue & J.R. Harrison (eds.), *Teaching Theology in a Technological Age* (Newcastle, UK: Cambridge Scholars, 2015), 147–166.
Smith, S. & L. O'Flynn	'Responding to Complexity', in L. Ball & J.R. Harrison (eds), *Learning and Teaching Theology. Some Ways Ahead* (Northcote, Vic: Morning Star, 2014), 123–127.

Southwell, E. 'A Proposal for the Integration of Information Literacy in Higher Education Coursework' (Unpublished paper, Australian College of Ministries, Sydney, 2020).

Taylor, S. & R. Dewerse 'Unbounding Learning Communities. An Educational Strategy for the Future of Life-Long Learning', in P.G. Bolt & P. Laughlin (eds.), *God's Exemplary Graduates. Character-Oriented Graduate Attributes in Theological Education* (Macquarie Park, NSW: SCD Press, 2021), 420–434.

Thormann, J. & I.K. Zimmerman *The Complete Step-by-Step Guide to Designing and Teaching Online Courses* (New York: Teachers College Press; 2012).

Williams, R. 'Interview with Benjamin Wayman, "Theological Education Is for Everyone"', reported in *Christianity Today*, April 2021. https://www.christianitytoday.com/ct/2020/august-web-only/rowan-williams-theological-education-for-everyone.html [accessed 1 April 2021].

Wright, D. '"Integration" in the Ancient World', in P.G. Bolt & P. Laughlin (eds.), *God's Exemplary Graduates. Character-Oriented Graduate Attributes in Theological Education* (Macquarie, NSW: SCD Press, 2021), 22–31.

Yount, W.R. 'Learning Theory for Christian Teachers', in M.J. Anthony (ed.), *Introducing Christian Education. Foundations for the Twenty-First Century* (Grand Rapids, MI: Baker Academic, 2001), 101–110.

INDEX

Index of Names

Abelard, Peter	22
Alexander, Irene	201
Allder, Bruce	18
Anderson, Lorin W.	68, 69, 70, 72, 103, 105, 107
Anselm of Canterbury	22
Aquinas, Thomas	9, 21, 22, 23
Arkwright, James	162
Astley, Jeff	140
Augustine	21
Australian Qualifications Framework	53, 54, 55, 60, 61, 64, 65, 103, 105, 194
Bailey, Mark L.	13
Bain, Andrew M.	28, 39
Bandura, Albert	120
Baur, F.C.	25
Belcher, Christina	45
Bingham, Murray	166–168
Blair, Edwina	103, 105
Bloom, Benjamin	67–75, 76, 129, 131–132, 199
Bolt, Peter	123–124
Brock, Vera	92
Brookfield, Stephen D.	6–8, 112, 114, 116, 127, 152, 169, 203
Budhai, Stephanie Smith	91
Budiselić, Ervin	8–9
Calvin, John	23–24
Chatfield, Graeme	28
Chihota, Clement	162
Coley, Kenneth S.	52
Cooper, Tim	153
Cronshaw, Darren	13
Cunningham, Shelly	145–146
Dahill, L.E.	112, 139–140
Dalziel, James	124, 161
Das, Rupen	96–97
Deininger, Fritz	36, 91
DeJong, Norman	14
De Jongh, Charles	64, 123–125, 176
Dewerse, Rosemary	150
Dockery, David	30
Eckel, Mark	45
Edgar, Brian	17–18
Erasmus, Desiderius	21, 23
Erikson, Erik	118–119, 126
Fleming, Dan	9
Forehand, Mary	130–131
Foster, Charles R.	112, 139–140
Francis, Pope	11–13, 19, 48
Freire, Paulo	26
Goldman, L. A.	112, 139–140
Guttierez, Gustavo	26
Hardy, Steve	99–100
Harkness, Allan	79–80
Harris, Dana M.	16
Healey, Stephen	137
Hull, John	27
Hussey, Ian	28, 39
Irenaeus	20
Jusu, John Kpaleh	160
Kant, Immanuel	24
Kendall, John S.	70
Kleemann, Catherine	166–168
Knowles, Malcolm S.	x, 146
Krathwohl, David R.	68, 69, 70, 72, 103, 105, 107
Laughlin, Peter	172

Lawson, Kenneth E.	30
LeFever, Marlene	133–134
Luther, Martin	21, 23
McEwen, Rhonda	91
Maddix, M.A.	172
Marquardt, Michael J.	165
Martin, Kara	124–125
Marzano, Robert J.	70
Maslow, Abraham	118, 121, 126
Miller-McLemore, Bonnie J.	151
Mudge, Peter	9, 72–76, 131–132
Newton, Gary	15–16
Norsworthy, Beverley	201
O'Flynn, Leon	150–151
Origen	20
Osmer, Richard R.	73–76, 87, 107, 149–150, 166
Ott, Bernhard	100, 117–118
Parr, Graham	45
Payne, Ian W.	134–135
Pazmino, Robert W.	5–6
Perry, William	120
Piaget, Jean	119–120, 133
Pietsch, James	152
Pullman, Ellery	119–120
Schleiermacher, Friedrich	24–25
Shaw, Perry	39, 199
Smith, Stephen	71, 74–76, 137, 150–151, 157, 166–168
Southwell, Emily	125
Strauss, David	25
Taylor, Steve	150
Thormann, Joan	174
Tolentino, B.W.	112, 139–140
Williams, Maureen	91
Williams, Rowan	1, 42
Yount, William Rick	133
Zimmerman, Isa Kaftal	174

Index of Subjects

assessment	14, 47, 52, 56–57, 59, 64–66, 71, 90, 105–106, 152–153, 173–174, 175–198
Bloom's taxonomy	67–69, 71, 72–73, 74–76, 199
revised	68–69, 103–106
variations on	70, 131–132, 199
conservator	38, 202–203,
critical thinking	55, 62, 87, 144–146, 168–209
entrepreneur	38, 202–203
formation	14, 16, 24, 39, 81, 82, 87–88, 90, 112, 116, 118, 150
and transformation	200–203
transformation	11, 16, 17, 137, 163
graduate attributes	14, 42–44, 49, 51, 78, 84, 89, 94, 149
Holy Spirit	10, 15–16, 18
integration	5–6, 12, 112, 125, 136, 156, 157, 158, 202, 205–207
domains of integrative learning	203
integrative curriculum	91–94
integrative learning	5, 9, 16–17, 29–31, 38, 44, 48–49, 51, 61, 80, 84, 89–91, 117, 130, 133–134
integrative pedagogy	159–174, 175–177
mathegenical teaching	ix, xii, 52, 56, 83, 92–94, 155–174, 184–193, 205–209
models of theological delivery	17–18
Athens	18
Berlin	18
Emmaus	18
Geneva	18
Jerusalem	18
nuances of terminology	45, 48, 56–57, 175, 178, 195

online learning	90–91, 105–106, 117, 122–126, 143, 148, 153, 171–174
peer learning	12, 90, 123, 163–166, 169, 173
perspectives on pedagogy	109–174
andragogical principles	x–xi, 146–153
curiosity based learning	166–168
focus on learner	118–129
focus on learning	129–135, 135–137
focus on teacher	116–118
group project based learning methods	159, 164–166
influences on pedagogy	111–115
inquiry based learning methods	159, 162–164
pedagogical principles	139–146
problem based learning methods	159–161
principles of curriculum design	35–94
characteristics of course levels	54–56
content-centred curriculum	40–41, 80–81, 82–84
course levels and curriculum	53–58
curriculum components	80–91
curriculum content and design	51–60
curriculum-pedagogy nexus	72–74
curriculum review and development	79–80, 95–107
curriculum structure and sequencing	91–94
learner-centred curriculum	41–43, 81, 89–90, 146–147
scaffolded curriculum	75–79
taxonomical curriculum	53, 67–72
principles of theological education	1–32
historical principles	19–30
philosophical principles	1–10
theological principles	10–19
processes	116–137
how learners learn	129–132
how teachers teach	132–137
understanding the learners	118–129
the learner in context	118–126
understanding the teachers	116–118
strategic alignment	47, 57–66, 103–107
learning activities and assessment	64–66
learning outcomes across the curriculum	58–63
team teaching	170–171
transformation, *see* formation	
world view	xi–xii, 1–32, 45–46, 77–78, 89, 92, 148, 206–209

www.ingramcontent.com/pod-product-compliance
Lightning Source LLC
Chambersburg PA
CBHW081333080526
44588CB00017B/2612